THE MAN IN THE MYTH MACHINE

The full story of the tragedy of Alan Ladd has never been told before. Here are the facts about the life he lived behind the legend Hollywood created: his lifelong love affair with his agent/wife Sue Carol, his "secret" son who became president of a major Hollywood studio...

And much more. For this intimate portrait of Hollywood's most enigmatic star also reveals the inner workings of the studio system itself. The deals and the mis-deals. The movie mags and the fan machines, the front office and the back lot.

How the myths are made. And the lives destroyed.

Ladd

THE LIFE, THE LEGEND,
THE LEGACY OF ALAN LADD

BEVERLY LINET

BERKLEY BOOKS, NEW YORK

LADD: THE LIFE, THE LEGEND,
THE LEGACY OF ALAN LADD

A Berkley Book / published by arrangement with
Arbor House Publishing Co., Inc.

PRINTING HISTORY
Arbor House edition published 1979
Berkley edition / March 1980
Second printing / September 1980

A BERKLEY BOOK® TM 757,375
Berkley Books are published by Berkley Publishing Corporation,
200 Madison Avenue, New York, New York 10016.
PRINTED IN THE UNITED STATES OF AMERICA

ACKNOWLEDGMENTS

Excerpts from Bosley Crowther's movie reviews of Alan Ladd's performances in *This Gun for Hire* and *Shane*, and excerpts from "Dual Addiction" by William Stockton, © 1942–1958/1978 by The New York Times Company. Reprinted by permission.

Lines from "Success" by Edgar A. Guest reprinted by permission of Hearst Publications.

Excerpts from *You Must Remember This* by Walter Wagner, © 1975 by Walter Wagner. Reprinted by permission of G. P. Putnam's Sons.

Lyrics from "Sweet Sue—Just You" by Victor Young and Will J. Harris, copyright MCMXXVIII. Renewed by Shapiro, Bernstein and Co. Inc., New York. Used by permission.

Excerpts from *Veronica* by Veronica Lake and Donald Bain, copyright © 1969 by Veronica Lake. By permission of Bantam Books, Inc.

Grateful acknowledgment is made to *Modern Screen* for permission to quote from articles on Alan Ladd.

Grateful acknowledgment is made to *Photoplay* for the excerpts from stories and articles on Alan Ladd appearing from 1950 to 1959, and for permission to quote from "The Man Who Came Back" by Kirtley Baskett from *Motion Picture*, February 1964.

Joshua Logan quote from *Mary Pickford & Douglas Fairbanks* by Booton Herndon. Published by W. W. Norton & Co. Inc. Copyright © 1977 by Booton Herndon.

Paramount photographs of Alan Ladd from the motion pictures *The Glass Key*, *Lucky Jordan*, *Wild Harvest*, and *The Great Gatsby* courtesy of Universal Pictures.

Photograph from the Paramount motion picture *Shane* copyright © 1952 Paramount Pictures Corporation.

Contents

Cast...
(IN ORDER OF APPEARANCE)

Mother   Ina Raleigh
Father   Alan Ladd
Stepfather   James Beavers
First Wife   Marjorie (Midge) Jane Harrold
Son   Alan Ladd, Jr. ("Laddie")
Agent/Wife   Sue Carol
Head of Paramount   Adolph Zukor
Paramount Production Chief   Buddy DeSylva

Director (This Gun for Hire)   Frank Tuttle
Leading Lady   Veronica Lake
Co-star   Robert Preston

Stepdaughter   Carol Lee Stuart
Best Friends (1)   William and Tess Bendix
Makeup Man   Hal Lierley
Daughter   Alana Ladd (Mrs. Michael Jackson)
Co-star   Howard Da Silva
Leading Lady (O.S.S.)   Geraldine Fitzgerald
Younger Son   David Ladd
Director (Shane)   George Stevens

Best Friend (2)   Van Heflin
Leading Lady (The Proud Rebel)   Olivia de Havilland
Best Friend (3)   Edmond O'Brien
Leading Lady (The McConnell Story)   June Allyson
SPECIAL APPEARANCES BY: Sophia Loren, Mona Freeman,
Shelley Winters, Gail Russell

FAMILY

Alan, Jr.'s Wife   Patricia Beazley
David's Wife   Cheryl Jean Stoppelmoor Ladd
Alana's Husband   Michael Jackson
Carol Lee's Husbands   Richard Anderson and John Veitch
Sue Carol's Previous Husbands   Allan H. Keefer, Nick
Stuart, and Howard Wilson

FORMER IN-LAWS

Mother and Father-in-Law   Olivia Wilson
and Robert Harold
Sisters-in-law   Barbara Harrold Grether and
Kathryn Harrold
Brother-in-law   Robert Harrold, Jr.

MARJORIE HARROLD'S FAMILY

Second Husband   William Farnsworth
Daughter Cynthia Farnsworth
Son   Darrick Farnsworth

ALAN LADD'S GRANDCHILDREN

Jonathan (Jody) and Jonna Veitch (by John and Carol Lee)
Kelly, Tracy, and Amanda Ladd (by Alan, Jr. and Patricia)
Jordan Ladd (by David and Cheryl)

A Note to the Reader

On the afternoon of September 28, 1961, I sat in the garden room of Alan Ladd's luxurious Holmby Hills mansion, where I had come to do a story for *Modern Screen* magazine about Ladd's teenage actor son, David. Teenagers were hot copy at the time, and there was particular reader interest in David Ladd. But I wanted to include something about Alan Ladd too. The magazines had neglected him during the previous four years, and he had always been wonderful to me. So I made him the subject of an "Instant Interview" featurette—a short quiz reserved for superstars who had long before said all there was to say about themselves.

The last question of what was to be my last interview with Alan Ladd was: "What would you change about yourself if you could?"

He replied tersely: "Everything."

Twenty-eight months later, at the age of fifty, Alan Ladd was dead.

For the next fifteen years, whenever one of his movies was shown on "The Late Show," I would think of that afternoon and wonder, *Why would a man who had everything want to change everything?*

This book is my attempt to find out.

I had thought I knew the basic details of Alan Ladd's life. I was wrong. I soon realized I was not just a researcher assembling facts for a biography; I was a detective unraveling a complex and often bewildering mystery. I found dozens of contradictory published statements, huge unchronicled gaps in time. There were people who had suddenly disappeared, others whose existence was impossible to prove.

Yet the many people I interviewed—Ladd's family, his friends, the majority of his co-stars—agreed on one thing: that they loved Alan Ladd.

Everyone loved him, it seemed, except Alan himself....

I spoke with the five people in Ladd's life who loved him the most: his widow, Sue Carol; his sons, Alan, Jr., and David; his daughter Alana (Mrs. Michael Jackson); and his stepdaughter Carol Lee (Mrs. John Veitch). I am grateful to them for allowing me to see Alan Ladd through their eyes.

I am particularly grateful to David Ladd, whose sensitivity, candor, and understanding of his father were invaluable.

I am indebted to June Allyson for frankly discussing—for the first time—an episode in her life which made her and Alan the subjects of gossip and scandal.

To Robert Preston, Virginia Mayo, Geraldine Fitzgerald, Olivia de Havilland, Howard da Silva—Alan Ladd's co-stars—my appreciation for the time they gave me and their opinions of Alan Ladd, both the actor and the man. Special thanks to Mrs. Tess Bendix, the widow of Ladd's closest friend, Bill, and to Hal Lierley, Ladd's longtime makeup man, for providing fresh and surprising revelations.

My conversations with the late Van Heflin took place shortly after Alan Ladd's death. They were too frank to be quoted then, but I'm sure Mr. Heflin would understand why I am using them now.

The opinions of Sophia Loren, Rod Steiger, Adela Rogers St. John, the late Veronica Lake, the late Leo Genn, the late Martin Rackin, the late George Stevens, and the late Frank Tuttle also provided fascinating insights.

My gratitude to writer Kirtley Baskett, Alan Ladd's trusted friend and confidant, for sharing his recollections with me and for generously allowing me to quote from his dozens of intimate interviews with Ladd, from which most of the information about the actor's early life was gleaned.

Albert Delacorte, past editor of *Modern Screen;* Henry Malmgreen, past executive editor of *Modern Screen;* Adele Fletcher, editor of *Photoplay* in its heyday—all personal friends of Alan Ladd and my former bosses—put themselves at my disposal. To Henry, a big hug for helping me solve some nearly insurmountable problems.

My gratitude extends also to publicists John Springer, Frank MacFadden, and Betty Goode; and to *Hollywood Reporter* columnist Robert Osborne; to New York *Daily News* reporter Don Flynn; to *Photoplay*'s current executive editor David Ragan; and to Joyce Jameson, Marilyn Henry, Harry Kroft, Ruby Boyd, and Germaine Deydier for the time and effort they invested. Thanks to my typist Jennifer Malahowski. And of course to my editors Jared Kieling and Deborah Prigoff for their assistance.

This book could not have been written without the assistance of two very special people: Joan O'Brien did much of my California legwork, never once failing to come through in spite of my difficult requests. I'd order, "Get me..." She'd shoot back, "Got you..." Among the many things she got me was contact with Barbara Harrold Grether, the sister of Alan Ladd's first wife, Marjorie Jane (Midge) Harrold.

It was Barbara, through countless hours of interviews, who helped me fit the final pieces of the puzzle in place. She created a powerful word-picture of what Alan Ladd was like as a young man, telling me in detail the poignant story of Alan and her sister Midge and correcting information put out by both the Paramount Pictures publicity department and some of the press. It was Barbara, too, who went through all her old family albums to supply photos of Midge—the first ever to be published—and who took me on a personally guided tour of all the places that figured prominently in Alan's and Midge's early life together. My deepest thanks to Barbara for ending her silence after so many years, despite the controversy her story may cause.

Barbara wanted her forgotten sister to have her day in the sun. Since she was responsible for part of the Ladd legacy, that would seem the least Midge—the mother of Alan Ladd, Jr.—deserves.

—Beverly Linet

New York
December 1978

My entire family felt the man had died, and that when a man dies you don't live in his legend. Yet major stars today— from Bob Redford, whom I consider one of the great actors, to Billy Dee Williams—were all inspired as actors by my father. Bogart, in death was a bigger star than he was in life, because he had found a renaissance. Perhaps my father will become a cult figure. Maybe this book will revive him....

—David Ladd

Preface

Since 1977, the name Ladd has made newspaper headlines, been featured on dozens of magazine covers and mentioned with ever-increasing frequency on all the major talk shows.

The Ladds referred to are Alan Ladd, Jr.—former president of Twenty Century-Fox, the man responsible for *Star Wars* and *Alien* and who is considered by many in the movie industry to be the last of the great Hollywood Moguls—and Cheryl Ladd, the blond beauty who replaced Farrah Fawcett-Majors in the television series *Charlie's Angels.*

In passing, writers and show hosts note that Ladd, Jr. ("Laddie"), is the son of the "tough-guy actor," and that Cheryl is married to David Ladd, the youngest son of the "late matinee idol, Alan Ladd."

Among contemporary audiences, *Alan* Ladd is thought of vaguely as someone whose movies appear on "The Late Show." Of his private life and career, they know nothing.

But to a generation who grew up during the movie-crazy days of World War II, Alan Ladd is remembered as everything a movie star should be.

Alan Ladd—he blazed across the screen like a young Greek god in the 1940s and early 1950s; his blond hair, rugged yet vulnerable looks, and performances in such movies as *This Gun for Hire, The Blue Dahlia, Two Years Before the Mast, The Great Gatsby* and the classic *Shane* capturing millions, putting him high on the list of the all-time-great box-office draws.

Yet on January 29, 1964, just a few months past his fiftieth birthday, soon after completing *The Carpetbaggers* —a film which he had hoped would launch him on the comeback he desperately wanted—Alan Ladd died alone and under ambiguous circumstances at his Palm Springs home. His once-beautiful face and strong athlete's body were ravaged by age, time, freak accidents, and a losing battle against alcoholism.

At the time of his death, Alan Ladd was already a forgotten man, because of a recent spate of bad movies and a press interested only in the newest fad stars. His memory would not be revived by the nostalgia craze of the early 1970s. When his widow, Sue Carol Ladd, who had been the keeper of the flame when it had burned so brightly, was asked by his biographer why she did not keep it burning—why, in fact, she refuses interviews with nostalgia scribes—she replied quietly, "I don't know. His death left such a void. I couldn't think about publicity."

And his son David Ladd theorizes: "Bogart, Tracy—they were surrounded by stars and their movies survived. But my father, who could carry a movie all by himself, didn't need a strong leading lady. He didn't need anything. He was enough. But his movies didn't necessarily survive. So during his final stages, he was not the most popular actor. And one of his greatest movies, *The Great Gatsby,* has not, in recent years, been reissued or shown on television—because of the remake. That was one of his greatest performances and one, I think, that would probably get his credibility back as an actor."

Some believe Alan Ladd never really lost his credibility. Of Ladd's early gangster roles, the distinguished *Time* magazine film critic Richard Schickel says, "Alan Ladd is probably the first male star to achieve fame by combining beauty and somnambulism like the female of the species. So unemotional was he, with his deadness of voice and feature, that in some movies he succeeded in reducing murder to an act as irrelevant as crossing the street. By this absence of emotion he created a wonderful commentary on violence. Similarly, his frozen good looks could be read as a symbol of evil's opposite, as in *Shane.*"

When an actor could personify evil and virtue with such impact, regardless of his talent, there *had* to be forces at work below the surface. He had to be more than just a face, a man with a perfect life. But the public devoured the lies and half-truths fed to them throughout Alan Ladd's career. He was the ultimate

Hollywood product—invented, manufactured, packaged by the film capital and sold for approximately twenty-five cents—the price of a movie ticket in the Forties.

Encouraged by an aggressive, ambitious agent-wife and a giant studio's high-powered publicity department, Ladd was a fan magazine editor's dream. He gave more interviews, posed for more photo layouts, answered more fan mail, sent out more personally autographed photos, and topped more personality polls than any other male movie star of the Forties. Only Frank Sinatra provoked more hysteria—but Ol' Blue Eyes stopped courting fans and the press once he had made it.

Yet at the height of Alan Ladd's fame, his wife Sue Carol commented, "Alan is a big star to everyone in the world except Alan. He thinks he's in the business on a raincheck."

That attitude—that vulnerability—was part of his appeal. Eventually it would contribute to his destruction....

Ladd's willingness to share every detail of his personal and family life with his public, his consistent affability, made him appear to be a relaxed and uncomplicated human being.

Not so. Like most extreme introverts, Alan Ladd was a complex, deeply private person. He liked people but was shy in any but intimate, familiar groups. Abidingly insecure, even through the peak years of public adulation, he went out of his way to please those who governed his life—his studio, his fans, his self-confident wife. Any resentments he might have felt were concealed, along with many of his other feelings, to fester and ultimately contribute to his own tragic and premature death.

When he died, Alan Ladd was a multimillionaire. An art collection valued conservatively at $600,000—including paintings by Matisse, Chagall, Braque, Noyer, and Utrillo—decorated his Holmby Hills mansion. His Palm Springs property, his Hidden Valley ranch near Santa Barbara, his stocks—all these had tripled or quadrupled in value since their purchase. As a lark he had once invested in ten wildcat oil wells. Nine came in. And eventual residuals on the six movies he owned outright were estimated at $6 million.

Ladd had not experienced financial hardship for more than two decades, but he could never forget the poverty of his youth. David Ladd, however, believes it was emotional deprivation—far more than not having enough to eat, decent clothes to wear, or toys with which to play—that affected his father's personality.

"I've heard all the stories about my father's poverty as a child," says David Ladd, "but I can say something about that in terms of my own wife. Cheryl came from a very poor background. She is going through the same things I think my father did. There is a major difference between the two. My wife came from a very happy, a very stable family. My father obviously didn't. Cheryl is gliding through her success very happily, very easily.

"A lot of people have attributed the drinking problem and the early death of my father to my mother. But in many ways, my mother kept that man together. If not for her, the end would have come years sooner. The problem was there years before. The unhappiness was there years before—having to do with *his* family, *his* background. . . ."

Prologue

On a hot July morning in 1963, Alan Ladd stopped his Cadillac a few yards from the huge, ornate DeMille Gate that opened into the Paramount lot. Trying to calm himself, he took a long look in the rearview mirror. But it wasn't the image of a "young Greek god" that stared back at him as it had on the autumn day twenty-two years before, when he had gone through the gate to begin work on the film that made him a star.

Although a strict diet and exercise regimen had gotten him back into what Mike Connolly of the *Hollywood Reporter* described as "his *Shane*-type fightin' and fittin' measurements" for his role as Nevada Smith in *The Carpetbaggers*, Alan Ladd's eyes were a give-away. Any excitement he may have felt about this first day before the Paramount cameras in twelve years was tempered by anxiety. Former colleagues would be expecting him the way he had been. Would he have to face their pity and shock? He braced himself, started the car again, and didn't stop until he pulled up beside his dressing room.

The studio executives who had been kind to him even when he had informed them that he wasn't renewing his contract were equally magnanimous about his return. They had given him back his old dressing room—the $110,000 bungalow especially built for him when he had returned from military service in 1943. Two stars had used it since then—Dean Martin and Yul Brynner—but around the lot it was still "Ladd's dressing room." Once, it had been furnished with all his favorite things. He'd taken them with him when he left and saw no point in dragging any of them back for what he knew would be a very brief stay. The days of long-term contracts, permanent dressing rooms, and one big studio family had passed and would never return.…

But with his fiftieth birthday just two months away, Alan Ladd was returning—to the place where he had once been king of the mountain in what was, at best, a supporting role. Without protest he was accepting third billing for the first time since 1942's *The Glass Key*. Only once after that—in *China*, when he had deferred to Loretta Young—had he ever dropped from the top spot.

"I'll go back to work when a good script comes along," he had recently been telling his friends. *The Carpetbaggers*, based on Harold Robbins' sensational novel, was hardly that. Still, the role of the aging Nevada Smith sounded promising, and the notion of working again for Paramount excited Alan—it was the first thing in years that had. It also scared the hell out of him.

He had just learned that Veronica Lake, after working as a cocktail waitress at a second-class woman's hotel in New York, was about to open the next month in an Off-Broadway production of *Best Foot Forward*, fittingly in the role of a fading movie star. Irony. Ladd and Lake—the team the Paramount ads had once touted as "so hot that they melt celluloid"—were now both fading movie stars playing the same parts three thousand miles apart.

There was a difference, of course. Veronica Lake had been so destitute that she had had to take a waitress job—and before that a factory job on Manhattan's South Broadway. Alan Ladd had left his old studio a superstar. "Mr. Paramount," they had called him then. He was returning, if not a has-been, then certainly a man whose professional future was a giant question mark.

This first day on the lot, Ladd stayed in his dressing room, going over his lines until an assistant director knocked on the door to tell him they were ready to shoot. Nervously, he set out for Stage 12. The technicians, the secretaries, the publicists who were still on the payroll all crowded around him—people he hadn't seen for years but who still remembered.

His fingers ached from handshakes, but he crossed two of them on each hand when he stepped into the first "take," which he was sharing with George Peppard. It was a short scene, but when it was over the sound stage shook with shouts and applause.

From the rafters a longtime studio grip shouted, "Now that you're back, Alan, Paramount will really get rolling again."

The reception was duplicated in the commissary. When Ladd dropped in during the lunch break, other diners called out and applauded too. The entire day must have had the dreamlike aura of a scene from a movie—the kind made in the Thirties and Forties. Only the strains of a Max Steiner score were missing to complete the image. Shane was back in the saddle. All was right with the world.

That was his image—the make-believe. The reality was another scenario....

Six months later Alan Ladd was dead.

Part One

1913-1939

Looking back, I'm grateful for the sparseness and the loneliness of my youth—my feelings of inadequacy, being "the kid behind the eightball." They were the most valuable assets I had going for me. They've been the force behind everything I've done, everything I've had, everything I've become. I couldn't slip back because I knew what I'd be going back to. Each slap made me struggle more.

—ALAN LADD

It was, in truth, to be a mixed blessing....

CHAPTER 1

In early autumn of 1913, Hot Springs, Arkansas, was a bustling resort town, proud of its Southern hospitality, its scenery, and the growing reputation of its natural spring waters, which brought the ailing from Oklahoma and Louisiana to seek relief from arthritis and other ills. Life for most of the town's residents was simple, sedate, and stable.

But not for Ina Raleigh Ladd, who never felt comfortable with her gossipy neighbors. She was a petite, reserved Englishwoman with wavy brown hair, warm brown eyes, and a flawless complexion.

On September 3, 1913, Ina gave birth to her first and only child: a tiny, beautiful blond boy named without hesitation Alan Walbridge Ladd. The birth was duly registered in the records at the Hot Springs Court House. (At least that's what Ina told Alan.)

Thirty years later, a reporter who went to Hot Springs to investigate the Ladd family background could find no one who remembered either Ina or her husband, Alan Ladd, Sr. But there were few in the community who didn't remember the night the courthouse caught fire and burned to the ground. Thousands of valuable documents were destroyed in the blaze. Officially there is, therefore, no record that Alan Ladd was ever born.

What Alan learned of his origins came solely from his
mother, and on that subject Ina was always vague or evasive. No
relatives ever came to visit, and no photos of kinfolk were ever
shown to Alan. He only knew that his mother was born on
November 25, 1888, in West Chester, England, and had come to
the United States in 1907 at the age of nineteen. That much was
duly recorded.

Of his father's background, he also knew practically nothing.
Alan Ladd, Sr., was reportedly American-born, of Scottish
ancestry. Period. His son would have only the fuzziest memory
of what he had looked like, recalling a "faceless figure" who was
always packing to go somewhere and then returning "tired and
travel-stained from trips" related to his job as a freelance
accountant. Alan Ladd never saw a photo of the man.

How and where Ina and Alan, Sr., met and the details of their
courtship are unknown. All that is known is that Ina told her son
they married in Hot Springs in 1912.

Alan's most vivid childhood memory was of the day in 1917
when he was four and saw Ladd Sr. tip over and die of a heart
attack. He was too young to grasp the significance of the event,
too accustomed to the man's absences from home to feel any
sense of loss—at least at that moment.

In time, the vagueness of his origins, the abrupt disappear-
ance of a strong masculine influence (if indeed there had ever
been one), and the lack of close blood ties were to make Ladd's
childhood lonely, unanchored, and insecure. The insecurity was
to become so deep-rooted that it would prove the overriding
force in his life. But for a little boy, the newness of having his
beloved mother with him *all* the time, of being able to crawl into
her bed at night, of sensing that her entire world revolved about
him alone, more than compensated for the lack of any other
family.

There was some insurance money—enough to last until Ina
decided what she wanted to do with her life....

The decision was made for her. On July 3, 1918, Alan and a
young friend, playing alone, found a box of matches and, with
no one around to stop them, decided to celebrate the Fourth a
day early. They burned down the ramshackle apartment
building the Ladds had lived in. Ina was too relieved to find her
son unharmed to punish him for the ruin he had caused.

There was nothing now to keep the two Ladds in Hot Springs—no friends, no family, no furniture, no possessions of any kind. Ina took what was left of her money and moved to Oklahoma City. The small boy made no friends at school in this new and hostile place. At seven, frail and the tiniest child in his grade, he was subjected to every cruelty his classmates could think of.

Inevitably his mother assumed the important role of best friend. Lonely herself, she'd tell him that he was her "fella," that together they were an unbeatable team. Ina, however, was still young enough to crave a "fella" in more realistic ways.

Alan was to learn that a boyhood trauma could play hell with a young man's memories. One day he would tell *Modern Screen* reporter Kirtley Baskett that he first learned of his mother's relationship with a house painter named James Beavers from their landlady, who carelessly remarked one day, "Well, sonny, I hear your ma is getting married. You're gonna have yourself a step-papa...."

When, Ladd said, he ran screaming to Ina, she tried to soothe him by saying, "Why, baby, of course you're still my beau. But you need a new papa, and you'll learn to like him a lot."

Fact or fantasy? Was it Ladd's imagination, or did a studio publicist try to put a little schmaltz into his life story to fill a huge gap with some concocted details? Like so much of Ladd's childhood, the courtship of Ina and Jim Beavers is a virtual blank. Ladd would talk kindly about Beavers, but he always managed to skirt the man's relationship with his mother, although they were married for fifteen years. Unimportant, perhaps. Still, Beavers was presumably the sole masculine figure of Alan's formative years....

Discussing his stepfather's eventual job as a movie studio painter, Ladd later said, "He could have become an executive. But he was too scared even to become a foreman." An ironic statement. Was James Beavers cursed with Alan's own self-denigrating feelings of insecurity? Or was Alan projecting those feelings onto the man who pre-empted his own cherished place with Ina? To this day James Beavers is faceless, disembodied—almost anonymous. And quite obviously his stepson preferred to keep him that way.

Alan Ladd's most vivid boyhood memories begin when

Beavers, newly married and unable to make a go of it in Oklahoma City, decided to pack up and start fresh in California.

In 1920 large sections of the country were experiencing a severe economic downturn. Farmers, lumbermen, coal miners and textile workers were affected. Most looked to California, the fastest growing state in the nation, as their last remaining hope.

Jim Beavers had an advantage over the others: he had a trade. New communities were springing up throughout Southern California, and he figured that skilled workers would be in demand to lay bricks, install pipes, paint houses.

First, though, the Beavers family had to get there. Alan later said that it took the three of them four months to make the journey in his stepfather's dilapidated 1914 Model T Ford touring car.

Their takeoff, as he described it, was a scene straight out of *The Grapes of Wrath*. The back of the car's front seat was split to recline so as to form a crude bed. A tent, tools, baggage and their personal belongings were roped to the sides and top of the car. For food, there was a grub bag on the back seat.

Each night the Model T would pull off to any convenient spot on the side of the road, since Beavers considered fifty cents for the cost of a tourist camp a luxury. Occasionally he'd earn a day's wages painting a house enroute, but the money always ended up at the nearest gas station—the car was constantly in need of repair.

It was hardly an idyllic honeymoon for Ina. Beavers was exhausted most of the time, Alan perpetually hungry and sullen at having to share his mother's attention. Eventually the house-painting jobs began to run out and in desperation Beavers sold his brushes in order to keep the Ford rolling.

The rigors of the trip, following three years of panic and struggle, took their toll on Ina. Her once-soft, wavy brown hair, now amateurishly bobbed in a Buster Brown style, hung limply against her neck. Her eyes reflected a sadness, a resignation that would never disappear.

Ina Ladd Beavers would never be young again. Or beautiful. Or happy. Just resigned. Her son saw what had happened to her.

A large potato farm outside Flagstaff, Arizona, needed harvest hands, and Ina was hired to do washing and cooking for the harvesters. Alan drew water and helped his stepfather dig tubers. At age eight he earned his first money and handed it to Ina with pride, promising that when he grew up he would make so much that he could hire people to wash and cook for her. From then on, Alan wouldn't let his stepfather pay his way.

At that age, Alan had every reason to believe that money was the answer to everything. He was to hold on to that belief for a long time to come. When he finally realized how wrong he'd been, it was already very late....

CHAPTER 2

The Beaverses finally arrived at a transient auto camp outside Pasadena, California, the Ford without tires, a kerosene lamp substituting for a headlight. Hundreds of people seeking work lived there, surrounded by their broken-down jalopies.

Beavers got a job almost immediately as a laborer, earning enough for a new set of paint brushes. He would work from twenty-four to forty-eight hours at a stretch and was soon able to move his small brood, first to a camp where the tents had wooden sides and wood stoves, then to a house which they shared with another itinerant family. Eventually he managed to save enough money to pay for a cheap pie-shaped lot, and with Alan's help built a garage on the property that the family lived in.

Alan would often look back on 1922 and 1923, ruefully remembering that "those were the rough days. I used to hike six miles to school. We got potato soup and cheap mutton week after week at home. I still turn green when lamb is served."

Beavers began to look for steady employment and was hired by the old FBO Studios to paint sets. The commuting distance to his home proved too great, so he found a small apartment within minutes from his job, put his land up for sale and moved the family into Hollywood.

Legend—and biographies emanating from Paramount, RKO, Warners, Columbia, Twentieth Century-Fox, Universal, and MGM for twenty-three years—has it that young Alan Ladd's new home was just a short distance from the Paramount-Lasky lot, that at night Alan would climb the fence and wander through the sets dreaming of the magic that went on there by day. It *could* have happened that way; maybe it did. . . .

When Alan was twelve, the years of struggle and malnutrition caught up with him and he became seriously ill with stomach ailments. A local doctor prescribed medicine and a special diet, but what the boy really needed, he pointed out, was "plenty of fresh air and sunshine and a place to run around in," and added that Alan was "a bundle of nerves."

The Beaverses decided on a move to the San Fernando Valley, where they bought a small house for a modest down payment. Though close to Hollywood, the Valley was a totally different world. It was one huge, sunny orchard. There were no streetlights, the roads were dirt tracks, and the town nearest the house was Lankershim, several miles away.

Physically, Alan showed some improvement from the move but his emotional problems still haunted him. At home, his dependency on Ina increased. At school, he was hostile and defensive.

The trip west had caused him to fall several grades behind his contemporaries. He was the oldest boy in his class, but at four-feet-nine he was still the smallest. Alan hated his classmates' nickname for him—"Tiny"—and reacted according-ly . . . "I guess I was a brat," he said later. "I had a lousy temper and the first day some kid pushed my head into the fountain. I started to punch him and found out he was twins, but I licked them both."

Because of the family's financial difficulties, Ina took precautions not to become pregnant again. Her husband apparently went along with her wishes. He had no desire to add another mouth to feed.

Not having to share his mother with siblings, Alan had neither the need nor the desire to seek friends, and the mutual dependency of mother and son for companionship continued to develop.

Although her own life had turned out a disappointment, Ina wanted Alan to be hopeful about his. "Son," she'd tell him, "in this state there are places to go. Never be satisfied with your position. Always look upward. Always improve yourself. Never forget ambition." ...

Movies were now making the transition to sound. Beavers would often talk of the frenzy at the studios to build "sound" stages to accommodate the demand for "talking pictures." This was fine with him; he didn't have an idle moment. He talked, too, of the panic that had gripped many of the actors. Those with poor voices were being put on the junk heap. Anyone with a good speaking voice, from age eight to eighty, was being snapped up like low-priced bank stocks.

Alan began to think seriously about earning some money as an actor. His voice had gone through the usual adolescent change, and his speaking voice and singing voice were superior. But he didn't have a way to bring himself to the attention of the casting directors. Jim Beavers had no pull and was not aggressive enough to approach those who did. Besides, he thought Alan's desire to act a teenage whim. So Alan dropped the notion—for a while....

When he was fourteen, Alan went to work for the Piggly Wiggly market chain, washing tomatoes, potatoes, and carrots, carting boxes and crates until dark—exhausting work which nonetheless built up his muscles and endurance.

Years afterward he said in an interview that appeared in *Modern Screen* magazine: "The only time I ever stole anything in my life was when I was working for Piggly Wiggly. I had never tasted an avocado and I couldn't understand why they should cost as much as seven cents *each*. So I stole one and took it in the back room and ate it. I still couldn't understand why they were so expensive." At the time he developed a mad crush on a local girl named Liz Swink. Between his job and dates with Liz, his school marks wavered around the failure point. ("I was a dummy in school," he later said.)

Alan enrolled at North Hollywood High School on February 18, 1930, five months after his sixteenth birthday. Although still

the smallest and youngest-looking of the freshmen, he
nevertheless moved his birthday ahead a year to 1914 on the
school records to avoid possible ridicule about his age. His
passion for Liz was tamped by his lack of money, and possibly
because he needed an outlet for his emotional frustration he
joined the school's track team. At the beginning, track and
shot-putting claimed his interest. He did the hundred-yard dash
in 9.8 seconds, the two hundred in 20.2. He scored a
considerable fifty-six feet for the twelve-pound shot put.

He also soon became interested in swimming and spent three
to four hours a day practicing strokes and dives. There was
nothing small about Alan Ladd when he took to the water.

And suddenly, he was a celebrity at North Hollywood High.

His accomplishments didn't escape the attention of the local
press. When he received his first notice in Len King's column
"Sportlight," he secured a dozen copies of the paper and started
what was to be his first scrapbook. The item was brief but left
little doubt that Alan was, indeed, someone worth watching:
"Alan Ladd, North Hollywood High School boy, is one of the
high point men of the Los Angeles Municipal pools. . . . Medals
and ribbons have been received by Ladd for winning and placing
in the following events: All City Swim, Interpool meets;
swimming and diving for North Hollywood High School which
netted him three places in diving. Swimming for H.A.C.
(Hollywood Athletic Club) against U.C.L.A. he took fourth for
diving, established a new record for the 50-yard at the
interscholastic meet. This is but a partial record of Ladd, who
hopes to make the American Olympic swim team."

Preparing himself to be eligible for the 1932 Olympics was
the uppermost thought in Alan's mind. The Great Depression
was engulfing the country when he celebrated his eighteenth
birthday, and he wanted to drop out of school to find a job. Jim
Beavers had trouble getting work at the studios, which were now
on an economy kick. "In those days you could have shaken the
Valley and not found fifteen cents," Ladd recalled. "But Ma
always found a way to keep going." Ina refused to hear of Alan's
leaving school.

Alan, however, was never to participate in the 1932 or any
subsequent Olympic competition. In his first magazine interview published in *Screenland* in August 1942, he told writer S.R.

Mook: "I lost my nerve. I hit my head once and knocked myself cold. From then on I found that every time I went to make a dive I was worrying more about whether I would hit my head again than I was about my form. A real diver never thinks of anything but form once he starts toward the board. When I couldn't concentrate on that anymore, I knew I'd never be any good again—so I quit."

The dream of becoming an Olympic champion died but the drive to be somebody remained and was channeled back into acting. During Alan's senior year at North Hollywood High, Isabel Gray, an English teacher, persuaded him to take part in the school's drama activities.

Recalling young Alan, Miss Gray said to a *Movieland* magazine reporter, "Alan always was willing to work hard. In school he'd often run through one scene as many as twenty times. Any teacher will tell you that rarely does she find a student who is willing to give so much effort. And his willingness inspired the rest of the cast."

He gained experience in a half-dozen trivial school offerings, proving himself a good enough actor and singer to be chosen for the role of Ko-Ko in Gilbert and Sullivan's *The Mikado*. Since the Japanese were then stereotyped as small people, his delicate physique gave him a built-in advantage for his characterization. Still, wanting to make something of his reputation as a star athlete, Alan planned to make his entrance swinging from the rafters. On opening night in May 1933 the rope broke and he landed on the stage head first, only to be applauded by the audience, which thought the "accident" was written into the script.

This was still another freak accident—not unlike the diving mishap. Alan, of course, couldn't know then that a life pattern was being established. . . .

A critic from a small local paper, *The Valley Times,* saw the play on closing night and wrote, "Ladd's interpretation of Ko-Ko . . . was acclaimed by critics as one that would have done much credit to a professional."

Universal Studios, located near North Hollywood High on Lankershim Boulevard, began putting together a stock company of young actors and actresses. Saved from bankruptcy in the early 1930s by the success of the *Dracula* and

Frankenstein epics but still unable to meet the salary demands of established players, the studio was hoping to develop its own stable of low-priced stars. (When they used this strategy again while under similar financial stress in the early 1950s, they discovered Rock Hudson, Tony Curtis, and Piper Laurie, among others.)

A few years earlier, "Uncle Carl" Laemmle, Universal's president and benign dictator, had listened to the advice of his eastern talent scout and signed a young Broadway actress to a movie contract for $300 a week. Considering Bette Davis a total disaster ("Her sex appeal simply ain't"), Laemmle decided to forego Broadway as a source and concentrate on local talent that could be seen before being signed.

Alan wasted no time applying to the Universal school—and got less than an overwhelming reception. He was considered too blond and too short, but Laemmle okayed him for a "provisional trial contract" that would enable him to train at the studio's new acting school and if he continued to show promise he'd be given a chance in front of the cameras.

Alan was ecstatic, Money was still a problem, but since his afternoons would be free—he had acting classes in the morning and scene development at night—he took on lifeguard duties at the North Hollywood public pool. It was an exhausting routine, but Alan entered into it with the same perseverance and enthusiasm he had given to his swimming.

It was while he was at the Universal school, during the summer of 1933, that he first met Kirtley Baskett, a writer-reporter for *Modern Screen* magazine who became an intimate friend a decade later. "I remember that meeting," Baskett says. "He wasn't even twenty-one then. The ambitious young Barrymores all wore blue linen coats and gray pants. Alan looked like a high school kid in his. He was only five feet four then and that's what finally eased him out of that start. 'You're too short,' they told him. 'Come back when you grow up.'"

Alan lasted four months. When the final votes came in from a panel of studio producers and directors who had seen the young hopefuls work, he was out. The fact that most of his fellow students felt the same ax was small consolation. The only lift to his sagging morale came when John Leroy Johnston, studio publicity chief at the time, told him, "You got what it takes, Ladd. You'll have your chance, remember that. Never quit trying."

Quitting was the last thing he had in mind, but he had to be realistic. In 1934, the Great Depression continued to paralyze the country and job-hunting was still a struggle.

Only the gods and goddesses of Hollywood seemed immune to the hardships that had brought an entire nation to its knees. Despite their economic problems, or probably because of them, Americans rushed to buy movie magazines filled with stories about Greta Garbo's mansion, Jean Harlow's new wardrobe, Norma Shearer's and Joan Crawford's priceless jewel collections. They read about parties which cost as much as it would take to feed a family of four for a year, and premieres of movies at which it seemed all the wealth in Southern California was put on full display.

On February 1, 1934, Alan graduated from North Hollywood High. He was twenty but looked sixteen—except for his eyes. They showed the hard-steel determination of a man who wouldn't be put down.

After working a time as circulation and advertising manager for a local newspaper, Alan somehow managed to borrow $150 to open a small hamburger and malt shop across from the local swimming pool. He was always vague about how he acquired the money. Whatever, the kids at North Hollywood High knew it was being run by the school's former star athlete, who named it "Tiny's Patio." (As though he were beating the wiseacres to the punch.)

The Patio served a dual function for Alan: he was his own boss and he was able to keep an eye on his mother, who worked with him in the shop, helping to cook fifteen-cent hamburgers.

Now in middle age, Ina was growing increasingly morose and becoming dependent on liquor. The Patio at least gave her a chance to be with her son and other optimistic youngsters, and keep her away from the bottle. For a while. And Jim Beavers, his health failing, offered little opposition. The fumes of cheap paint, the years of worry and struggle, the regrets over his wasted life all combined to wreck both his body and spirit.

Tiny's Patio provided welcome relief from this atmosphere of family gloom, but the prospect of spending the rest of his life

over a grill or behind a counter was hardly an attractive one to
Alan. He had gotten a heady taste of being a celebrity during his
days as an Olympic contender. He fantasized that a scout from
Warner Brothers, located in nearby Burbank, would come into
the Patio, offer him a screen test and he'd be on his way. James
Cagney, Edward G. Robinson, and Paul Muni were "short"
men, and they had made it. . . .

By the end of the year Tiny's Patio had become a losing
proposition. Alan was forced to look elsewhere for work and he
turned toward the studios—but not at all in the way he had
daydreamed. Warner Brothers was short of grips and was hiring
men at $42.50 a week. Alan convinced the union he was
qualified, but after eight months he quit his job for one
overriding reason: he still wanted to be an actor and his
ambition intensified each time he watched the stars courted as
though they were royalty. He'd hoped that an imaginative
producer or director at Warners would bring him down from the
"catwalks" and put him in front of the cameras, but since no one
ever looked up he decided to try it another way—*any* other way
he could dream up.

With an almost childlike naïveté he applied for admission to the Ben Bard School of Acting. After hearing him
read, Bard—a former vaudevillian and stock film actor—
assured him he had what it took to qualify for enrollment.
Actually, all it took was the tuition fee. A friend of Ina Beaver,
learning of Alan's desperation, agreed to advance the money.

None of this sat too well with the parents of the girl he was
planning to marry—Marjorie Jane (Midge) Harrold.

Alan had been dazzled by beautiful seventeen-year-old
Midge months before they were introduced.

In the spring of 1933 when he was a senior in high school he
had taken a job as an usher at the El Portal Theater on
Lankershim Boulevard to see free movies and earn some pocket
money. He would stare at Midge whenever she came to the
theater, never thinking he'd have the chance to meet her.

Barbara, the baby of the Harrold family and the sassy one,
recalls, "Both my sisters were very popular in the local society of
North Hollywood. They were big fish in a small puddle, but at
the time it was considered a big deal to be part of the Harrold

crowd. Marjorie Jane was nicknamed Midge as a child because she'd always been tiny and never got beyond five-one as an adult. Her health was rather delicate, she had asthma as a child and hay fever later on. For this reason Dad had her attend private school up to the first year of college. She was blond with very dark brown eyes and olive skin, which tanned beautifully. Cheryl, David's wife, bears a very strong resemblance to Midge as a young girl. When Cheryl first joined *Charlie's Angels*—before all the publicity she's now getting—old friends of ours in the Valley all thought she might have been Alan's daughter by Midge. It's funny how the Ladd men seem to prefer the same type of woman... Midge was introverted but extremely intelligent and quick-witted. She was a perfectionist, and everything she undertook she could do well. She loved to cook and was one of the best, had excellent taste in clothes, though she was not a clothes-horse. Midge was also very loyal to her friends and family. She was much loved and she in turn loved people."

The elder Harrolds brought their children up carefully but with love. The father, Robert, was born in Bloomington, Indiana, and as a practicing attorney came to Los Angeles early in 1912. Soon after his arrival he met a pretty Texas girl named Olivia Wilson, and they were married in January 1913. They had four children: Kathryn (called Kay), Marjorie Jane, Robert, and Barbara.

Kay was active in the drama club at North Hollywood High. One afternoon, shortly after Alan's triumph in *The Mikado*, she invited him back to her house along with some other friends... "I remember that afternoon as though it was yesterday," says Barbara. "The family had seen Alan as Ko-Ko—he was really wonderful—and we all wanted to meet him. Especially me. I was only ten at the time but I was snoopy. Whenever Kay brought friends home from school I managed to stay in the thick of things. It was fun time—Cokes and music and dancing—all of the things teenagers found pleasure in back in 1933. We were better off than most of the families in the Valley. Dad, now an insurance executive, was extremely successful even in those days. But the Depression was a great equalizer, and none of my sisters' crowd gave much thought to who had what and who hadn't..."

Alan was delighted by the invitation to the Harrold house. He had never been able to get Midge out of his mind, and this, of course, was the perfect opportunity to meet her. He turned on his charm, and after that first afternoon neither Alan nor Midge wanted to see anyone else.

"Alan was truly something else in those days," Barbara says. "He had a beautiful face. All the girls in school were daffy about him and he surely liked them. But after he broke up with Liz Swink he played the field until he met my sister. We loved having him at the house. In a group of people Alan was the life of the party—a good dancer and very outgoing. He was like an athlete, just filled with energy and fun. He was very very funny, he could have you in stitches sometimes. We'd have barbecues and play silly games like hide-in-the-dark...I remember Alan always being terribly attached to his mother, Ina Beavers, at the time. Sometimes she'd call the house and for some reason or other demand that he return home. And no matter *what* he was doing, he'd just take off. Ina was like both a father and mother to him, and even though Alan may have liked Beavers, his devotion was obviously to his mother.

"And Alan loved kids. He never treated me like a pesky kid-sister type. He was always very kind to me. I remember many times when I was sick and he'd come to my room and spend hours reading to me. I'd just love it. He had a beautiful voice, even then, and he used to read to me all the time.

"Alan had one aim in life, to be an actor, and none of us doubted that he would succeed. I think he felt he would make it as quickly as he had made his high school accomplishments, but Hollywood was a new ball game...."

When Alan was trying to make a success of Tiny's Pafio, Midge would come by and take Barbara along for company.

"By then," recalls Barbara, "the two were madly in love. The whole family loved him, but my parents, especially my father, took a dim view of his marrying Midge. My father would have preferred him in a nine-to-five job—not the movies."

For years Robert Harrold discouraged Midge's talk of marrying Alan Ladd until the young man "made something of his life."

"Midge's belief in him, though, never wavered," Barbara says. "When he appeared in his first play at the [Bard] school she was in the audience, of course, and delighted in sending him his first telegram. It read: A SUCCESSION OF SUCCESSFUL SUCCESSES."

The Beaverses had now decided to leave the Valley and they bought a small house at 969 South Serrano Avenue—a short distance from both the Ben Bard School and Paramount Studios in the heart of Hollywood. In those pre-freeway days it was a long trip to North Hollywood.

Nonetheless Alan and Midge still found ways to see each other. By now both were willing to defy Robert Harrold's opposition to their marriage though they were hesitant about facing it, so they decided to elope immediately after Midge's twenty-first birthday party, coming up on October 25, 1936, and then keep the marriage a secret from the family until Alan started making a steady living.

Then Jim Beavers suddenly died of a heart attack, but neither Midge nor Alan Ladd wanted to change their plans... "Midge told me much later that they felt if they did, they'd never get married," Barbara says.

One afternoon, in late October 1936, Alan Ladd and Midge Harrold were married. That night, Midge returned to her parents' house alone.

A few months later the Harrolds moved into a new house on Cahuenga Boulevard, and Alan left Serrano Avenue to share an old house with an old school friend named Bill McCann, a small and unpretentious place on Fair Avenue. It was close to Midge's house, and Bill was gone often enough for the newlyweds to spend some time together—away from Robert Harrold's overprotective presence.

Alan soon managed to talk his way into some acting work at KFWB, a small radio station in Hollywood, but he still did not feel certain enough about the future to confront Midge's father and say, "Look, I'm married to your daughter and am in a position to make a good life for her."

In April Midge's doctor confirmed that she was pregnant. Alan's excitement at the news he was going to be a father was considerably tempered by his frustration at his inability to meet his financial responsibilities and his panic at facing the Harrolds with the news... "I can't keep it from them much longer," Midge told her husband. "They'll have to know. I'm sure my father will understand."

But Robert Harrold couldn't understand why Midge had deceived him. Although he at least didn't invoke the old vaudeville routine of "never-darken-my-door-again," he let it be known that he wouldn't accept Alan as even a house guest, nor did he ever want to see him until he got a responsible job. So Midge left her parents' comfortable home and moved into the shabby quarters Alan shared with McCann.

Ina Beavers accepted the news of Alan's marriage and impending fatherhood with apparent indifference. She had found a new man and had some secret plans of her own. With the $2,000 insurance money she had received on Beavers' death, she took off to join her friend in San Francisco.

Alan and Midge Ladd, concerned with their own problems, struggled through the next six months. From his meager earnings Alan, determined that his first child would not be born in a charity ward, and too proud to go to Midge's father for assistance, tried to put enough aside to meet the forthcoming medical and hospital bills.

Early on October 22, 1937, he drove Midge to Hollywood Hospital. At 11:50 P.M. Alan Ladd, Jr.—if not the "once and future king" at least the future president of Twentieth-Century-Fox—was born.

Pooling their money for the first month's rent, the Ladds' friends went apartment hunting while Midge was in the hospital and found a pleasant little place at 11271 North Morrison Avenue. They then solicited secondhand household goods from other friends. The Harrolds bought a layette for the baby and other needed furnishings. No longer angry about his daughter's elopement, Robert Harrold was concerned only with her happiness. And she *was* happy.

By the time Midge was well enough to come home the apartment—the Ladds' first real home as man and wife—was habitable.

"It's the three of us now," Alan told Midge. "The first time we've really been alone together."

A few weeks later Ina, distraught and disheveled, returned from San Francisco. Her insurance money was gone and so, it seemed, was her lover. There was nothing for it except to have her move in with her son's family. (Five years later Alan told

Kirtley Baskett that Ina had offered him her insurance money to
keep him at Bard's and then "soon Mom left to visit friends.")

Alan's "official" life story by Kirtley Baskett in *Modern
Screen* magazine would read:

> Then, just as he stacked up a failure—when his fortunes
> were the lowest—right then his mother died. Of all people
> who had faith in Alan it was his mother. She was the one
> who never admitted defeat—who always held her head up
> high and instilled in Alan the faith that he would someday
> be somebody. And she went to her grave when he was a
> nobody, worse than a nobody. Alan thinks maybe she
> understood though, maybe she knew what he was trying
> for, what he was up against even when no one else did.
> Maybe he thinks that faith was part of what made him go
> on, when his last friend was gone. Because he had few
> others now....

Until 1978, when Barbara Harrold Grether related the story,
only Alan and Midge Ladd and the Harrold family would know
the details of Ina's death—not even the Ladd children would
ever hear them.

CHAPTER 3

On Thanksgiving Day in 1937, Ina Beavers marked her forty-ninth birthday with persistent complaining.

"What do I have to be thankful for?" she said to her son. "My life is over. What man is going to want a woman of my age? Nobody is going to marry a grandmother."

Since her return from San Francisco Ina had been paranoid about her age, her appearance and the burden of being a grandmother.

Needing a scapegoat, she took her frustrations out on her son and his young wife. "You never knew what it was like to starve," she'd carry on. "You never had to go without."

In the late stages of menopause, looking older than her years, Ina was unable to cope with her loneliness. She was now an incurable alcoholic, spending every penny she could lay her hand on for beer or cheap wine.

"I took care of you," she'd yell abusively at Alan. "I could have put you in an orphanage. Now you're just going to have to take care of me!"

Alan wanted to. He had hoped that having a grandson would take Ina's mind off her troubles. It didn't . . .

A few days after Thanksgiving—on November 29—Ina was

sullen throughout dinner, whining, as usual, about her meaningless life, about how everyone would be better off if she were dead.

Marjorie was washing the dishes when Ina demanded of Alan: "Give me some money. There's something I want to buy at the store."

Alan hesitated, certain that Ina wanted money to get a small bottle of cheap wine. "Don't you think you've had enough?" he asked quietly.

"I'm not going to the liquor store," Ina insisted. "There's something else I need. Something personal. Will you give me the quarter or won't you?" Her voice was at a hysterical pitch now, waking the baby, who had been asleep in the next room. "Laddie," as they later called the child, began crying.

Resignedly Alan reached into his pants pocket, found a quarter and handed it to his mother. "Buy what you want," he said angrily. Anything to quiet her down.

Clutching the quarter tightly in her hand, Ina went to a late-night grocery store where she made her purchase. Then she hurried back to the house on Morrison Avenue.

She didn't, though, return to her son's apartment. She headed instead to his old car parked in front of the building. She sat in the back seat, opened a small can, and gulped down the contents.

Screaming hysterically, in pain, she staggered out of the car and, vomiting uncontrollably, managed to make it to the front steps.

Alan and Midge heard Ina's screams and managed to get her back into the apartment, where she continued to vomit all over the living room.

Alan begged his mother to tell him what had happened, but by now her eyes were glazed and no words came out of her mouth. Midge ran to get help from her father, who phoned for an ambulance. When Midge and Robert Harrold returned, Ina was catatonic. By the time Ina was brought to the Georgia Street Hospital, it was too late to save her.

Stunned by the suddenness and the mystery of Ina's death, Alan agreed to an autopsy. The three Ladds spent the night at the Harrold house, and on Tuesday morning Alan walked back to the apartment for a change of clothes. The back door of his car was still open. It was then that he noticed the small metal can resting on the floor.

The autopsy, performed by Dr. S. T. Wagner of the Los Angeles County Coroner's office, confirmed what Alan had found: "Arsenic poisoning by ingesting ant paste"—one of the most horrible and agonizing methods of suicide.

Robert Harrold took care of the funeral arrangements. Alan had to rush off for an audition for "Lux Radio Theater," which the producers had refused to postpone. He had told Midge a few days earlier, "I think I'm going to get the role. I'm going to make it, Midge—and then it will all be worth it . . . Nothing is going to stop me. Nothing. I want it too much."

Alan barely managed to get through his audition.

He didn't get the job.

He later told Kirtley Baskett, referring to the audition without mentioning Ina, "Multiply that scene ten thousand times and you'll have some idea of what I went through. Add in being steadily broke, hungry and panicky—and it's only part of the picture."

That, no question, was the way it was.

CHAPTER 4

In mourning throughout the Christmas holidays, Alan was guilt-ridden by the thought that it was he who had given his mother the money to buy the fatal ant paste.

He reproached himself for not taking Ina seriously the times she had threatened suicide. Nothing either Midge or her family could say would change his conviction that he might have prevented the tragedy if he'd been more understanding of his mother's problems.

He also reproached himself for having run off and eloped so soon after Jim Beavers' death and for being too preoccupied with his own life and career to be aware of the extent of Ina's disintegration. But typically, he hid his feelings about his mother's suicide and would not discuss them even with Midge. Midge, too, kept her emotions to herself, but she had a physical reaction to Ina's death: her milk dried up, and she could no longer breast-feed Laddie.

Alan was now almost desperately anxious to return to work. From the movie people he still got the usual bromides—"too short," "too blond," "not the right type." Because there were no such limitations in radio, he set out on a private self-improvement program to progress from undemanding local

27

shows—even they were hard to come by—to the more lucrative network dramas.

His speaking voice was good, he needed no further assurance about that after hearing his playbacks. And he had a range and command of dialects that made him salable. But he wanted to be more—in a class with the likes of Orson Welles, H. V. Kaltenborn, Gabriel Heatter and the other eastern broadcasters who were making names for themselves on the airwaves. As a start, he at least had to eliminate the flaws he knew existed . . . "I used to notice," he said in his first interview (with S. R. Mook), "when I was on the air a lot my throat and vocal chords got tired. It didn't seem to me it should be that way. So I started experimenting. I didn't know much about the technical end of voice culture, but I began imagining the roof of my mouth as a sort of sounding board. I thought, if instead of trying to force words and sounds out through my mouth, I could just make them hit that sounding board, they would bounce out. It worked. So then I began watching the clock to see how long I could read without tiring myself. It was good for my diction and gave me nuances of intonation—because if you don't vary your tones even you can get pretty tired of your own voice."

Many evenings after Laddie had been put to bed Alan would read passages from the Bible or the local paper to Midge, who would listen to the improvement in his voice. "Alan's goals were Midge's goals," sister Barbara recalls, "and all efforts were bent in one direction. Midge had never known want until those struggling years with Alan, but she made do with what little money he brought in. And I never heard her complain. Nor did she want to accept help from our parents, who certainly were able to afford it. There was, however, a period not long after Ina Beavers' death when things got very rough and they couldn't make the rent on Morrison Avenue. At that time they moved in with our family for a while—but just until Alan started working regularly again. Midge never doubted for a minute that Alan would make it. None of us did. But he was terribly ambitious and was disappointed that it was taking so long to happen. Still, at twenty-four, he had his whole life ahead of him. There was no reason to panic."

There *was* no real reason, but nevertheless Alan was panic-stricken. Convinced that failure and deprivation had caused both Jim Beavers' death at fifty-two and Ina's addiction to liquor and subsequent suicide, he now had an almost demonic drive to get ahead. *His* son, he promised himself, wouldn't be selling papers or cleaning up candy stores. (And he was right.) *His* wife wouldn't become a worn-out shell before she turned forty. Living with the Harrolds, even for a brief period of time, was a blow to his macho-image, although the Harrolds neither said nor did anything to undermine him.

Alan had just about reached his breaking point when the calls began coming in again. Gradually he began to gain a reputation on Radio Row as a competent actor with an extraordinary voice. He got leads in lesser programs and supporting roles on network favorites like "Hollywood Hotel," the "Texaco Star Theater" and "Lux Radio Theater."

In mid-1938 he and Midge moved to a guest house hidden behind a plumbing store off Ventura Boulevard in North Hollywood. It had a small yard, where a child could crawl safely. Things were looking up for the Ladds.

And then, one afternoon before leaving the station where he had just completed a radio drama, Alan was summoned to the phone. The call was from the co-owner of the new Sue Carol–Bruce Shedd Agency. Sue Carol had liked what she had heard that afternoon, she told him, and if he was available for representation, she'd like very much to speak to him in person. She was so persuasive that Alan impulsively made an appointment to drop by on the way home.

Driving on Sunset Boulevard, he began to regret the decision, and as he entered the Norma Talmadge building in which the office was located, he thought of polite ways to excuse himself... "That's all I need," Ladd later recalled saying wryly to himself. "An ex-movie starlet, playing agent, to manage my career."

Actually, that *was* all he needed.

Part Two

1939-1943

He came into my office wearing a long white trench coat. His blond hair was bleached by the sun. He looked like a young Greek god, and he was unforgettable.

—SUE CAROL LADD

CHAPTER 5

...Every star above
Knows the one I love
Sweet Sue, Just You.
No one else it seems
Ever shares my dreams
And without you, dear,
I don't know what I'll do...

"Sweet Sue—Just You"
    —written for Sue Carol in 1928
  by Will J. Harris and Victor Young

Evelyn Lederer was a nice Jewish girl from Chicago.

Born on October 30, 1903, adorable, dark-haired Evelyn grew up pampered and protected, her every wish granted.

A Jewish Princess, she'd be called today.... It was not an accident that four-year-old Evelyn was posed sitting on a paper moon surrounded by stars when she was taken to a local photographer's studio.

From childhood Evelyn showed, as they say, an aptitude for dancing, and at dancing school didn't lack for little boy partners. She was cheerful, pudgy, and vivacious.

The Lederers were not affected by the economic pinch of the early 1920s but were in a good position to benefit by the upsurge in the economy that followed. They sent Evelyn to the best schools, of course, and took for granted that her future would follow the same preordained course as other well-brought-up young girls of the time: a trip to Paris, a well-to-do husband, a comfortable home and several children.

If Evelyn had any secret ambition to break out of that mold she showed precious little of it.

In 1925 she married a handsome young man from Chicago named Allan H. Keefer. Within a year, however, she left him. In 1927 she left with her mother, for what she expected would be a brief vacation in Los Angeles.

The last thing in her mind, she always insisted, was the thought of becoming a movie actress. A chance meeting with a young actor named Nick Stuart changed all that. Nick introduced her to a casting director at the old Fox Studios who saw in Evelyn a possible competitor for the "It" girl, Clara Bow, the darling with the cupid-bow mouth that had driven strong men wild in the cinemas across the nation.

With the pert new name of Sue Carol, she was before the cameras a few weeks later—as one of the slaves in *Slaves of Beauty*. She found the work fun and, most important of all, she and Nick had fallen in love. No reason at all now for her to return to Chicago.

Slaves of Beauty, in which she received next-to-last billing on the credits, was released in June 1927. After that Sue went from one picture to another, her billing improving until she either starred or co-starred, her salary increasing with each role. In 1928, she made seven films.

Her reviews as an actress were mixed. About the early "B" programmers the *New York Times* kept dismissing her work with the same four words: "Sue Carol is pretty."

In his review of the silent film *Girls Gone Wild* (in which Sue was teamed with Nick), the *Times* critic generously upped his praise a notch, noting that "Sue Carol is attractive, vivacious and capable." But for the subsequent *Why Leave Home?* (in which Sue also acted opposite Nick), the best he could manage was, "She sings the theme songs winningly."

Sue, however, seemed to suffer when she appeared with a

stronger leading man. As William Boyd's co-star in *Skyscraper*, she was totally ignored. After commenting on Boyd and Alan Hale, the *Times* critic said, "The less said about the rest of the cast the better." When she shared billing with Grant Withers, then the husband of actress Loretta Young, in something called *Dancing Sweeties* in August 1930, Sue was dismissed in the *Times* as the dance partner who "lisps her way ineffectually through her scenes."

This was the last Sue Carol movie the *Times* was to review. In 1930 Sue and Nick Stuart were married.

Reminiscing about her acting days with author Walter Wagner, in *You Must Remember This*, Sue commented, "I never made much of my career—it wasn't important to me. My stardom ended when I was supposed to do a picture on loan-out to Warner Brothers. It was called *Nikki and Her Birds*. They brought this director from Germany, William Dieterle. We were practicing some dance sequences on the set when he walked in with white gloves and a cane. He kept knocking the cane on the floor saying 'Faster, faster. Tempo, tempo, tempo.' It scared me so much that I went home in tears and never came back."

(This 1931 film was retitled *The Last Flight* and starred Richard Barthelmess, Johnny Mack Brown, and Elliot Nugent in the male leads. The sole female lead, Nikki, won rave notices for Helen Chandler, a fragile blue-eyed blond.)

With her fling in the movies over and no longer so concerned about watching her figure, Sue began to think about having a family. Her best friend Dixie Lee, a starlet with whom she had worked in Fox Movietone's *Follies of 1929* and *Why Leave Home?*, had become the bride of a young singer named Bing Crosby. Like Sue, she too had decided to forego her career for family. The two women were together constantly, planning and dreaming about the future. Neither apparently missed working, having time now to enjoy the glamorous social life of Beverly Hills.

Sue became pregnant first, and on July 18, 1932 her daughter Carol Lee was born. The name was a combination of her and Dixie's movie surnames.

Shortly after the child's birth, though, Sue's marriage began to disintegrate. By May 1933 she and Nick had officially separated. Still, Sue did not want to return to Chicago. Men found her enchanting. Her social life was thriving, and now that Dixie Crosby had given birth to her first son Gary and was pregnant again, the two women were closer than ever—Sue was a frequent guest at the Crosby home. And little Carol Lee—too young to be affected by Sue's separation from her father Nick Stuart, who visited often—was a healthy, cheerful child.

Although the gossip columns speculated about a possible reconciliation between Sue and Nick, they were divorced on August 24, 1934—with Sue telling a sympathetic judge that Nick had thrown a crossword puzzle book at her.

On November 20, 1936, Sue tried marriage again—for the third time. Her choice, however, was not a Hollywood glamour boy or film executive, as many had predicted, but a writer named Howard Wilson, whose only claim to fame was a book titled *Hollywood Doctor*—considered quite scandalous at the time.

In 1937 Sue made one final attempt to return to films—in still another forgettable "B" called *Doctor's Diary*. At that point a friend suggested she try the agency business. "It was a natural, easy, obvious thing to do," Sue says. "I knew everybody in the industry. I had helped several people get jobs when I was still an actress and I enjoyed doing that. However, I didn't want to use my friendship with Bing Crosby or other big stars to get them as clients, so I decided to sign impressive young people and build a stable of promising young players. I went into business with a partner named Bruce Shedd in late 1938." A year later Shedd had left the scene; the agency was now called "Sue Carol and Associates."

There have been many versions of what happened next. In the most recent one—probably closest to the truth—Sue recalled: "Someone said I should listen to a radio show that had a talented fellow on it who was so versatile that he played two parts—an old man and his grandson. I was intrigued, and tuned in. That was the first time I heard Alan's voice. I thought he was remarkable. I had no idea what he looked like or what his personality was like. I didn't know a thing about him except that he was a good radio actor and I wanted to meet him, so I phoned the station and asked him to drop by the office."

And Alan told it this way: "She thought I'd be sixty years old. We were both glad I wasn't."

Sue's first impression would be indelible: "He was very shy, but he had a wonderful smile. His eyebrows and his eyelashes were pitch-black over level green eyes which were deep and unfathomable—an actor's eyes. He was for me."

No matter how flattered Alan was by Sue Carol's immediate interest and willingness to sign him, he wasn't too sure *she* was for him . . . as an agent, that is. Nor, as he always insisted, did he have the slightest premonition that this meeting would change his private life as well.

For the rest of that day, for the rest of that week, in fact, she couldn't get him out of her mind. "I thought he was great. I never doubted he'd be a star. But," she remembers with a sigh, "it was a struggle."

And a challenge. And perhaps that was what made Alan Ladd so irresistible. Up until then, for Sue Carol, née Evelyn Lederer, most things had come easy.

This one would be the hard way.

CHAPTER 6

"Are you going to sign with her?" Midge asked Alan after he told her about his meeting with Sue Carol.

"I don't know. I don't think so. I told her I'd let her know in a few days. She hasn't been an agent very long. Maybe if I had met her two or three years ago. Now I have you and the boy to think of, and I'm not a kid anymore. It's your future as well as mine that will be affected—whichever way it goes."

Accepting Sue's offer, he knew, would be like starting from scratch again, and that hardly made sense. Not at this point in his life. He had established himself on Radio Row as a capable, dependable actor, and there was the possibility of a contract with the Columbia Broadcasting System in the near future. If that came through he would have a comfortable, steady income, and he'd be working in his chosen profession, in a medium that was blind to his height, hair color or age.

Yet in back of his mind there was always that fantasy of becoming *somebody*, and radio actors were the most anonymous of all performers—unseen and unpublicized. Only name singers or comedians—or a dummy named Charlie McCarthy—got singled out for attention.

After two weeks of soul-searching Alan opted for security.

He would accept the network's offer if he received it and forget about his bigger dreams in movies. He had endured enough rejections, enough humiliations. Why reopen old wounds?

It was in that frame of mind that he finally decided to call Sue Carol, thank her for her interest and forget the whole matter. Instead, he found himself driving up Sunset Boulevard to her office...Later he told Frank Tuttle, the director of the movie that made him famous, "I wanted to tell her personally why I had to reject her offer. Instead, once I saw her again, I heard myself saying 'Where's the contract?' There was something about her—I couldn't get her out of my head. I kept seeing her in my mind's eye, the funny way she had of tipping her head on one side when she was listening. Things like that..."

Sue, recalling those initial meetings in Walter Wagner's *You Must Remember This*, says, "Other than his potential, the thing I sensed most strongly about Alan was that he was so terribly unsure of himself, that his childhood poverty and the unhappy relationship he had with his mother and stepfather had given him the insecurity that would stay with him all his life. I'm no psychiatrist, but it was obvious to me as we talked that day in my office that Alan was searching for something. He felt rejected, and maybe he was looking for an anchor of some kind. Life hadn't dealt him a very good hand, though he didn't complain, and wasn't bitter. Alan always held much of himself back. He was friendly with people, but didn't confide in them easily. I think he also had a premonition that he would die young."...She didn't explain that this premonition may well have had something to do with his father's relatively early death when he was a child, or with Ina Beavers' violent death twenty years later. She *never* referred to the fact that Alan had a young, gentle wife who worshipped him, or a baby son. Publicly, she never acknowledged Midge's existence, although for the first two years of her association with Alan she did everything possible to try to convince Midge that she was her good friend....

Because Sue had a great many contacts at Paramount, including the Crosbys, she immediately proved she could deliver what she had promised. She persuaded Paramount director Frank Lloyd to cast her new find as a seasick voyager in *Rulers of the Sea* for $250 a week. Douglas Fairbanks, Jr., and

Margaret Lockwood were the stars, and Alan's role consisted of two short scenes. In the first, he bunked down in the ship that would carry him to Scotland. In the second, he had a short conversation with his screen wife on quayside, and Fairbanks. By a quirk of scheduling Alan's scenes were the first and last shot, so he was carried on the payroll for sixteen weeks. The money was an unexpected windfall for the young Ladds, and more than that, now Sue had some film to show to casting directors.

Alan's spirits were definitely on the upgrade. Neither Midge nor her family had seen him so buoyant since the days before Ina Beavers' death. When Sue wasn't making the rounds with him, he'd drop by her office for talks about his career. Feeding his ambitions, she would reiterate her conviction that she could make him a star—perhaps one of the biggest in Hollywood. She beguiled him with stories about her famous friends Bing and Dixie Lee, Jack Dempsey and Estelle Taylor, who during her early days in Hollywood often invited Sue for evenings at the swank Mayfair Club. Alan was especially impressionable at this time—starstruck, in fact. Because he still had a family to support he continued accepting radio work whenever a good job was offered, one of which was in a "Silver Theater" production opposite Bette Davis, and when *she* complimented him on a fine performance he rushed out and bought Miss Davis a gift—grateful as much for the source as the substance of the compliment.

As his agent, Sue had many legitimate reasons to call Alan at home frequently, and in the process she grew friendly with Midge. According to her sister Barbara, Midge was grateful to her husband's dynamic agent for taking such an interest in him. (The three-way relationship was itself becoming like a script.)

Sue enjoyed giving parties, and within a short time the Ladds became regular guests at her little house on Cromwell Avenue. (Occasionally Barbara trailed along.)

Sue's husband, Howard (Bill) Wilson, was usually there, as was her young daughter Carol Lee. Sue was always the impeccable hostess, extending herself particularly to make sure Alan's shy, pretty wife was not uncomfortable in a group that included some of Hollywood's better-known personages.

Midge, however, was overwhelmed by this powerful woman.

She had little in common with Sue except their mutual desire to help Alan's career. It never occurred to Midge that Sue's interest in her husband was anything other than professional. (True, so far as one can determine, if a strain on credibility.) Midge's brother, Bob, was not as naive. He recalls: "I kept warning Midge that Sue was after Alan. But Midge was incapable of understanding such duplicity in anyone."

On the strength of Alan's work in *Rulers of the Sea*, Sue got him his second job—a five-day quickie filmed as *Goose Step* but eventually released as *Hitler, Beast of Berlin*. Everything was so rushed that Alan, after appearing as a young anti-Nazi, could be spotted by attentive filmgoers in an entirely different role later in the movie, digging a grave for another Nazi victim.

The role of Joe Bonaparte in *Golden Boy* was the most coveted of that year—to young male actors what Scarlett in *Gone With the Wind* was to women. Rouben Mamoulian's announcement that he wanted to cast an unknown in the part was all Sue had to hear. She succeeded in getting Alan an audition at Columbia and alerted him to come in looking as Italian as possible.

Reluctant to expose his hair to the then-primitive home-coloring kits, Alan sent Midge to a nearby drugstore for several cakes of Meyer's Mascara. As he sat in a kitchen chair with dishtowels protecting his clothing, Midge painstakingly applied the dissolved, homemade hair dye to a few strands at a time. When the treatment was completed Alan Ladd still didn't look terribly Italian, nor was he likely to fool anyone into believing black was his natural hair color. Still, it was the best they could do under the circumstances.

In a guest column for *Daily Variety* in 1950, in praise of agents, Alan related the ensuing *Golden Boy* fiasco: "It was one of the hottest days of the year. While reading the test scene I began to feel a dripping down the back of my neck. I was taking a shower in black ink. Thanks to Mamoulian's tact, he pretended not to notice. Sue and I laugh to this day because, after our frantic efforts to be a true Italian type, another blond actor landed the role—William Holden." (Over the years Midge's partnership in the deed had somehow become Sue's.)

Alan delighted in telling dozens of similar Sue stories: how Sue kept different outfits in the car, found out what the studio wanted and had him make a quick change of clothes to be the type required. One that remained foremost in his memory was about the time a producer named Billy Gordon called from MGM about the lead in *The Mortal Storm*. There was one big problem, as Alan recalled it... "He had to see some film on me immediately. I had only that one picture, *Hitler, the Beast of Berlin*, in which I had a part big enough to impress anyone. It was then my Susie pulled the coup of the year. Have you ever tried to borrow a picture from an exhibitor that he was running for cash customers? Well, she did. While he was running the last half, Susie had the first half under her arm and we were speeding to Metro. But with all that, we arrived fifteen minutes too late and I lost the job. But I still contend it was quite a trick to talk a theater manager into lending a couple of strange kids the only print of his current picture."

There wasn't a stunt Sue wouldn't pull if she thought it would result in a job. Her agent-friends from the old days—like Joe Rivkin and Henry Willson (who later discovered Rock Hudson)—amused at her tenacity, called frequently with tips about what might be "an Alan Ladd-type part."

"I tried for better roles," Alan said, "over and over again, but directors or producers just kept saying I was too young or too old, too slight or too blond. Or else my name lacked prestige for the part. It was always something."

Sue, however, wouldn't admit defeat. At least her protégé was becoming known around the studios, and she also worked out a clever monetary scheme. If the roles were small, she charged $250 a week for Alan's services; if larger, she would ask only $150. "Our idea was to get a lot of film to show producers."

So from 1939 to 1941 Alan Ladd chalked up a long if unimpressive list of "credits." He managed a semi-lead in a Universal serial, *The Green Hornet*, and appeared as a cowboy in a remake of Zane Grey's *Light of the Western Stars*, billed twelfth. In *In Old Missouri* he played the spendthrift son of a local scion, who invited a cabaret troupe to stay at his father's mansion. *Those Were the Days* found him misspelled in twenty-second position as *Alan Laird*. He had an unbilled part in *Wild Cat Bus*. In a Victor Mature whizbang called *Captain Caution*, about prison ships and privateers, he was called on to do little more than drag a ball and chain around a ship's deck.

He was also used ingloriously in *Gangs of Chicago* and *The Howards of Virginia;* actually one of his biggest roles during this period was in an insurance company commercial film in which he aged from eighteen to eighty.

If the major studios were reluctant to cast him in romantic roles, those in "Poverty Row" would. He was Edith Fellowes' beau in *Her First Romance*, a movie worth remembering only because it was directed by Edward Dmytryk, who was to give Alan his chance for a comeback in *The Carpetbaggers*. No matter... Sue's primary concern was to keep Alan working. Although constantly reminded by friends that "bit" players on Poverty Row actors almost never made it to the majors, she refused to give up her plan.

The roles kept coming, and Sue went on accepting them. Her young hopeful had one line—"A package of cigarettes, honey"—in Laurel and Hardy's *Great Guns*, in which he played a soldier who flirted with actress Sheilah Ryan. He was Clark Gable's commanding officer in *They Met in Bombay*, did a sequel to *Meet the Missus* called *Petticoat Politics*, was seen in *The Parson of Panamint* with Charles Ruggles, and was billed along with Basil Rathbone in *The Black Cat*, appearing as a romantic juvenile. Somewhat more exciting was a spot—though billed thirteenth—in the live-action sequences of Walt Disney's *The Reluctant Dragon*. (Unfortunately only the cartoon section was retained in subsequent reissues.) He was also a cadet in *Cadet Girl*—at least half of the title role—and a reporter in *Paper Bullets*.

Working steadily now, he rented a charming little house on DeWitt Drive for himself and his family, and Sue persuaded Midge to allow her to help select furniture she felt would be suitable for Alan—and to help Midge shop for new clothes for herself. Midge dutifully hid her resentment, not wanting to antagonize the woman who was doing so much to help her husband. "She treats me like a child," she complained privately to sister Barbara, "not like Alan's *wife*." (She still seemed to miss the point.)

Alan was even more optimistic about his big chance not being far off—just one good role, just one major film, and he'd make a name for himself, and once he had that, the rest would come easily... But when the bigger roles in better pictures were cast, Alan Ladd continued to be odd man out. Though not for lack of Sue's trying. Her connections were still strongest at Paramount and RKO. She had no problem obtaining auditions or even screen tests, but the important roles still always went to someone else . . . At RKO, Alan was up for a lead in *The Devil and Miss Jones*, but the studio decided on a name—Bob Cummings. They signed Dennis Morgan for *Kitty Foyle* and Regis Toomey for *Meet John Doe*. At Paramount, William Holden again got the part—in *I Wanted Wings*. (The fair-haired, six-foot Holden would continue to have an edge on Ladd for years to come.)

By early 1941 the gag circulating in studio casting offices was that the only role Sue had not submitted Alan Ladd for was the lead in *Charley's Aunt*.

There were some other comments being passed around about the two, but Alan and Sue seemed oblivious. Alan naïvely told reporter S. R. Mook: "People used to ask me what I did when I wasn't working—if I played golf or tennis, if I went out at night and with whom. I'd fallen head over heels in love with Sue by that time. But she was married. If I couldn't go out with her, I didn't want to go out at all. So I used to sit home nights and read. The only chance I had to see her was during the day. I used to chauffeur her around the studios and wait while she called on casting directors. Everyone knew she was promoting me, and if anyone saw me, they thought I was with her on an interview. And I used to coach her other clients when they were going out on tests—kids who had no experience. Anything to be with her."

Actually, of course, they were fooling no one. Even Sue would reluctantly admit that in the first magazine story she issued under her by-line (authored by a professional writer). About her early relationship with Alan, she "wrote" in the December 1942 issue of *Photoplay*:

I was sitting in the office of a prominent casting director talking about Alan's ability.

He listened for a while, then his eyes narrowed with shrewd amusement.

"No woman could be that enthusiastic about a man," he said, "unless she was madly in love with him. You're in love with this Alan Ladd, aren't you, Sue?"

Vehemently I denied it, not only to him but to myself. In love with Alan? The idea was absurd. My only reason for being so interested in Alan was purely a business one. So I told myself.

Even when Alan told me he was in love with me, I felt it was just a temporary passing emotion. "You'll get over it," I promised him.

I didn't think it was love he felt for me. I was sure that he was just so grateful for the help I had given him in his career that he was mistaking gratitude for love. It took many months, even years of knowing Alan before I was sure that this was no passing emotion on either of our parts and that neither of us would get over it.

It's hardly possible to pinpoint the moment in their lives when the professional relationship turned into an affair. But the general feeling of those who knew the two was that Sue was clearly the aggressor. And Barbara, who was always fond of her brother-in-law and still bears him no ill will, says, "You must remember that Alan wasn't doing very well. He was always very ambitious to make it big in films, and she offered him his dream of being a star. My sister Midge was not a fighter. Besides, she was too young, too guileless to cope with a woman of Sue's experience. Sue had money, though not a great fortune. But what she really had was power. She had a way of getting what she wanted and what she wanted was Alan."

So while Midge remained home, trying to quiet her fears that she might be losing her husband and busy rearing an active youngster, Sue was devoting herself to taking care of Midge's husband.

In the summer of 1940 the big excitement at RKO, indeed throughout the motion picture industry, centered around Orson Welles' production of *Citizen Kane*, considered one of the most controversial movies ever made. Although Welles recruited his main cast from his New York-based Mercury Theater regulars, there were enough secondary and bit parts available to have every agent in town seeking auditions for his or her clients.

"*L'enfant terrible,*" as Welles was called, had just turned twenty-five. Alan, a year and half his senior, was intimidated— like everyone else—by the boy genius (today they call them "Baby Moguls") who towered over him during the interview Sue had arranged. Alan never talked about this incident publicly, but Barbara recalls his ordeal. Welles said to him, "Tell me about yourself, Pretty Face. With that pretty face you think you're something of a hot shot, don't you?"

Welles, who had total control of casting and every other phase of the movie, continued in that fashion for a few more minutes. Alan felt the blood rushing to his face, and to keep from telling his tormentor where to shove his movie, he turned and started to walk out of the room.

"Hell, come back! Where do you think you're going?" Welles' Orsonian voice boomed after him. "You've got the part!"

A veteran radio performer and director who had starred in *The Shadow* when he was twenty and scared millions of Americans with his simulated Martian invasion in *War of the Worlds* when he was twenty-three, Welles had been sufficiently impressed with Alan Ladd's radio background to use him. He was, in fact, totally unconcerned with the prettiness of this Ladd's face or the color of his hair, since he planned to cast him as one of the faceless "News on the March" people. According to Pauline Kael in *The Citizen Kane Book* (Atlantic Monthly Press/Little, Brown): "Among the 'News on the March' men, there were some bit players who had potential faces (Alan Ladd was one of them), but they weren't presented as personalities... Welles probably thought it didn't matter how bad these actors were, because they should be colorless anyway; after RKO gave him the go-ahead on the project, he didn't reshoot the test scene he had made of the projection-room sequence."

Lost in the darkness, Alan was identifiable only by his white collar, his porkpie hat, and by his voice. He received no billing in the credits. Though Joseph Cotten, Agnes Moorehead, and Everett Sloane would work steadily for decades, of the huge cast, Alan would be the only one to go on to achieve an enormous popular success....

He was still living with Midge while working in *Citizen Kane*, but being torn between two women was beginning to take its effect. And by now Midge knew she was in a losing battle. Aware of how much Alan's career meant to him, she couldn't demand that he stop seeing Sue, and she was too proud to use their son for leverage. For her, it was a matter of waiting helplessly until he made the decisive move... Looking back on those last days of her sister's marriage, Barbara comments, "His conscience must have troubled him, because he struggled with himself for three months before he walked out on Midge in the spring of 1941." But he did walk out. Midge told him she would put no obstacles in the way of his getting a divorce, nor would she do anything to prevent him from seeing his son as often as he wished. If her family had misgivings about her submissiveness, they said nothing. It wouldn't have mattered if they had. Midge simply would not involve Alan in a messy divorce case that could hurt his chances.

Attempting to explain her sister's remarkable selflessness and lack of vindictiveness, Barbara recalls, "She was very much like the sweet, gentle character Joan Fontaine played in *Rebecca*. She had the kind of love for Alan that meant she wouldn't stand in his way. You might say when it came to how she reacted to Sue, she did it her way. It took courage and class, but being the type of person she was, she could act no differently. Most of us scream our rage outside. Midge screamed inside. She was a very private person." Almost as private as her husband. But in this case, likes obviously did not attract. Alan needed someone more confident and secure than he was himself to supply the "anchor" Sue said he was forever searching for—and the push Sue alone could provide.

Midge even failed to protest when, according to Barbara, Sue hired the lawyer to represent Midge. In July 1941 the case came up on the calendar, and Midge was quietly given the divorce she never wanted but refused to contest. The judge granted her custody of Alan, Jr. ("Laddie"), three and a half then, but allowed Alan visitation rights. "However," remembers Barbara, "aside from twenty-five dollars a week child support for the boy, Midge got practically nothing—one hundred dollars a month. Well, Alan didn't have much at the time."

Alan was, however, on the brink of a career breakthrough.

A few weeks before receiving his interlocutory divorce decree, free from guilt for the time being and deeply in love with Sue, he had sailed through still another test at RKO. With no hesitation or excuses Robert Stevenson, who had just completed directing Margaret Sullavan and Charles Boyer in *Back Street*, had cast him as Baby, a fugitive British flier, in the Michèle Morgan wartime adventure-romance, *Joan of Paris*. Ladd was given billing, and because there had been some early indecision as to whether the character was to be Scots, Welsh, or Lancastrian, he had begun working on dialects as diligently as he had on his voice range a few years earlier.

Sue had gotten his salary up to $750 weekly for freelance parts, and Baby was a young actor's dream role. His final moment was a scene in which he died heroically in a Paris sewer as Thomas Mitchell recited the Lord's Prayer. There wasn't, as they say, a dry eye on the set when it was completed, and studio executives started thinking of a contract. A few months earlier they could have gotten Alan Ladd without lifting a finger, or more importantly, spending a hard dollar.

There was, however, something considerably more exciting cooking across the square at Paramount. Sue would repeat the story many times: "Bill Meikeljohn called to tell me that Frank Tuttle was looking for an unknown to play Raven in *This Gun for Hire*. Alan and I went over to see Frank, who said that Alan looked like someone who would say 'Tennis, anyone?' 'He'd be perfect for a part like that,' Frank told us, 'but this script needs an actor who can play a cold-blooded killer and still come off sympathetically.' Luckily I'd brought along some mood stills of Alan—you know, with him looking sinister, smoking a cigarette with smoke curling out of his nose. They were quite effective. Alan photographed beautifully. Frank Tuttle studied the stills for a few minutes. Then he looked up at us and didn't say anything for what seemed like ages. Finally he said, 'Let me test him.'"

Robert Preston, who had earlier been considered for Raven but had been rejected as too tall, had known Alan casually for a couple of years. "I guess he was between wives at the time," Preston says now. "But I don't recall his mentioning ever having been married. I worked with him on his screen test. This was when we didn't know we'd both be in the same movie. But he was obviously going to have the role—even without the test. He was an awfully good actor. People never realized just how good he was. I just ran over the lines with him. I didn't do the actual test. So it came as a pleasant surprise when I was cast in the romantic lead in *Gun for Hire*."

Possibly because of the confidence he felt after rehearsing the lines with Preston, an actor whose talent he admired, Alan was remarkably calm the day he was tested. Everyone was impressed, and when the film was run in a small projection room, Tuttle assured Sue, "This picture is going to make your client a star."

By coincidence, on the same day Paramount decided to give Alan the part and a starting contract at $300 a week, RKO, impressed with his work in *Joan of Paris*, offered to put him under contract at a hundred dollars a week more.

According to Sue, "After reading the script of *Gun*, I would have persuaded Alan to do it for nothing. I didn't even try to pit Paramount against RKO to get more money. I guess I wasn't a good agent, but I desperately wanted Alan to play Raven. I agreed with Frank Tuttle that he'd come out of the picture a star. And I felt that Paramount at this time was the ideal place for Alan to be."

As usual, Sue's judgment proved out.

CHAPTER 7

If there was ever a perfect pairing of aspiring actor and studio, the Ladd-Paramount teaming was it. For several good reasons, Alan Ladd might never have risen to stardom at any other time or at any other studio.

First and most important, a Louis B. Mayer (MGM) or Darryl F. Zanuck (Twentieth-Century-Fox) or Jack Warner (Warner Brothers) or a Harry Cohn (Columbia) would not have put up with Sue Carol's ideas or interference regardless of how intelligent or sound they appeared: agents, mates, mothers—all were expendable.

Paramount, in 1941, was not under one-man rule. B. G. (Buddy) DeSylva, a former Broadway producer and songwriter *(Panama Hattie, DuBarry was a Lady, Louisiana Purchase)*, ran the West Coast operation informally but efficiently. As long as he kept the costs down and the profits up, there was little intervention by the legendary Adolph Zukor (founder of the company), Y. Frank Freeman (Zukor's strong right arm), and Barney Balaban (president of the studio from 1936 until 1964). All three men wielded power from the New York home office and made only occasional trips to the Marathon Street lot in

Hollywood to take a look at "product" and to meet both new and established actors.

Zukor, who had made movie history in 1912 by presenting Sarah Bernhardt in the four-reel *Queen Elizabeth*—the precursor of the feature film—was also responsible for America's first movie star: Mary Pickford. The legend went, "He built her a million-dollar studio and paid her a one-million-dollar salary to keep her there—for a while."

Also in 1912 Zukor, together with Broadway showman Daniel Frohman, had formed the Famous Players Film Company to produce "famous plays with famous players." Zukor kept a jump ahead of the other burgeoning motion-picture companies by engineering mergers and consolidations—the first with Jesse L. Lasky's Feature Play Company under the banner of Famous Players-Lasky. He continued these shrewd operations, and in 1917 the Paramount Pictures Corporation was formed to distribute their films. Two years later the new company bought one hundred thirty-five theaters in the Southern states from the Publix Corporation, adding to them regularly, and in 1926 Zukor built and opened the magnificent New York Paramount—considered by many a personal monument to himself. In time Paramount-Publix controlled some two thousand theaters as well as production and distribution of films.

Zukor's motto (and the title of his 1953 autobiography) was "The Public's Never Wrong." He always allowed moviegoers to determine the type of stars he picked and the stories he filmed rather than subject them to artistic whims.

Throughout the Twenties, Paramount and Paramount-Publix thrived and built a dazzling list of stars. William S. Hart became the greatest Western star of his time. Gloria Swanson and Clara Bow skyrocketed under Zukor's banner, as did Marlene Dietrich a few years later.

Indulging in a rare bit of self-aggrandizement, in April 1930 the studio released a revue titled *Paramount on Parade* in which it displayed the talents and voices of Maurice Chevalier, Helen Kane, Mitzi Green, William Powell, Jack Oakie, Nancy Carroll, Ruth Chatterton, and the "It Girl" Clara Bow.

By now, the movies had found their voice. The Paramount-Publix Theaters were all wired for sound, and on the Paramount lot those players who had survived the initial shock of unfurling their vocal chords were joined by such dynamic "talkie" personalities as the Marx Brothers, Fredric March, Jeanette MacDonald, Claudette Colbert, Cary Grant, Gary Cooper, W. C. Fields, Sylvia Sidney, Jack Oakie, and that original—and eternal—sexpot, Mae West.

Although the Depression was to force mighty Paramount-Publix into bankruptcy in 1933, Miss West saved the day with her quadruple-entendre films. Reorganized as Paramount Pictures Corporation, the company began to prosper and for the next decade and into the mid-Forties it set a pattern of moviemaking style.

In a class by himself, Cecil B. DeMille rewrote history and the Bible and produced—or overproduced—for Paramount epics which the critics mocked but the public lapped up. More enthusiastic critical receptions were accorded the polished comedies directed by Ernst Lubitsch, the madly satirical efforts of Preston Sturges, and slyly mischievous scripts by the team of Charles Brackett and Billy Wilder.

Oddly, Paramount, which won the first Oscar with its 1927 production of *Wings*, with Richard Arlen, and had many pictures in contention over the years, was not to be honored again until 1944's *Going My Way*—a humiliation quickly forgotten when it won again the following year for *The Lost Weekend*.

Awards were gratifying, but Adolph Zukor's major concern was always making and saving money for Paramount. One way was to encourage the signing and training of attractive young people at the lowest possible salaries. The best of these were co-starred with established names. If the neophyte caught on, Paramount had a million-dollar personality for pennies. If the youngster failed to ignite, he or she was dropped after six months or a year of the so-called seven-year contract, at a minimal financial loss.

At the tail end of the Depression the million-dollar salary was a thing of the past—and the future. Susan Hayward was happy to sign with Paramount for $200 a week after losing out in the Scarlett O'Hara sweepstakes: Veronica Lake was ecstatic when her salary was upped to $350 a week after she had created a sensation in *I Wanted Wings* and *Sullivan's Travels*. Salaries for contractees usually ranged from $150 to $300 a week to start, with guaranteed raises at "option time."

Sue Carol was well aware of the advantages of a Paramount contract for Alan Ladd. She liked the people at the studio, whom she knew from her own acting days, and she had been impressed by the studio's techniques in that mysterious process known as "star-building." There was a comfortable, informal atmosphere at the Marathon Street lot, from the executive offices down to the commissary, where a salad or a sandwich named after a star was a better indicator of his having finally "arrived" than billing above a movie title.

But it was more than Paramount's proud history, the ambience of its studio, or even the potential power of the Raven role in *This Gun for Hire* that convinced Sue that only here could Alan Ladd's potential be properly developed.

Zanuck liked his men tall, dark, and handsome—the Tyrone Power type. Harry Cohn preferred the "boy next door"—Glenn Ford, William Holden—and when his Columbia needed a male powerhouse he "borrowed" a Clark Gable or a Jimmy Stewart. Louis B. Mayer favored the "matinee idol"—pretty, like Robert Taylor, or rugged, like Gable.

Paramount was the only major studio where a blond leading man was not anathema—sexless, spineless, not worth the risk of a stock contract. And Paramount was ripe for a new blond leading man, having lost their giant, Sterling Hayden, to the army.

Alan Ladd's height was hardly a hindrance there either. Zukor—himself so diminutive that visitors never knew whether he was sitting or standing when he greeted them from behind his huge desk—was secretly pleased that he was finally getting a leading man under six feet tall. And Veronica Lake, supposedly the box-office lure of *This Gun for Hire*, was a wisp of a girl, barely five feet two and one hundred pounds.

By now, Europe had been at war for more than two years. But on the other side of the DeMille Gate fantasy prevailed, as cutting rooms and sound stages hummed with such productions as *Louisiana Purchase, Reap the Wild Wind, The Great Man's Lady, My Favorite Blonde*—and the inexpensive little melodrama about a psychopathic paid killer named Raven.

So, on a sunny October day in 1941, Alan Ladd rode through

the gate to join Veronica Lake, Robert Preston, Paulette Goddard, Gary Cooper, Loretta Young, Dorothy Lamour, Bob Hope, Bing Crosby, Fred MacMurray. Ray Milland, Eddie Bracken, William Bendix, Mary Martin, Susan Hayward, Macdonald Carey, Diana Lynn, and Marjorie Reynolds as a member of the Paramount family.

He would appear with most of them in the Paramount all-star entertainments, *Star Spangled Rhythm, Duffy's Tavern*, and *Variety Girl*. Preston, Carey, and Bendix would play second fiddle to him. He would eventually co-star with Lamour and Young, but the names Lake and Ladd would always be linked in the public's mind.

The legendary directors/producers on the lot—DeMille, Brackett, and Wilder—would have no influence on Alan Ladd's career, nor would he be given the opportunity to work with them.

But on this day Alan wasn't thinking of the great stars and directors he was soon to meet. All he could think of that first exciting day at Paramount was justifying Sue's belief in him.

He was finally a part of the world he had fantasized about.

He had found, finally, a home.

CHAPTER 8

Alan spent hours before the mirror perfecting the "Raven look," as it was called. Driven by the same determination that enabled him to gain control of his voice a few years before when he had practiced until it had the resonance he demanded, so now he worked on the look for the chilling effect he wanted. He had already brought it off for the screen test. Now he had to sustain it throughout an entire performance.

The key to Raven's character is revealed early in the script when Ladd reports to his employer, played by the overpowering Laird Cregar, to be paid for a cold-blooded murder he has just completed.

"How do you feel," asks the employer, "when you're doing a job like this?"

"I feel fine," Raven mutters in a monotone, without a twitch in his pretty-boy face.

The look had to be conveyed by the steely-cold eyes, empty of all guilt or compassion; the trim mouth; the icy smile. It was the look of a psychopathic killer who enjoyed his work.

But there had to be something else, something which would make the audience fear the Raven—and yet reluctantly regret his inevitable (dictated by the Hays censorship office) fate. It would be that reaction which would set him apart from the small but deadly stock Hollywood heavies like Elisha Cook, Jr. (also in the cast), Martin Kosleck, and Paul Guilfoyle.

The makeup department at Paramount added a dimension by dying Alan's hair black. Despite the studio's partiality to blond stars, the front office had decided in a burst of literary fidelity that a fair-haired killer could not be called by the name of the sleek black bird Edgar Allan Poe had immortalized. The wardrobe department contributed the worn-looking trench coat and wide-brimmed felt fedora to complete the illusion of menace. (The hat would be discarded by mid-script, but the trench coat would become a lasting symbol.)

Before shooting began in October, Alan was summoned to the studio's publicity department to provide material for the standard new contract player's biography. His story, carefully prepared and rehearsed with Sue, was a publicity man's dream. From rags to riches, he was Horatio Alger in Hollywood's own backyard: loss of father, loss of mother, years of struggle. The "bio" was so good, in fact, that the studio flacks didn't even bother to invent a great-great-grandfather with a royal crest or *Mayflower* heritage—standard practice at the time. They sensed too that the public, now jittery over the inevitability of becoming involved in World War II, was no longer buying that variety of moth-eaten bull.

Sue, it was decided, would be referred to only as Alan Ladd's agent. The studio was aware that they were lovers, and feared repercussions from Sue's husband. Midge suddenly ceased to exist, as did the now four-year-old Alan, Jr. In the initial releases, Alan was a bachelor and a loner—moody, elusive, a mystery man.

This Gun for Hire, considered by all a routine film, was rushed into production mostly to provide Veronica Lake with a starring vehicle. Veronica Lake was happily married to John Detlie and had a three-month-old baby girl, which wiped out any chance of turning her and Alan into an offscreen affair—even if only for publicity purposes.

The studio might have been openly antagonistic to Sue if the situation had been otherwise. Sue was, moreover, still close to the Crosbys and had other good friends on the lot from the "old days." So the Paramount brass decided that as Alan's agent she could be reasoned with to do what was best for him—if by some fluke *This Gun for Hire* took off.

Twenty-five years later Sue told the *Hollywood Reporter*, "They didn't want him to marry. Actually, I was against it too, at first. In those days all the publicity could have been geared to Alan Ladd, the single lover. I thought marriage might hurt his chances with the fans. But we were in love. Actually, Alan said that if his studio contract revolved around him being single, he'd rather not have the contract."

At the very beginning, however, both Sue and Veronica Lake's husband stayed far enough in the shadows for Ms. Lake to say in her autobiographical *Veronica*, published four years before her death in July 1973, "Naturally the public linked us romantically, but neither of us cared what the public conjured up about us. And we were just as indifferent to the studio's sly attempts to spread romantic rumors. It was all part of the game in enticing the public into the theater, and the Ladd-Lake billing proved to be a powerful lure."

The association lasted and grew through their co-starring in three films after *This Gun for Hire: The Glass Key, The Blue Dahlia,* and *Saigon*—plus guest shots in two Paramount "all-star" trifles.

In her autobiography Veronica Lake also wrote:

There is no actor with whom I'm more closely connected than Alan Ladd. And yet we had less to do with each other than most other acting teams.

We'd arrive on the set early each morning. Alan would nod and say, "Good morning, Ronnie."

"Hi, Alan."

We'd go to wardrobe and makeup, play our scenes together, and go back to our dressing rooms to take off the makeup and wardrobe.

"Night, Ronnie."

"Night, Alan, see you tomorrow."

Alan was a marvelous person in his simplicity. In so many ways we were kindred spirits. We were both professionally conceived through Hollywood's search for box office and the *types* to insure that box office. And we were both little (in size) people.

It was true that in certain films in which his leading

lady was on the tallish side, Alan would climb onto a small platform or the girl worked in a slit trench. We had no such problems working together.

Both of us were very aloof.... We were a good match for one another. It enabled us to work together very easily and without friction or temperament.

Actually, in *This Gun for Hire* Robert Preston was Lake's romantic vis-à-vis and the actor to whom Paramount entrusted the honor of giving her her first screen kiss. Nowhere in the script was there a chance for Ladd to receive as much as a friendly pat on the head.

However, poster art and publicity shots, combined with a thirty-year time lapse, tend to play deceptive tricks on the memory. Veronica Lake wrote, "Alan Ladd died in *This Gun for Hire* with his head resting in my lap, and *Variety* would comment, 'Better men have died with their heads in less pleasant places.' I always meant to ask Alan about his feelings on the subject but never got around to it. He probably wouldn't have answered me."

He probably wouldn't have, considering that his Raven died in no such manner. At the fade-out, after disposing of the traitors who were involved in selling poison gas to the enemy, the cold-blooded killer with a newly acquired patriotic streak, lies full of bullets in solitary splendor on an office couch as Lake stands clutching Preston with romantic fervor. With his last breath, Raven asks for reassurance that she didn't turn him in to the cops. Then, after receiving it, he expires with a heretofore unrevealed, heartbreakingly contrite little-boy smile.

In today's movies, such an ending would bring forth derisive hoots, and any actor participating in it—be he Robert De Niro, Al Pacino, or Robert Redford—would doubtless be laughed off the screen. But the closing scene known as Redemption of Raven, as it was called on the Paramount lot, was the imaginative touch that turned a B film into something memorable. And it was responsible for the electric effect this young newcomer would have on his audiences....

After the first day's shooting director Frank Tuttle looked at the rushes and realized he'd gotten even more than he'd hoped for when he decided to take a chance on Ladd. He decided to favor Alan at every opportunity, adding more close-ups than the script demanded and touches designed for effect.

A good example is Ladd's introduction to the audience. Shooting in near darkness, the camera catches a fleeting glimpse of Raven's mutilated hand taking in the milk for a pet cat. Then it pans and lingers on an unshaven face, catching the cold fanaticism behind the eyes. For what seems an interminable time, still under low-key lighting, Raven prepares for his latest assignment and slowly the viewer becomes aware that it is an assignment to kill.

The opening sequence left little doubt about either the director's or the studio's intentions. This was a star buildup. No young actor could ask for more. But still, Alan would have to deliver. Tuttle was convinced he could. The director later recalled the day he wandered into what he thought would be a deserted rehearsal room during a lunch break: "Alan was initially oblivious to my presence. There he was, in full costume—Raven raincoat, hat pulled over one eye, crossing the room to pick up a telephone. He did it once, he did it twice—and a third time. He was improvising, experimenting. Each trip to the telephone was slightly different. Finally he became aware of my presence, and was more than a little embarrassed, almost apologetic. 'Just trying to get into Raven's skin,' he said. 'After a guy has killed a man and is going to make a date to pick up his pay, how would he get to the telephone booth? He doesn't want to be recognized, so he would try not to be conspicuous in any way. He knows there are people outside, so he wants to guard his voice. Yet he doesn't want to whisper to the telephone. This is a pretty delicate scene, don't you think?' "I was impressed," Tuttle said, "by Alan's eagerness and comprehension. The test of any screen actor worth his salt is the way he handles a telephone scene. Adolph Menjou's scene in *The Front Page* was an example of this, and of course, Luise Rainer's in *The Great Ziegfeld* won her an Oscar."

The opening scene, the closing scene, the telephone scenes—they were really all that were needed. But Alan was given a great deal more. Robert Preston, who only appeared man-to-man with Alan in the final shot, was wiped out. Veronica Lake got the feeling that Tuttle wanted to get her solo scenes out of the way and was irritated when he had to spend too much time on any of the sequences in which she did not appear with Ladd. According to the cast sheets and billboards, *she* was the star of the picture. After a few weeks into shooting, however, she began to suspect that she was being used mainly for decorative purposes.

She consoled herself with the thought that it wasn't much of a movie and would be forgotten in a year.

In her autobiography she admitted, "As I look back, I view the film with mixed emotions. Surprisingly it has fallen into today's mysterious realm of minor film classics. [It] became known as a 'sleeper' in the trade and even compared with much of Hitchcock's success in the suspense medium. The chase scenes were exciting, to the credit of editor John Sietz. But . . . I had obliterated any inroads I had made as an actress in *Sullivan's Travels*."

Ms. Lake never credited Alan for the success of *This Gun for Hire*, though she grudgingly agreed that he was "a superb psychopathic killer. He could be cool, placid, all-observing and knowing, or just plain nasty." For Frank Tuttle she never had a kind word, and although she was forced to work under his direction again in *The Glass Key* and *The Hour Before Dawn*, she did so with misgiving. Years later she dismissed Tuttle as "that jerk who never considered me anything more than a sex-zombie whose only purpose in movies was either to cause mass masturbation and heavy breathing in darkened theaters, or provide a lap for Alan Ladd's last screen moments."

But to Ladd, Tuttle, at forty-nine, was mentor, friend, idol, and father. "He is," he told Sue, "the only man I've ever known who really believes in me." The two men remained close friends for two decades. Although discreet about the personal side of their relationship on the set, since technically they were still both married to others, Alan and Sue were uncharacteristically honest in admitting to Tuttle just how "wildly in love" they were. When Tuttle invited Alan to weekend barbecues around his pool, he was including Sue as well.

Maintaining her agency made it impossible for Sue to spend all her time on the Paramount lot, but she'd never fail to drop by at least once on the days that Alan was working. Between her and Veronica Lake there was no communication at all. The world might consider Veronica Lake a sex symbol, but Sue had long since dismissed the tiny twenty-two-year-old as a threat. Alan's and Sue's evenings were spent together, discussing the next day's scenes or the rushes she had seen. She would reassure him, "Nothing can stop you now."

Something almost did.

More than halfway through production, Alan collapsed. He was rushed to a hospital with a one-hundred-four-degree temperature. The diagnosis: a severe case of pneumonia, and there was no penicillin in those days.

On the surface there hardly seemed anything too surprising about Alan's collapse. He had been working himself beyond the limits of endurance, his resistance lowered by nervous tension and improper diet. Both Sue and Frank Tuttle had urged him to eat more, but he'd tell his director, "It's a funny thing about me. I don't have any interest in food most of the time now, although when I was a kid I was always hungry."

Tuttle and Buddy DeSylva assured a worried Sue there was no risk of Alan's being replaced. The footage in the "can" was too sensational to be discarded, and they could shoot around him until he was well enough to return and complete the picture. The worst that could happen would be a shutdown of the production for a couple of weeks. However, since everyone involved in the final shots was under contract, any additional expense would be minimal. The important thing was for Alan Ladd to get well—as soon as possible.

This was more than just an ordinary set-to with illness. Coming as it did at the most crucial point in his career, the pneumonia was significant as the first of dozens of unpredictable illnesses and accidents that would continue to afflict Alan Ladd for the rest of his life. (It also left him with a slight case of pleurisy, which, combined with the lingering problems from his old diving accident, classified him 4-F in the draft—at least for the time being.)

Alan was still confined to his hospital bed that Sunday morning of December 7, 1941, when he heard that the Japanese had just bombed Pearl Harbor and that Roosevelt would officially declare America's entry into World War II the following morning. One report had it that "though weak as a fly and still burning with fever, Alan jumped out of bed yelling, 'I got to get out of here, they'll be needing guys like me!'"

Which made smashing patriotic reading for Ladd fans, but it's somewhat more likely that Alan was relieved that he had been disqualified from military service for a year. He had spent ten years of his life scrambling to get where he was, and only a martyr or a lunatic could calmly watch everything slip through his fingers.

Alan Ladd was neither. He had no intention of dodging his patriotic duties—*if* and when he was needed or wanted—but he was human enough to welcome the reprieve in secret.

The Paramount executives were equally pleased. A number of their younger players had been classified 1-A, and many of the actors who remained in Hollywood were either closet homosexuals or older family men.

By now there was no doubt in anyone's mind about Ladd's potential. The only question: How would a film about a professional killer be received now that the country was at war? The plot twist which had Raven turning against the traitors who sold poison gas to the enemy was a reassuring plus for the picture, but it was the cops-versus-bad-guy aspect of the movie that worried the studio. Would anybody really care about all that now that there were far more important good and bad guys?

The release date was moved up to keep the film from being too dated, lacking as it did extras in soldier and sailor uniforms. And Alan Ladd was immediately re-teamed with Veronica Lake in a remake of Dashiell Hammett's *The Glass Key*—Brian Donlevy was the nominal star by virtue of both his role and contract, but every effort was made to allow Ladd to outshine him in the footage the two had together in this rather complex melodrama. Following completion of the film Paramount planned to send Alan to New York to introduce him "officially" to the Eastern press in conjunction with the opening of *This Gun for Hire*. They had hoped to send him as a bachelor, but Alan and Sue had plans of their own.

While Alan was absorbed in his role, Sue established six weeks' residence in Las Vegas. On March 8, 1942, she was granted a divorce. A week later, she and Alan quietly went to Tijuana, Mexico, and were married. When the newlyweds returned to Los Angeles, Alan said, "When Sue became my wife I realized that at last I had everything in life that I wanted."

He would continue to repeat those words, at times sounding like a well-programmed computer, for the rest of his life.

CHAPTER 9

Two months after their wedding, Mr. and Mrs. Alan Ladd checked into a twenty-eighth-floor suite in the plush Waldorf Towers in Manhattan for a combination publicity trip and slightly delayed honeymoon.

The local press had already attended screenings of *This Gun for Hire* and were eager to meet the young man Paramount had been touting as their next major star. Even *The New Yorker* magazine conceded, "He seems to be a rather agreeable killer; his felt hat pulled down at a frivolous angle; his mouth only a trifle sullen. A different kind of mug, smooth and with even a parlous manner, he may start a vogue for a new species of melodrama—stories of nervous and gentle gunmen without a trace of human kindness anywhere about them."

At 1501 Broadway, a half mile southwest of the Waldorf, Adolph Zukor was happily anticipating the grosses. From the window in his executive suite high above the Paramount Theater, he could see the lines forming at the box office on opening day, and his instincts told him that they weren't for the high-powered stage show that shared the bill. He was right—*Gun*, which cost less than half a million dollars to make, eventually grossed $12,000,000.

The studio had asked the hotel to provide the Ladds with top-priority celebrity treatment. The rooms in their suite were filled with expensive floral arrangements. A bar was set up, loaded with a variety of top-brand liquors. The hotel phone operators were alerted to screen all calls. The Duke and Duchess of Windsor, who had a permanent apartment in the Towers, had never received better treatment. All expenses were on Paramount.

This was the first time Alan Ladd had been out of California (other than the elopement to Tijuana) since the day he had arrived in Jim Beavers' jalopy some twenty years earlier. New York during the first few months of World War II may have had its signs and streetlights browned out at night, but the kaleidoscopic patterns made by the Park Avenue traffic were a scenic wonder from the twenty-eighth floor of the Waldorf.

Looking back on the first trip two decades later, Sue told writer Walter Wagner (in *You Must Remember This*): "The picture was a blockbuster in New York and Alan was mobbed everywhere he went. But crowds scared him. He should have loved the attention, he should have enjoyed his stardom, but it frightened him. The studio publicity department set up so many interviews for him that he got to hate New York. Inside he was in turmoil. The childhood insecurity was still there. He wanted to be a star, but he never expected to make it. When it happened, he couldn't handle it easily."

Outwardly, at least, Alan did manage to fake it convincingly, though the contacts with the press had a nightmarish quality. He wiped beads of perspiration from his forehead as a steady stream of interviewers came in and out of his suite on an almost regimental schedule. He stumbled and muttered as he tried to answer a barrage of questions under the hawklike gaze of a Paramount press agent. Had he said too much—or not enough? Had the reporters found him at all interesting, or would they go away thinking he was just a stupid new actor who'd gotten a lucky break, a one-picture wonder who'd been cleverly directed?

Endlessly, wearily, he had been coached by both the studio and Sue on the art of facing the press: Be charming and cooperative, hype the film, be modest about his own performance, stick to the "facts" already spelled out in the official biography; above all, avoid any mention of Midge and young Alan, Jr.

If the questioning got too complicated, the studio press agent would come to his rescue. The latter would be the "heavy" if need be, but Alan must at all times be a paragon of charm. It would be smart, he was told, to drop in a few references to his experiences as a "cub reporter." This would give him a brotherly in with the men. To the women, he'd express his appreciation of "bright, hard-working ladies." And, of course, he would say he *loved* New York and explain apologetically that he was only rushing home to California after a scheduled appearance on the "Kate Smith Hour" because he had an appointment with his draft board.

Despite his anxiety, Alan succeeded in making an almost unanimously favorable impression on the press. His personal apprehensions seemed to provide an appealing contrast to the nervelessness of Raven.

He was still, however, apprehensive about his appearance on Kate Smith's show. Each week the ample Miss Smith would present a short sketch, using a top Hollywood name as a gimmick to break the routine of an all-musical hour. Because her show was among the most popular on the air, she rarely lacked for important names. The show was presented before a live audience at CBS Playhouse #2, a converted theater on West Forty-fifth Street at eight P.M. and repeated live again for the West Coast at eleven.

The size of the theater and the audience worried Alan, not to mention the fact that he was the least known of the celebrities who had ever appeared in this "spot." His radio performances in Hollywood had taken place in small studios with technicians as his only audience. Now, before the eight o'clock show, he had a bad case of stage fright.

Still, once he was introduced and the audience responded to both the build-up and the rapidly blinking APPLAUSE sign, he sailed through the performance. At the end, excited by a new discovery, no one needed the sign to respond with enthusiasm.

During the hour-and-a-half break between shows, to Alan's astonishment a huge and somewhat hysterical crowd had gathered in the alley that led from the stage door to the street, where a car was waiting to take him to a nearby café. Dozens of people were shoving scraps of paper and pencil stubs in his face, begging, "May I please have your autograph, Mr. Ladd?" But before he could do anything the studio publicity people and the CBS ushers had positioned themselves between him and the fans. He was appalled at the treatment the autograph-seekers were receiving. It was his first experience of mob hysteria, and although a bit frightening, it was also very exhilarating.

When the Ladd entourage came back to Playhouse 2 a few minutes before eleven o'clock, the late-night audience had all been seated and only a few die-hards remained in the alley, but once again a single autograph... "Please, Mr. Ladd," one small blond boy said, "I've been waiting for hours." To Alan, that could have been himself, fifteen years earlier. He started to turn back but the broadcast executive whispered, "No time, no time, we're on the air in a few minutes." All Alan could do was call out, "When I come out I'll sign for all of you, I promise..."

His confidence boosted by the reception he'd received during the first show, he breezed through the repeat, giving an even stronger performance for the West Coast. Once again the APPLAUSE sign was a superfluous prop. At the end of the show Kate Smith, her director, and the station executives were full of praise and congratulations.

Outside the theater the crowds were as thick as before. The chief usher, not wanting to risk a foul-up, steered Alan and Sue out a side door and into a car, but the fans, aware of what was happening, chased the car west toward Eighth Avenue. Looking out, Alan spotted the blond boy's face. "Mr. Ladd, you promised..." Remembering too well all the broken promises he'd had as a youth from older men—and being just twenty-nine years old and in many ways still idealistic—Alan felt like a damn monster. That evening he made a promise to himself—no matter what success lay ahead, he would never pass up anybody who wanted to talk to him, he would never refuse an autograph or snub a fan.

It was a promise he would keep.

Back at the Waldorf Towers Alan was uneasy again and anxious to get home, but before he did he had some shopping to do. For Sue he bought the beautiful platinum fox fur coat she had always wanted. For Laddie he sent back a toy from F A O Schwarz. And, despite his discomfort in New York, there was one night he'd always remember with a special happiness—when he and Sue walked the eleven blocks from the hotel to the Paramount Theater to stare at his name on the marquee—"Like a couple of kids let loose in a candy store," they recalled. (Years later, when Sue talked of that evening, she'd "remember" the thrill of seeing Alan's name up in lights blinking on and off. Actually, the Paramount didn't have that type of marquee, and even at theaters that did, the "brownout" forbade any such display. But the name Alan Ladd was to become almost a permanent fixture on the Paramount marquee—all but five of the twenty-four movies he made while under contract to Paramount found a berth at the flagship theater.)

It was the New York reviews that really provided the biggest thrill. *Variety*, the *Herald Tribune*, and the *Daily News* acclaimed Alan Ladd as the most exciting new star of the year. Bosley Crowther's review in the *Times* on May 14, 1942, was a rave. A conservative-minded critic who could, and sometimes did, destroy a film he considered inferior, Crowther, mostly on account of Ladd's performance, let out all stops in his appreciation of the picture:

> One shudders to think of the career which Paramount must have in mind for Alan Ladd, a new actor, after witnessing the young gentleman's debut as a leading player in *This Gun for Hire*. Obviously they have tagged him to be the toughest monkey loose on the screen. For not since Jimmy Cagney massaged Mae Clarke's face with a grapefruit has a grim desperado gunned his way into the cinema ranks with such violence as does Mr. Ladd in this fast and exciting melodrama.... Mr. Ladd is the buster: he is really an actor to watch. After this stinging performance he has something to live up to—or live down.

Crowther would ask in a subsequent article, "Is it [Ladd's popularity] that youngsters see in him some vague implications of themselves? That is, beyond the obvious romance attached to a handsome tough guy, do they see imaged in him their own insecurities, a sympathetic rebel against the problems and confusions of modern youth?" (The modern youth Crowther was referring to was that generation preparing to go out to be maimed and killed in World War II. Those who survived Bataan, Iwo Jima, Anzio, and Bastogne would later be at the older end of the generation gap: the fathers considered too square to understand their rebellious children who defiantly tore Berkeley and Columbia apart.)....

After the bedlam of New York the Ladds welcomed the long train ride home—the privacy that allowed them to relax and plan for their future. And at the same time some other rather powerful folks were also laying their plans for the new star.

MCA (Music Corporation of America), then Hollywood's most prestigious talent agency, wanted to buy Alan Ladd's contract, but Sue couldn't bring herself to sell. She decided to give half to an agent friend, Bert Allenberg (who could then represent Alan's interest without nepotism); Alan insisted she keep the other half herself.

Paramount raised Alan's salary to $750 a week, but the newlyweds wanted to stay in Sue's house on Cromwell Avenue because, as Sue ruefully put it, "Every picture Alan made from then on, he thought was going to be his last one." This rather dismal conviction was to influence his career almost as much as Sue herself did.

For his stepdaughter Carol Lee, Alan had great affection. Having had a stepfather of his own, he went out of his way to try to avoid the dangers of such a relationship, although he still felt a bit self-conscious about seeming to usurp Nick Stuart's paternal role.

Laddie, his own child, was a frequent visitor to Cromwell Avenue. Midge would call Sue, or Sue would call Midge, to make arrangements. "Midge," says her sister Barbara Harrold Grether, "maintained a speaking relationship with Sue—for Laddie's sake. She didn't want the boy torn up between two hostile families."

Midge, however, was considering leaving California and returning to Chicago with her son at the time. Among those who came to look at her house was professional football hero Tom Harmon and his college friend William Farnsworth, who had come west with him. By the time the men decided they were interested, Midge began having doubts about leaving. Farnsworth, however, asked if he could take her to dinner, and within a short while the two were spending a great deal of time together.

An expert aircraft technician, Farnsworth was employed by Lockheed in the San Fernando Valley while waiting for his induction orders from the government. He wanted to marry Midge before he went into the service, and eventually she accepted his proposal and they made plans to marry.

Although Sue and Alan's Mexican marriage was legal, they too were looking forward to Alan's final California divorce decree. They were eager to marry again in California, to be on the safe side. Sue, although she was thirty-nine years old—ten years older than her husband—wanted to bear Alan a son as soon as possible....

CHAPTER 10

In early June 1942 American naval forces were definding Midway Island from a massive assault by the Japanese; the strategic Crimean seaport of Sevastopol had been overrun by the German Army; and Buddy DeSylva, Y. Frank Freeman and Adolph Zukor were counting the box-office receipts from across the country for *This Gun for Hire*. And worrying about how long they could keep Alan Ladd from being reclassified by the draft.

Paramount was taking no chances with their new low-salaried star. They planned to keep Alan working with such frenzy that they would have a stockpile of his films to release—no matter what the vagaries of the military.

Alan was given a hero's welcome following his return from New York: a $5,000 bonus as a gesture of appreciation, and a starting date for *Lucky Jordan*. He was glad to be back among his friends—for the first time in his life he felt he really *had* friends... During an earlier interview with S. R. Mook, the writer accused him of being defensive. "Pretty sensitive, aren't you?" challenged Mook. "I guess so," Ladd admitted uncomfortably. "You can't be put through a wringer all those years the way I was with no one to play around with—no one to talk to, to confide in—and not be sensitive. When you don't mingle with people you don't understand them and you imagine insults and snubs when none are intended. You get your feelings hurt over nothing. But now I have Sue and I can only be hurt by her or through her, and Susie wouldn't hurt a fly."

Actor William Bendix wouldn't hurt a fly either. Not offscreen. However, one of the more violent sequences of *The Glass Key*—filmed after *Gun*, shortly before the Ladds' marriage—called for Bendix, in the role of "Jess the bodyguard and beater-upper," to pick Alan up off a bed, slam him down, pick him up again, throw him up against a wall, back down on the bed and then pull a couple of chairs apart to finish him off with. When finally ordered to stop, Bendix retires to a corner petulantly murmuring, "Aw, you mean I don't get to smack baby no more." Director Stuart Heisler, anxious to film the scene in as few takes as possible, asked the men to spend some time rehearsing until they got the timing right. Finally the cameras were ready to roll. Bendix, instead of grazing Ladd's jaw in a way that would make the fight look just enough like the real thing, accidentally caught Alan flush on the button and knocked him cold.

"Cut, print," yelled Heisler. A few moments passed before either he or Bendix realized that Alan was unconscious. Tough guy Bendix's face became rigid. "God, what have I done?" he said, and promptly burst into tears. When Alan came to, the first thing he saw was Bendix's face crumbled in despair . . . Bendix's widow, Tess, now living in Arizona with her children, recalls, "From that moment on the two men became close friends. Alan was very affected by the fact that Bill could be so concerned. After that you'd have thought they had been friends forever." . . . Alan insisted that the Bendixes, who had been living in a rented bungalow, buy a house in the Los Feliz section. "As a matter of fact," says Tess Bendix, "Alan found our house for us. It was just across the way from Sue's on Cromwell Avenue and was exactly what we were looking for: an unpretentious but comfortable two-bedroom house, just right for Bill and me and our daughter, Lorraine."

An Easterner like her husband, with no other friends in Los Angeles at the time, Tess liked Sue and was appreciative of her help in making her feel at home. The two families became near-inseparable. Sue was not threatened by the attractive brunette—it was obvious that Tess (then happily married for fourteen years) worshipped Bill. If Sue felt any resentment that Alan had found someone else to spend time with or to confide in, she was shrewd enough to keep it to herself. And if she felt that Bendix was not yet in the social or professional stratum she wanted Alan associated with (Bendix received eighth billing in *The Glass Key*), she kept those thoughts to herself too.

Bill Bendix and Alan Ladd made a very odd couple, indeed. Physically, the rugged six-footer with the broken nose was the antithesis of the then slender-faced Ladd, who was seven years younger. With his New York stage background, Bill Bendix could and eventually would play everything from the leads in Eugene O'Neill's *The Hairy Ape* to *The Babe Ruth Story* to the farcical Chester Riley in TV's *The Life of Riley*. Ladd was good-naturedly envious of his friend's versatility, but was also pleased that such a talented actor admired his work. At Paramount, the friendship caused some raised eyebrows, because of the great personality differences between the two men during working hours. Bendix was impulsive; Ladd was always thinking twice about everything. Ladd was serious; Bendix full of the devil. But Ladd's association with Bendix also brought out a playful side in him—the two men were constantly thinking up new gags to play on each other . . . Because of his radio training, Alan was able to affect dozens of different voice changes and he'd rarely phone Bill as himself but rather as "Mr. Fish of Pacific Canneries" or "Mr. Wood of Consolidated Toothpicks." Tess Bendix fell for it every time, but not her husband. "You know," he'd say, "what you can do with those toothpicks, Mr. Wood, m' Ladd" . . .

The relationship with Bill Bendix was the kind Alan had never had with another male when he was growing up. He thrived on it, and was grateful for it. He thought of the Bendixes as family, and he was always on the lookout for ways in which to show his appreciation. Having a considerable amount of money for the first time in his life, he delighted in being able to buy gifts for those he loved—and those he felt loved him . . . Tess mentioned that she'd been hunting for some old beer steins to decorate a Dutch shelf they had built around an alcove in the kitchen. Unable to find them, she had given up, and then one day

Bill came home to find a collection of mugs on the shelves. "Alan brought them," Tess said. "The son-of-a-gun—" "That's what *he* said. 'They're for you, Tess, and that son-of-a-gun from Sue and me.'"

To the Bendixes, the newlyweds seemed genuinely in love, and even those executives at the studio who may have found Sue a pain in the neck had to admit that the marriage had been good for Alan—beyond the strong sexual pull on both their parts.

Of course, this softening of attitude toward Sue may have been at least partly because Alan was now receiving a record nine hundred fan letters a day. After seeing *This Gun for Hire* the public was demanding that Alan Ladd be in a movie in which (a) he got the girl; (b) he smiled; and (c) he was alive at the end.

So if DeSylva and Freeman couldn't quite figure out the common denominator in the camaraderie between Ladd and Bendix, neither was particularly concerned about it either. They had a new success on their hands. Besides, it was 1942; there was a war going on and it was a time when men could be buddies, brothers and constant companions without being victims of slanderous assaults.

Lucky Jordan was completed in late July, and from the rushes and rough cut, Paramount was convinced it had another winner. Leading lady Helen Walker, fresh from a Broadway success in *Jason*, was an unknown quantity. Alan had solo star billing above the title. The success of the film was therefore dependent on his charisma. Appearing with his natural blond hair for the first time, he was, in fact, extraordinarily handsome. And although the Jordan character was less than admirable throughout most of the story—a combination con man, racketeer, draft dodger and then Army deserter—his reformation toward the end made him, as intended, irresistible. His final speech, after he foils the insidious scheme of some local Nazi spies to get hold of some vague secret plans, was a classic of good-guy patriotism that, at the time, could not fail to be effective:

"Listen," Lucky says, "as far as I'm concerned, the Nazis were just another mob of gangsters trying to horn in. But maybe I don't like guys who beat up old women. I'm selling those plans to an outfit that will pay me fifty a month and throw in a uniform free."

Bill Bendix had recently given a dynamic performance in a heroic role in *Wake Island*, which Paramount rushed into production shortly after the invasion of that Pacific island. Although there was nothing suitable for him in *Lucky Jordan*, he was penciled in to co-star with Alan in *China*. This time, however, he'd appear not as Alan's brutal nemesis but as his trouble-shooter and pal: two tough guys, bucking the dirty yellow Japs who went around raping and rampaging in China prior to the attack on Pearl Harbor.

Loretta Young was given the romantic-interest role of an American schoolteacher working in the Orient. At the peak of her career, she demanded and received top star billing. But this would be the last time Paramount would make such a concession while Alan remained under contract.

China was scheduled to start shooting in late fall. In the meantime the studio dropped Alan into a cameo role in their *Star Spangled Rhythm*, a sappy musical grab bag that starred Betty Hutton as a Paramount switchboard operator and Eddie Bracken as a sailor under the mistaken impression that his father, the gateman (Victor Moore), had been made head of the studio. The flimsy plot was merely a peg for an all-star roster of players to be put through a series of vaudeville turns. Dorothy Lamour, Paulette Goddard, and Veronica Lake did a ditty about sarongs, sweaters, and peek-a-boo bangs. Resisting the temptation to team Lake and Ladd, the studio had Alan do a parody of his trench-coated tough guy with Macdonald Carey. Bob Hope and Bing Crosby had separate but equal parts, and Dick Powell—on the lot to co-star with Mary Martin and Betty Hutton in the musical *Happy Go Lucky*—was recruited for another duet with Mary Martin for this opus.

In August, a few weeks after Carol Lee's tenth birthday, Sue's gynecologist confirmed that she was pregnant—the baby due the following April. Approaching forty and in fine health, Sue would have the tie to bind Alan even closer to her. She was certain that fatherhood, like his marriage, would not damage Alan's image—particularly if the forthcoming event were shared with his fans.

Carol Lee and Laddie had been carefully kept out of the spotlight up to this point. In his earliest encounters with the press Alan had let slip that there had been a brief marriage in his past but he had not mentioned a child. Naturally, all of Sue's Hollywood friends knew about her daughter, but the old chestnut of wanting the little girl to have a "normal childhood" was persuasive. Carol Lee, too, was omitted verbally and pictorially from the "Alan and Sue" stories that were now being printed regularly in movie magazines. (When Carol Lee finally appeared publicly in the late Forties her surname had been changed to Ladd. Nick Stuart, who remained friendly with Sue, permitted the name change but would not agree to the formal adoption of his child.)

Alan, overjoyed when Sue told him she was pregnant, rushed to inform the Bendixes before they learned about it in Luella Parsons' column.

Midge, however, learned the news from the paper. According to Barbara, she was later horrified to read that "If the baby was a boy, he'd be called Alan Ladd, Jr." Angrily Midge protested, "She can't do *that*. There already *is* an Alan Ladd, Jr." But it never occurred to her to call Luella or even speak to a local reporter.

In the fall, after the best summer of his life, Alan received word that he had to begin his military service early in 1943.

China was completed in mid-January, but before Alan put away his civilian clothes another of his fantasies came true.

Lux Radio Theater now asked for him. And to get him they adapted *This Gun for Hire* for his first starring appearance and hired Joan Blondell to co-star.

Alan would then get a royal send-off to the wars.

CHAPTER 11

The great Cecil B. DeMille himself was recruited to give
Alan Ladd a hero's farewell on Monday, January 25, 1943.

When the red OFF THE AIR sign flashed, the "Lux Radio
Theater" orchestra played a chorus of "Auld Lang Syne" and a
spotlight played on an American flag which rippled in the breeze
from a wind machine.

After the screams and yells and whistles from the packed
theater had quieted some, DeMille stepped to the footlights and
announced, "Tomorrow night at this time the star of this show
will be Private Alan Ladd of the United States Army." The
audience rose to their feet as one, drowning out DeMille's
remaining words. Alan was speechless, his eyes filling with tears.
He might have been Douglas MacArthur giving his memorable
"I will return" address.

A few days earlier Buddy DeSylva, Alan's boss, had taken
him aside and said: "Alan, you'll never have to worry when you
come back. With the start you've got and the talent you've
shown, you're in for keeps."

Indeed, Paramount had insisted on giving a luncheon in his
honor. The elite of the studio had attended and embarrassed him
into giving a speech. Still self-conscious and inhibited, Alan,

who always hated making speeches in public, kept it brief: "Like every other guy I am going into the Army because there's a job to be done. When the job is finished—in the right way—I'll be back. Thanks to every one of you for all the swell things you've done for me. I'm no good with words but I'll find ways from time to time to show you how grateful I am. That's all. I'll be seeing you."

He sat down to another standing ovation. It was as if he were headed straight for the Allied Air Force bases in England, where the first round-the-clock bombing of the industrial cities of Essen, Dusseldorf, Solingen and Mulheim had just begun. He was, in fact, bound for Fort MacArthur, just outside of San Pedro, California.

Alan's good friends, Davy Clyde and his actress wife Fay Holden (known for her role as Mickey Rooney's mother in the Andy Hardy series), drove him and Sue to the induction center during a rainstorm. Knowing he'd be returning home frequently on leave, Alan took with him only the toilet case with his Air Force identification number given him by Bill Bendix as a farewell present.

The Paramount publicity department had been careful in building his image as the average G.I. Joe. Stories flooded newspapers and magazines: about how he avoided any special privileges; how the other men in the outfit accepted him as one of their own; how he had to stand in line with a hundred others to wait his turn at the phone booth to put in a call to his bride; and how, in fact, when he got his first liberty pass, he had to catch a streetcar to get back to his Susie. Girls away from their guys or girls who had no guys of their own lived vicariously through Alan and Susie. They believed every word when Kirtley Baskett wrote in *Modern Screen* that "since Alan has been in the army he is a changed man. He can make a bed as tight and smooth as a snare drum. He can scrub a lovely floor, peel potatoes in artistic style, manipulate the business end of a broom with amazing results, wash clothes without tattletale gray, and rise and shine without a grumble anywhere from four A.M. on."

In short order Alan Ladd became more than the typical Army rookie...he became the idealized rookie, and mail flooded the base. Some enterprising admirers got his Cromwell

Avenue address. The less sophisticated wrote him at Paramount, asking: PLEASE FORWARD.

Although the studio had taken him off salary when the Army Air Force claimed his services, they allowed Alan $200 a week to keep on four secretaries to answer the fan mail, which by now was beyond their control. Sue made sure *every* letter was answered and wrote personal notes to G.I. wives and expectant mothers who identified with her. In March the Air Force sent Alan on his first official mission—to Camp Callan outside San Diego to appear on a Bob Hope broadcast being performed before the men at that center.

In April they granted him a furlough so he could be in Hollywood for the birth of his child. On April 20, the Ladds felt it would be safe to attend a sneak preview of the movie *Stage Door Canteen*, but by eleven P.M., before the movie was over, Sue got her warning signals. They left the theater and went straight to the hospital.

By two-thirty A.M. on April 21, six-pound, eleven-ounce Alana Sue Ladd was sleeping soundly in the nursery. Sue had no problems with the delivery, and Alan assured her that he wasn't in the least disappointed that the baby was a girl. He stayed with Sue most of the night, attributing his flushed face and dizziness to excitement. But when the nurse came by to take Sue's temperature, Sue asked that she also take Alan's. The new father was running a 103-degree fever, and the doctor who was called in ordered him home and to bed immediately.

He was forced to stay in bed for three days, and on the second he sent his wife a huge box of flowers with a card reading, "Because our happiness is now complete and because I love you so terribly much." On the fourth day, recovered, he rushed back to the hospital loaded down with gifts for Sue: a satin comforter; a white wool robe; and blue-gray sports coat; a brown clipped beaver coat; and a tiny gold heart for Sue's charm bracelet, accompanied by a note reading, "To my mommy from Alana Susan."

After six days in the hospital, Sue and Alana were allowed to return home. Alana, in her blue-and-white bassinet, was placed in a nursery decorated in yellow, white and blue. The sunlit room contained a small bed, a tiny dressing table, a play table, a rocking chair and a gleaming bassinet with a card attached: "To Alana from Dad, with love." There were toys everywhere—gifts from Alan and Sue's friends, his Paramount co-workers and from fans throughout the country. Albert Delacorte, *Modern Screen* magazine's young editor, who became a father himself a few days earlier, sent a three-foot-tall teddy bear that wound up to play a lullaby.

Midge wished the new mother the best when she spoke to Sue to make arrangements for Laddie's next visit. Happy now in her second marriage, Midge made no attempt to get Alan to raise the $100 a month child support he had agreed to but she did suggest that in fairness to her husband, who was also in the service, Alan pay for the growing boy's wardrobe.

Hearing about the newest Ladd's luxurious nursery, seeing photos of doll-like Alana in all the magazines, Midge, as she told her sister, couldn't help remembering that October morning five and a half years earlier when she had brought Alan's son to the dingy apartment on Morrison Avenue, put him in a secondhand crib with the secondhand bedding and the dime-store toys donated by their friends, and bathed him in the kitchen sink....

Before she returned home from the hospital Sue had hired a nurse, a Dutch woman named Rinsje, to help care for Alana. Tess and Bill Bendix, who had paced the floor with Alan the night the baby was born, were also constantly on hand to make sure Sue wouldn't be lonely, bringing fruits and vegetables from the "Victory Garden" they had planted in their backyard.

The Air Force, at this time, was using Alan's services for training and propaganda films, and the government would borrow him to launch war bond drives, apparently considering him more valuable in that capacity than behind a gun—the Ladd name would bring out the crowds, the crowds would excitedly buy bonds and the money would support the war effort.

But Alan had in common with the average G.I. a tendency to gripe about conditions at camp. Home on a weekend pass, he half-kiddingly voiced his grievances to Bendix.

"Aw, c'mon, Laddie," Bendix said, laughing. (In 1943, many of Alan's close friends and some of the press began to call him "Laddie.") "Stop griping. You know you're living a plush life down there in San Diego." Before Alan could respond, Tess Bendix remembers, "Sue turned to Bill and said, 'You're a fine one to talk—considering you're not rushing off to join up.' Bill was stunned. He just got up from his chair and walked right out of Alan's house without saying a word. And he'd never go back. You see, Bill had asthma badly when we first went to California, but he was very patriotic and he did want to volunteer. They wouldn't take him. With just a little remark like that Bill thought Sue felt he was a dodger. Sue knew Bill had asthma, but she didn't give it a thought that they would turn him down for that. Bill, being so patriotic and so sensitive—well, his feelings were terribly hurt. It was so ridiculous—the whole thing. Because we were so close, just like sisters and brothers."... Bill had half expected that Alan would come rushing across the street to make amends or at least phone a few minutes later, but Alan thought Bill had been rude to Sue and that the apology should come from him. "Bill and I felt so awful about it," Tess recalls. "Here we were, living right across the street from each other and not talking. It was a very uncomfortable situation, so Bill just went looking for another house in a different neighborhood. Then we moved. And with Bill being so busy, we just didn't take the time to get the thing straightened out."

Many years would pass before they did.

Shortly after the incident with Bendix, Alan was transferred to the air base at Walla Walla, Washington. Sue planned to join him there, taking Alana and Carol Lee with her, but houses suitable for a family with children were impossible to find anywhere near the crowded base. So Sue, leaving the children in Rinsje's capable charge, took the train there alone. The Ladds set up housekeeping at a small hotel in a nearby town and Alan rode the bus daily to the base. Whenever possible, Sue planned picnic parties for Alan's Air Force friends, borrowing a neighbor's kitchen to do all her own cooking. (It was a kind of obsession with her to see that Alan's friends ate well—one that would continue throughout their married life. As though she were somehow anxious to win them to her ...)

At the end of Sue's second month in Walla Walla, Alan received a furlough and they trained back to Los Angeles for a real vacation. They promptly packed the family into a car, drove to Malibu Beach to visit Brian Donlevy and his wife, and then, on an impulse, rented a house close to the Donlevys, the Crosbys and the Andy Devines.

Alan would remember this as the perfect furlough—one in which he spent sun-filled days lazing on the sand, playing catch with Bing Crosby or rummy with Brian Donlevy, sleeping ten hours a night. Certainly he never looked more attractive—like Sue's Greek statue now done in bronze—or even healthier.

But he wasn't as healthy as he appeared.

Shortly after he returned—alone—to Walla Walla, Alan was hospitalized for what would be described as "a recurrence of an old stomach ailment." In mid-November, the Army Air Force gave him an honorable medical discharge "due to a double hernia." His height on his discharge papers was listed as five-feet-nine—Army life stretches one, they say. (Alan's height has been quoted by friends, family, and press—from 1942 until today—as ranging from five feet four to five feet nine. When questioned about it, Sue has always referred to his discharge papers, insisting on five feet nine as official.)

When Alan stopped at a newsstand at the crowded Walla Walla Station to buy a pack of cigarettes, his face smiled back at him from a row of *Modern Screen* covers. If he had had any fears about his popularity diminishing during the less than eleven months he had been in uniform, his first appearance on the fan magazine's cover put an end to them. This was proof positive that he was a "hot property"—much hotter even than before he had left. . . . Thirty-five years later Sue Carol would say that Albert Delacorte (then editor of *Modern Screen*) "was responsible for a lot of Alan's success. He loved Alan very much." Delacorte, remembering those days, smiles and says, "Alan Ladd sold magazines."

The 1943 schedule for *Modern Screen* shows what he meant:

January:	"Alan Ladd's Christmas List"; "What 1943 Will Bring to Alan Ladd" (Horoscope)
February:	"Her Heart Belongs to Laddie" (Marriage Story)
March:	Candid photo
April:	Fictionalization of film *Lucky Jordan* plus production notes on making of movie.
May:	"To Laddie, with Love" (*Modern Screen*'s Farewell Party to Rookie Ladd)

June:	Alan Ladd's Book-Length Life Story—Part I; Fictionalization of film *China* plus production notes on making movie. And a *China* contest awarding a $1,000 war bond to the reader sending in the best congratulatory wire to Alan Ladd for joining the American Air Force.
July:	Alan Ladd's Life Story—Part II
August:	"Alan's New Girl" (Birth of Alana Ladd); Analysis of Alan Ladd's handwriting. (The magazine's price jumped from 10¢ to 15¢, the cost blamed on wartime inflation.)
September:	Full-page color portrait in civilian clothes—suitable for framing.
October:	"The Best Friend a Guy Ever Had" (Bill Bendix—Alan Ladd story)
November:	"Don't Tell Laddie, But..." (*Modern Screen* revealed what everyone was saying about their newest idol, plus full-page color portrait suitable for framing of Ladd—in uniform.)
December:	Corporal Alan Ladd on the cover with accompanying story: "Reunion in Malibu—Alan's Romantic Furlough With Sue."

CHAPTER 12

It seems to me that as long as my pictures go into theaters and we ask people to pay to see what I do on the screen, I should not object if customers want to know what kind of man I am, how I live, what I do with my spare time. It seems only reasonable that the people have a right to know virtually everything about the personality they are buying each time they put their money through the box office.

—Alan Ladd

In 1943, *Modern Screen*—then the country's number one fan magazine with an average monthly circulation of 1,750,000 during that year of the war—carried sixteen Alan Ladd features in twelve issues. No other star had ever achieved such coverage. Nor would anyone ever equal it—not Frank Sinatra, not Elizabeth Taylor, not Elvis Presley. And as *Modern Screen* went, so went every other fan magazine in America, playing follow-the-leader to make Alan Ladd a household word.

To appreciate this, it's perhaps helpful to understand the psychology of the times and the esteem enjoyed by the two biggest publications in the fan field, *Modern Screen* and *Photoplay*. Today most magazines of this genre are considered rather trashy, with their sensation-seeking cover blurbs and often undocumented stories. Few stars are actually interviewed, and the studios ignore these once-powerful fan bibles, seeking coverage, instead, on television talk shows. In the 1940s, however, every major studio maintained a department for the sole purpose of servicing fan magazines. Appearing on the cover of *Modern Screen* or *Photoplay* was considered a coup. It was a sure indication that a newcomer had "made it," that an established star was maintaining his or her popularity. Combined monthly circulation of these two publishing giants totaled nearly four million, which according to surveys came to an average readership of some twenty-five million people each month. Such an awesome-sized audience could easily insure an actor or actress's stardom, and justify the publication's constant promotion. It could also send him or her to oblivion, not by the magazine's commission of some scurrilous story but simply by omission of any story at all.

Although they advertised their films heavily in fan magazine stories, studios got nowhere trying to pressure editors into hyping a movie or a star who was a dud. They could and did, however, make something of a mockery of the First Amendment. Magazine censorship during the Forties and Fifties was even more stringent than the wartime security clamp-down imposed by the military. Betraying a star's secrets was considered high treason, punishable, if not by death, then certainly by blacklisting the writer or withholding advertising from the offending publication.

Modern Screen's Kirtley Baskett was to write the stories on Ladd which Paramount later adapted for its official biography. Though he has recently acknowledged that he knew about Ina Beavers' suicide (but not about the ant paste) and Alan and Midge's marriage back in the Forties, he kept those confidences off the record—even from his boss. Midge was swept under the rug, as was Alan, Jr., together with Sue Carol's first and third husbands—Alan H. Keefer and Howard Wilson. It wasn't a matter of lying . . . it just wasn't exactly the whole truth.

Sue, because of her own Hollywood background, was of course keenly aware of how vital fan magazines could be to a performer striving for recognition, so early in Alan's career, along with the Paramount publicity department, she mapped out a game plan. The Ladds would go beyond mere cooperation with the major editors and writers. They would become their close friends and hosts, catering to their editorial whim. Publisher Irving Mannheimer, who gained control of *Photoplay*, and his wife Ruth considered themselves devoted friends of Alan and Sue. And George T. Delacorte, founder of the Dell Publishing empire, enjoyed the Ladds' hospitality when he was in California and suggested that Dell's movie magazines were responsible for making Alan a star.

Albert Delacorte (George Delacorte's son), however, says, "It would have been nice to have believed at the time that I made Alan Ladd a star, but I didn't fool myself for a minute about that. After *This Gun for Hire* was released, he started to make a strong enough showing in our reader poll to justify a full-length story. I told Kirt Baskett, one of our best writers, to get on the guy. The introductory story called 'Killer Diller' was scheduled for the October 1942 issue [out in September], and the first week's response was so overwhelming that we realized we had stumbled on potential dynamite—and decided to make the most of it."

Actually Paramount had tried—at Sue's suggestion—to arrange a meeting between Albert Delacorte and Alan when the latter was in New York the previous spring. But young Delacorte, just back from his honeymoon and inundated with a backlog of work, was at first indifferent to the studio press agent's pitch.

It was left to Baskett, who had established Alan's personality with the readers, to sustain the carefully constructed characterization. Although the Ladds spent hours amounting to days providing Baskett with material, it was his pen that fashioned the offscreen image. Just as Cyrano wrote the poems which captured Roxanne's heart for Christian, so did Baskett, with the first-person dialogue attributed to Alan, help capture America.

Creating an image of Alan Ladd was one thing. Sue presented a somewhat different problem. Says former executive editor Henry Malmgreen about the flood of Ladd pictures that began pouring into *Modern Screen*'s offices at that time, "You've got to remember that Sue was years older than Alan.

And she looked it. There was no way the cameras could lie about her matronly figure and dress. The sexy young starlet who had stubbed her dancing toes on a movie career was now a plump, hard-headed, liberated businesswoman thirty years before Women's Lib was born. By no stretch of the imagination was she the idealized version of "the girl he left behind" when Alan went off to war. How much easier if he had married someone like Lieutenant Ronald Reagan's adorable 'button nose,' Jane Wyman! Or think of the photogenic combination he might have made with either of those blond cuties, Gloria DeHaven or June Haver. Sue was a problem to image-makers and editors alike. But talented fingers at a typewriter can perform miracles." Perhaps Mr. Malmgreen overstates, but in any case, contradicting the chestnut that one picture is worth a thousand words—it depends, of course, on the picture—writers called thousands of words into service to create a portrait of Sue Carol presenting her as the warmest, wittiest and wisest wife a man could hope for.

And with Alana's birth came an avalanche of reader mail demanding to see photos of Alan Ladd's heiress. When Alana was four weeks old the nursery doors were opened so the magazines could get the pictures of mother and child that fans were impatient to see. Stories accompanying the photos spared no detail of the happiest day in the life of the world's most perfect couple—except that Sue already had a daughter. The publicity script called for fans to be informed that Alana was Sue's firstborn. There was no mention of Sue's previous marriages. If, in 1943, the public had become aware that Alan was Sue's fourth husband, the Ladd boom might just possibly have become a bust.

No one wanted to kill the proverbial goose. Too many golden eggs remained to be laid. Albert Delacorte says today that if he had been offered the Midge Harrold story he would have turned it down: "We were busy building an image of Ladd and of our magazine."

And in the movie magazine offices as well as at Paramount, plans were being made for Alan Ladd's return from the wars.

Part Three

1943-1952

I never fail to feel let down when I see myself on the screen.... Maybe I can't act, but I know the gimmicks. I studied acting all my life and I know what's good for me.... I just want to make pictures that are entertaining. I'll leave the scenery chewing to someone else.

—ALAN LADD

Alan Ladd is a big star to everyone in the world except himself.

—SUE CAROL LADD

CHAPTER 13

In November 1943 Paramount rolled out the red carpet for ex-Corporal Alan Ladd.

The studio built and furnished a luxurious wood-paneled star dressing room suite complete with kitchen facilities and all the modern conveniences. Anything Alan wanted, Alan got. Anything, that is, except a raise commensurate with his drawing power.

"In time, in time," stalled DeSylva. "After all, there's still a war going on. And we have big plans for you."

On Alan's immediate schedule was Rachel Field's tearjerker *And Now Tomorrow*, a tale about a young doctor who cures a rich deaf girl and, surprise, falls in love with her in the process. Once again Alan Ladd was co-starred with Loretta Young, and while waiting for filming to start the two were asked to repeat their *China* roles on the November 22 "Lux Radio Theater" broadcast. Bill Bendix, too, was in the cast, but both men were too stubborn to make the first move toward a reconciliation.

Two months later Alan was back on "Lux Radio Theater" again, this time with Hedy Lamarr and John Loder in *Casablanca*. He had once struggled so hard to land even a bit role on the program; now they couldn't seem to get enough of him.

Although *China* had been released the previous April (1943) and Alan's weekly mail was reaching new highs with fans begging him and the studio to rush his first post-Army movie into the theaters as quickly as possible—Paramount decided to hold *And Now Tomorrow* for its gala Thanksgiving 1944 attraction. Both the publicity and advertising departments of the studio were ordered to plan spectacular campaigns heralding Ladd's "return to the screen" in a way that would build anticipation for the event to what was known as "fever pitch."

By the time the film opened nothing could stop the stampede to the box office—not even the *New York Times'* critic Bosley Crowther, who said that "this is a very stupid little movie," and dismissed Alan Ladd's return from service by noting that he "plays the doctor with a haughty air that must be tough on his patients—and is likely to be equally tough on yours." Loretta Young got even worse, with Crowther observing that her performance could be compared "to Fanny Brice's imitation of a glamorous movie queen. Whatever it was that this actress never had, she still hasn't got it."

Fortunately, when that review appeared Alan had already completed a light piece about racing called *Salty O'Rourke* and was immersed in the filming of the epic Paramount promised would be his most important picture yet: the film version of Richard Henry Dana's *Two Years Before the Mast*. And in spite of his dissatisfaction with his paycheck he was pleased about the way things were going. He was in fine health throughout the year. Alana was thriving, his popularity was increasing. Whenever he had time off he sold war bonds or visited army hospitals, doing as a civilian pretty much what he had been called upon to do as a soldier. In early April 1944 he did a second radio broadcast of *This Gun for Hire*—this time for the "Screen Director's Playhouse," and this time, of course, with Veronica Lake. Later that month he co-starred with Dorothy Lamour on "Lux Radio Theater's" presentation of *Coney Island*.

Wherever he went he was mobbed. Sometimes his presence nearly caused a riot. When author Charles Samuels, writing an article for *Motion Picture* magazine, questioned the wisdom of subjecting himself to possible injury, Alan replied, "I hear about stars being torn to pieces by fans. It never happened to me and I never saw it happen to anyone else. I never was in a crowd I couldn't push my way quietly through. I think any movie star who refuses autographs has a hell of a nerve." This was Ladd speaking for Ladd, and it rang—and rings—true . . . truer than the copy manufactured by studio and magazines.

At the Lux Radio Theater broadcasts, where pandemonium was standard among the studio audience and the fans outside the station building, he did more than sign autographs. He couldn't resist the pleas of fans who stood outside the CBS Vine Street studios without tickets and rarely arrived backstage without fifteen or twenty young girls he passed through as his guests. When fans who'd discovered his home address came to Cromwell Avenue, he'd go outside and pose for pictures; if there wasn't too much of a crowd, the fortunate girls—and sometimes boys—would be invited in for Cokes. On one occasion, arriving home at one A.M., he noticed a group of teen-agers walking by the house, apparently hoping for a glimpse of him and an autograph. Learning they had missed the last public transportation both he and Sue insisted on driving them home. He spoke to every fan clever enough to get his private number. He insisted on signing every photograph in spite of the studio's suggestion he use the hand stamp made for such purposes. Kirtley Baskett once asked him if he wasn't carrying his obsession about the fan mail a bit far. Alan took out a special folder, the contents of which damn near broke that rather cynical reporter's heart. There was, Baskett remembers, "the despondent young man in the South who planned to end it all and wrote Alan that life wasn't worth it, and the air-mail special Alan subsequently received from the guy thanking him for a display of friendship when one was so badly needed. There was the boy in a New York school for the mute who couldn't hear him on the radio and who asked for a picture so he could see him when everybody else heard him, and the six young female patients in the TB sanatorium at Santa Barbara, who formed a fan club and called him their Hollywood 'doc,' and the Gold Star mother who, having lost her own son in the war, asked if she could 'adopt' Alan as a son through the mail." And there were the thousands of letters from G.I.'s stationed all over the world. Alan showed Baskett one such letter:

Dear Al: Thanks for your swell letter. It did me a lot of good because I get plenty blue sometimes. It isn't exactly a picnic here in this hospital. But I've got a confession to make. I didn't write you that last letter myself. My pal did it for me. I hope you don't mind but, you see, I can't write them myself. I haven't any hands.

"Whenever I hear anyone say, 'How can you take the trouble to write?'" Alan told Baskett, "well, I just think of that guy. Was it trouble for him?"

All of this, of course, sounds precisely like the stuff of which fan magazine stories are made. The stories, indeed, made their way into the magazines and enhanced the public's image of Ladd. In this actor's case, they just happened to be true. He still identified with the underdog, was still astonished that he evoked such interest and response—and was still convinced that "it could all go up in a poof of smoke."

In late 1944 Alan reported to Paramount to begin work on *Two Years Before the Mast*.

Today nautical films—whether for theatrical or television release—are usually shot on real ships on real water. In 1944 the Pacific islands were battlegrounds, the Atlantic was infested with submarines, and moviemaking was such that sea films were usually shot in a studio tank designed for that purpose.

Howard da Silva, who played the tyrannical captain of the hell-ship *Pilgrim*, recalls: "It was very interesting with the ship actually being four sections of a ship mounted on double rockers, and we all found ourselves getting seasick in the process shots. And it was interesting, too, working with Alan. He was a star, he was a *star!* But he was different from any Hollywood star at that time. He behaved least of all like a Hollywood star than anyone I had ever met. From the first I felt an aura of melancholy about him.... There were a group of people in Hollywood whom I worked with and who were maligned by cynics for being not at all talented. The talented ones, in my opinion, were people like Alan Ladd, like Gary Cooper. In Ladd's case, I felt he was so gifted and they were using only a small portion of his talent and ability. There was enormous potential in that man, yet he was playing almost the same role all the time. Anyway, my fondness for Ladd wasn't just because I felt an element of sympathy for him. Although the script of *Two Years Before the Mast* called for a great deal of antagonism between us, our personal relationship on the set was very easy. He wasn't a chatterbox, he wasn't a practical joker, and he never pulled the 'I-am-the-star' routine. I think we liked and respected each other. There were no battered egos."

Da Silva spent much of his time on the set with Bill Bendix, and says, "Bendix was such fun and had such humor. He and his wife Tess, who gave me the most marvelous lasagna, were such simple, straightforward, unphony people. But I was very unaware of the fact that Ladd and Bendix had been best friends. After their scenes together they each went their separate ways. I don't recall Bendix ever discussing Ladd at all. Sue was on the set, all the time, it seems, and would invite a group of us into Alan's dressing room for snacks and such. I may have wondered why Bendix never joined in, but obviously I didn't make anything of it."

Paramount delayed the release of *Two Years Before the Mast* for nearly two years, in favor of war-related films. By the time it opened in New York in September 1946, the world had been at peace for more than a year—and there had been some drastic changes in Alan Ladd's life-style. . . .

CHAPTER 14

Sue Carol finally put late hubby Alan Ladd's famed ranch in Hidden Valley up for sale. Don't call me, etc.

—Hank Grant
The *Hollywood Reporter*
May 22, 1978

The price tag for the ranch in 1978 was $825,000.

In 1945 it had cost Alan a fraction of that. By 1957 it was valued at $200,000.

This lush, verdant land nestled among the rolling hills south of Santa Barbara was the retreat where he had once dreamed of spending the later years of his life. It was to be, he said, "the place that's going to give me security when I get too old to work in pictures or when they don't want me anymore." But most important of all, he planned it as something that would provide his children and grandchildren with a sense of permanence.

He had found the ranch by accident, bought it on impulse. Preparing for the film *California*, he had learned to ride and had become crazy about horses. Although he could have hired a few horses for his weekend gallop through Griffith Park in Los Angeles or have had the studio supply them, he decided to buy his own animals and rent stable space.

He acquired Salty (for *Salty O'Rourke*) for Sue, Lucky (for

Lucky Jordan) for himself, added Jonesy as a spare, and considered the notion of breeding his own horses someday. It was actor Joel McCrea—working at Paramount at the time, with a beautiful place of his own in Hidden Valley (to which he would eventually retire a millionaire)—who initially put the notion into Alan's head. "What you need is a ranch," he'd insist. "There's no better fun than plain outdoor work."

Alan was thinking seriously about it when a good friend named Chet Root, a Beverly Hills antiques dealer, asked if he'd drive out to the Valley one Sunday afternoon and help him deliver a desk to a country estate some forty-five miles north of town. While Root was winding up some business, Alan walked around the area, spotted a FOR SALE sign some distance down the road and went to take a look at the place. It was an abandoned ranch with a series of stables set into the side of a hill. There was a decrepit windmill, a dust-covered garage, a sagging barn and a stone foundation of what had once been a house that had burned to the ground years before. Moreover, the ranch stood on twenty-five acres of good California land.

Alan found the owner and, as he would delight in telling people, "Fifteen minutes later I was a land baron." He'd sealed the deal with a handshake, and Sue was horrified when she learned that he had committed himself to buying the property without a thorough investigation into the value of the land. Her apprehension wasn't entirely unfounded. In his fervor for acquiring the place Alan hadn't given much thought to such mundane items as water and electricity. Water had come to the Valley, but a large portion had been siphoned off by the Hearst ranch at San Simeon, leaving the other ranchers with a meager supply. There was a well on Alan's place, but the windmill that pumped it took weeks to fix. Finally, though, he had sufficient water flowing into a small cement reservoir to supply the additional heads of horses he had immediately purchased and to irrigate some of the grazing land. He'd learned, too, that it would cost a small fortune to get electric power at the site, but by now the place had become an obsession with him.

"Alsulana Acres," the Ladds decided to call it—a combination of the names Alan, Sue, and Alana. Alan had one of the studio carpenters carve out a pistol with a warning to trespassers: "This Gun *Not* for Hire!"

Early in February, 1945, he and Sue piled their car with cots, canned goods, a coal stove and lanterns, and after driving north to Hidden Valley set up housekeeping in the old garage. That night Alan remembered a similar structure that had been his home nearly twenty-five years earlier. Now things were different. For the first time since childhood he felt he had roots. No matter what happened to his movie career, he had somewhere to go, something tangible to leave his children . . . He would tell Baskett, "What I want to do is make the ranch self-sufficient. I'd like to build a little future security here. Suppose I'm lucky enough to last in pictures another ten years. That's about all I can expect unless I turn into the Grand Old Man of Gower Gulch. By then, if this farm is producing horses, hay, vegetables and milk—well, what's wrong with that for an ace in the hole?"

Actually, with each passing week it was Alan who was getting more into a hole. Stables had to be converted into a house. New board-flooring had to be put in and the room fumigated, painted. A flagstone extension was added to the front of the living room and decorated like an Early American country farmhouse. Another small extension was built onto the main room for a three-burner kerosene stove, icebox and sink.

Alan and Sue, though, never considered giving up the house on Cromwell. It would have been impractical to commute from Hidden Valley to Hollywood when Alan was on a film; difficult, if not impossible, to find a proper school for Carol Lee. They decided to spend only weekends and vacations on the ranch, and hired a young helper and experienced hands to run the place. By coincidence Howard da Silva bought forty-two hillside acres overlooking the Ladd spread in Hidden Valley, "but," he insists, "it couldn't compare with his. He had the prime property, the grazing land. It was one of the most beautiful bits of acreage in the area." . . .

Since *The Blue Dahlia* wasn't due to go into production until the first week in March, Paramount arranged schedules to allow Alan to accept Eleanor Roosevelt's invitation to help launch the annual March of Dimes drive at the White House on February 26, 1945. For Alan this meant a cross-country train trip at the height of the wartime travel crush—when even such luxury streamliners as the Twentieth Century Limited and Super Chief were halted in order to allow troop trains priority—but he turned down the government's offer to arrange accommodations on either a commercial or military airplane flight. "Sorry," he said, not faking a man-of-the-people stance, "but you just won't get me up on one of those things."

At the White House Mrs. Roosevelt was gracious and hospitable and gave no indication to Alan or the other guests of her concern about her husband's health. Instead she apologized for FDR's absence and expressed her hopes that they'd all be together the next year when, she hoped, "this awful war will be over." (The weekend Ladd was at the White House the ailing President was attending the Yalta Conference. There would be no "next year"; in two months Franklin Delano Roosevelt would be dead.)

Excited by the visit, Alan was in good spirits when he reported to work on *The Blue Dahlia*. As always, he didn't look at the script, which was by the celebrated mystery writer Raymond Chandler. This was not because he had no say about the contents; it was a habit from his early years in pictures... Whenever he was being considered for something important and would get the book, play or script, he'd be—to quote himself—"a dead duck." He wouldn't get the part. The fact that *The Blue Dahlia* was, in effect, written for him couldn't affect the habit of his dour thinking. Never mind. There were no computers in the mid-Forties, but if there had been one and it was programmed to come up with the perfect Alan Ladd movie, *The Blue Dahlia* would have been it.

The story was a combination of dark melodrama and suspense in which Alan plays Johnny Morrison (a macabre coincidence—in no way could Chandler have known about the Ladd tragedy on North Morrison Avenue), a war veteran who returns from the Pacific to find his wife had been unfaithful. He walks out in a rage, but his presence there and his anger are enough to make him the prime suspect when the woman is found slain in her bungalow a few hours later. Morrison is then chased through raffish Hollywood dives, fancy hotels and police chambers, helped by an affectionate and nervy blonde, hindered by a powerful and sinister nightclub owner until, a step ahead of the police, he catches the real culprit.

Chandler included a goodly amount of violence and action to

satisfy a public numbed by newsreels exploding with scenes of mass killing in Germany and Japan. About this, Bosley Crowther noted in the *New York Times* (May 9, 1946): "... bones are being crushed with cold abandon, teeth are being callously kicked in, shocks are being blandly detonated at close and regular intervals. Mr. Ladd ... goes into action like a hawser that had suddenly snapped. One adversary is nothing. Two thugs make a fair and equal match. The low art of knuckle-duster fighting is elaborately displayed in this film."

All by careful design.

When Paramount had bought *The Blue Dahlia* (the title refers to the name of a café), it was an unfinished manuscript of a novel, about one hundred twenty pages long. So, with a substantial portion of the work completed, and with the knowledge that it would be Alan Ladd's next vehicle, Chandler was able to turn in half his screen adaptation in three weeks and include the kind of material that would fit Ladd's personality and temperament. The role of Joyce Harwood, the sympathetic, all-helpful blonde, was tailored to showcase Veronica Lake without putting too great a burden on her capacities.

John Houseman, a renowned Broadway figure previously associated with the WPA Federal Theater and Orson Welles' Mercury Theater, was set to produce *The Blue Dahlia* as his first picture under a newly signed Paramount contract, although the film was billed as "A George Marshall Production," directed by George Marshall. Bill Bendix was reunited with Alan Ladd for the fourth time—and upped to a star billing—in the role of his "slug-nutty pal." And Howard da Silva, Doris Dowling and Frank Faylen, represented as "the three famous finds from *The Lost Weekend*," completed the cast. For additional box-office insurance the studio created a provocative advertising campaign that read: "CROSS LADD ... AND YOU'VE DOUBLE-CROSSED YOURSELF! Fool around with Ladd's woman ... and you're a fool! For Ladd's gun and Ladd's fists say you can't get away with that, brother—not in his territory!"

This may have had very little to do with the movie, but it certainly enhanced the Ladd image, and *The Blue Dahlia* was considered a "can't lose" from the day it went into production.

Perhaps the only downbeat note came from author Chandler, who, less than enthusiastic about Alan Ladd, remarked, "Ladd is hard, bitter, and occasionally charming, but he is, after all, a small boy's idea of a tough guy."

Chandler not withstanding, filming of *The Blue Dahlia* went smoothly. Ladd and Lake continued to maintain their aloof but friendly rapport, and Ladd and Bendix worked well together, although their earlier offscreen camaraderie was once again missing.

Through it all, Alan remained true to his insecurities. Tailor-made for him though *The Blue Dahlia* might be, his old feelings of inadequacy were intensified by a conviction that he was being taken for granted by the studio . . . after all, his weekly salary was not on a par with his ratings on the popularity polls, nor with the fortune his films were making for Paramount. So with Sue's blessings, indeed encouragement, he rebelled, telling his bosses that he was quitting movies entirely and would take up ranching as a full-time occupation—unless some changes were made.

The *Hollywood Reporter* of August 23, 1945, front-paged the impasse:

> Paramount announced Alan Ladd was suspended yesterday when the actor refused to report for work in anticipation of the filming of the picture *California*.
>
> Unofficial cause given for break is the issue of money. The actor is said to receive between $150,000 and $200,000 annually for his work. He contends he should be paid a salary commensurate with his high box-office position.

Since his suspension prevented him from working on radio, Alan, together with Sue, two-year-old Alana, and Carol Lee, left for the ranch to sit things out until, hopefully, Paramount came around. Carol Lee, now thirteen but kept as much in the background as Laddie, volunteered to get a job to help out with the family's finances. That, however, was hardly necessary. There was enough money on hand to enable Alan to make his stand, and Sue was behind him one hundred percent.

The Ladds' togetherness no longer astonished Hollywood cynics, and even Louella Parsons and Hedda Hopper began to believe the rather gushy items they themselves wrote about the

Ladds. Certainly there was no phoniness about the way Sue's eyes lit up whenever her husband entered the room. And his devotion to her surely seemed genuine enough. (His refusal to remove his wedding ring for films in which he was obviously playing a bachelor drove more than one of his directors crazy, though the makeup department finally did devise a flesh-colored cover for the ring.) Every other word out of Alan's mouth seemed to be "my Susie..." or "you'll have to ask Susie about that..." or "Susie says..." or "Susie knows best..." He readily admitted that he turned all his checks over to Sue because "figures bore me and I couldn't balance a bank statement if a gun was held at my head." To everyone who knew him, Alan Ladd was a man very much in love with his wife, or totally dependent upon her—or both. Certainly he never flirted with any of the beauties who wandered seductively around the Paramount lot....

Shortly after his thirty-second birthday he received word at the ranch that he had come in fourth in *Modern Screen*'s reader poll. (Bing Crosby came in nineteenth, the only other Paramount star to make the top thirty-five.) Preceding Ladd in order of reader popularity were Van Johnson, Frank Sinatra and June Allyson, and following him in fifth and sixth positions were Peter Lawford and Robert Walker. All these were MGM stars.

Ladd's suspension from Paramount lasted four months and received little or no publicity other than mention in the trade papers. The fan magazines kept clamoring for interviews, but the Ladds were far more interested in the joys of bringing up little Alana than in bringing down the wrath of studio executives... They'd already done enough of that.

Fan mail kept coming in huge canvas bags. There weren't bins big enough to hold the thousands of letters addressed to either Alan or Sue that flooded the studio weekly. A remarkable number came from men stationed overseas or in veterans hospitals, recovering from or coping with injuries received in battle. Perhaps because of the easy time he had had in service, Alan felt compelled to make frequent visits to the hospitals, and answering fan mail was still an obsession. (At the height of his fame, taking care of the mail cost him about $60,000 a year—for secretarial help, postage and stationery.)

Salty O'Rourke, which had been released in April 1945, proved a powerhouse at the box office. Neither Sue nor Bert Allenberg, first to capitulate, and even Alan, despite his jumpiness and eagerness to return to work, had a surprising (for him) feeling of confidence.

The edict came west from the home office. Mr. Zukor wanted the kid back on the payroll. The studio couldn't afford *not* to keep him working, and Buddy DeSylva remarked, referring to Sue, "You can't fight pillow talk."

Alan got his pay hike—a substantial one guaranteeing him $75,000 a film—and, as Sue was to say later to Walter Wagner, "When Paramount was making big money on him on a cheaper contract, they treated him like a little boy who had never grown. Now he was given the treatment he deserved, the dignity and respect that were his right as a star."

The respect, however, stopped short of giving him approval of scripts, co-stars, and directors. Whether because of that or because he couldn't shake the memories of what once had been, Alan apparently still didn't feel like a star. Parties, other than those Sue gave, continued to terrify him. He admitted that he was often taken for a snob at gatherings because, "I'm shy and can't for the life of me barge around and slap people on the back. I sit in a corner by myself and am tickled to death when anyone comes over to talk to me."...Jack Benny later recalled discovering Alan leaning up against a pillar in the empty foyer of a flood-lit mansion where a Hollywood soirée was taking place. Inside, the celebrities were mingling noisily, happily. "What are you doing out here by yourself?" Benny asked. "I don't know any of the guests," Alan truthfully told him.

Sitting at a dinner table in a jacket—formal or otherwise—was also something he tried to avoid at any cost. "I hate it," Alan told a friend. "If I had my way I'd do all my entertaining on the front steps." ... In part, his aversion to large or formal dinner parties could possibly be related to his own chronic lack of appetite. No amount of persuasion by Sue, for example, could get him to have anything but black coffee—and lots of it—for breakfast (which no doubt was another reason she took pleasure in feeding his friends who loved to eat). He frankly admitted: "Once I was about to buy a certain house when I walked in and smelled lamb cooking. The kitchen was right off the entrance hall and I realized that I'd smell that lamb forever every time I walked in. I liked the house in every other respect, but I backed out of buying it for just that reason." ... Obviously he never could get over memories of the early Twenties, when he was served cheap mutton every day at home. He did, though, encourage his wife to have friends over for dinner regularly. "It means a lot to me. Being a good host sort of offsets the deprivation and loneliness of my youth." As the guest he felt as if he were getting a handout. As the host he was in control ... as he imagined back when he presided at Tiny's Patio. The sight of lamb, though, in any form continued to make him physically ill—as host or guest. Not only was it never served at the Ladds' but Sue tactfully informed friends whose dinner invitations they did accept of Alan's almost psychopathic abhorrence of it.

At the time their small group of close friends consisted of the Frank Tuttles, Joel McCrea and wife Frances Dee, orchestra leader Kay ("Kollege of Musical Knowledge") Kayser and his wife, the Bill Demarests, and Sonny Tufts—Paramount's newest blond male star—and his wife Barbara, a nonprofessional. Of them all only Tufts, just a year older than Ladd, was a contemporary, though that seemed the extent of what they had in common; Tufts—born Bowen Charleston Tufts III—was the scion of a socially prominent Boston family and educated at Phillips-Exeter Academy and Yale College.

A pattern was beginning to emerge. To newspaper and magazine interviewers and to casual acquaintances, Alan Ladd made much of the fact that he preferred the company of studio technicians—grips, wranglers and the like ... "They're my kind of people," he'd say, and mean it. However, from the time he was discharged from the service, he (or he and Sue) seemed to seek out those people who could contribute to his growth. They were the powerful actors (though not necessarily of his star caliber), the educated elite, and—not surprisingly—often those actors and directors who represented dominant father-figures. According to Boonton Herndan, author of *Mary Pickford and Douglas Fairbanks* (W.W. Norton, 1977), producer-director Josh Logan, in discussing his therapy, revealed his discovery that a man who has lost a father at an early age "subconsciously expects every male associate to be the understanding, indulgent, permissive parent he believes his father would have been. These associates can hardly know they're expected to be someone's father, much less play the role, and the father-seeker, who doesn't know what's going on in his subconscious either, may well feel rejected by some perfectly normal action, and crack up."

It was Paramount, though, that was the ultimate father-figure. And Paramount opened its arms wide to its prodigal son. . . .

In December 1945, leaving Alana and Carol Lee in the care of Alana's nurse, Alan and Sue went on a tour of army hospitals in the Midwest. Their itinerary included Camp Joseph P. Robinson and the Army/Navy General Hospital in Arkansas. On an impulse Alan traveled to Hot Springs and tried to track down his origins—or anyone who might have known his parents during the early years of their marriage. He drew a blank, and the brief odyssey served no purpose other than to revive painful memories of Ina Beavers. Eight years had passed since her death, but at holiday time in particular Alan was haunted by memories of that dreadful Thanksgiving weekend.

Christmas 1945 was the first in six years that the world was at peace. There was a feeling of excitement in the air, with special jubilation in Hollywood as stars and technicians returned home after long absences.

There were few losses of personnel and no maimed or wounded among the Hollywood elite. At Paramount, the welcome mat was spread for Sterling Hayden, who had served with the O.S.S., and Robert Preston, who came back with the rank of major after more than four years with Air Force Intelligence. William Holden was also back, and the studio teamed him with six-foot-four Sonny Tufts and six-foot-five Hayden in *Blaze of Noon*. Bill Bendix and Howard da Silva were also featured in this aviation adventure about four barnstorming brothers. Casting Alan Ladd with these blond giants would have been ludicrous.

As his *own* welcome-back present, Alan was starred in an interesting but hardly prestigious spy thriller, *O.S.S.*; Geraldine Fitzgerald, who had just left Warner Brothers, was cast as his leading lady . . . Ms. Fitzgerald, today considered one of the finest living actresses, had worked with Laurence Olivier, Orson

Welles, and Gregory Peck, among others, before meeting Alan. She still remembers him as one of the finer actors she has worked with during her long and distinguished career. "And yet," she says, "he really didn't believe in his talent. I remember one afternoon when we were talking and he said to me, 'I don't know what I'm going to do if this all gives up on me . . . at least I used to be a swimming instructor and now I couldn't do anything. I can't really act, and if I had to leave the film world, I'd have to go back to I don't know what—because I couldn't even go back to swimming instruction anymore.' So you see, he felt quite badly about himself, because he believed the press he had received, and the critics just didn't understand that they were dealing with a man—an artist—who needed to be brought out. Alan had such an odd opinion of himself . . . He kept on saying, 'I was never trained for anything.' Somebody must have fed him a lot of——!

"Although we were so chummy and I know he liked me, he never invited me to his home or anything like that. I didn't feel . . . rejected, because a lot of people are like that, and I thought Alan was a very private person. We'd often talk about acting, but he never told me anything about his life other than the fact that he had been a swimming instructor, and I just knew Sue to say hello to when she came on the set.

"Alan and I only did that one picture together, but all my impressions of him are very positive and affectionate. I really loved him and had great respect for him and couldn't help responding to his physical beauty, which was fabulous. He had a beautiful face with these luminous eyes—I think they were greenish hazel—with all these lights in them, like sequins on the irises; very large eyes and very pale skin. And then this brownish golden hair. . . . He was not tall, but that's inconsequential. He had a beautiful body. I think that's why the jokes made about his height must have hurt him a great deal. Making fun of a person destroys his defenses in a way he finds difficult to compensate for. That's why it's worse than an open attack. If someone attacks you openly, you can attack back. But if someone laughs at you and you attack back, then the world says, 'Oh, you can't take a joke,' so you're really caught in a vise.

"I never knew Alan to make fun of anyone. He wasn't the type of man who'd laugh at someone slipping on a banana peel; he'd had far too much of that himself—of people laughing at him. But he had a satirical sense of humor, an ironic sense of humor, and if you said something that was funny he'd be the first to appreciate it. But in many ways he took himself too seriously. When we were working on *O.S.S.* Alan was offered the idea of doing *Gatsby* and I said, 'Oh, do. Do Gatsby, you're perfect for it. You're exactly what Scott Fitzgerald had in mind.' Alan *was* the perfect Gatsby. But he said to me, 'I won't be able to do it because I can't act, you know.' And I said to him, 'Of course you can act. You're a wonderful actor. Just try to get yourself a director who understands you.' Maybe he didn't have a choice. I just don't know what happened.

"Alan needed to get with an *actor's* director who understands the problems that some actors have.... Then he could have learned that he had a real skill, a real profession that no one could ever take away from him. And he *didn't* know that. If he had had a director who was very warm to him, that would have supplied him with the confidence he needed. But Elliott Nugent, who directed *Gatsby*, is himself an inhibited person. However, I think that Alan felt he was made by publicity and his charisma—which was a thing he thought he had no control of. He thought that just came with him and there was nothing he could do about it. But the fact was that that charisma was *talent*, and it could have been chained; it could have made him feel that nothing could ever happen to his acting career.... If he had felt that way I think he would still be alive today. His inability to believe that—I think that's what did him in. And it is sad. Because Alan was very talented. He was one of our lost talents.

"I kept hoping and hoping that someday he would find himself with a great director, and when *Shane* came out I thought he had. I was so happy for him, and I was hoping that there would be a continuity to that. But I guess he wasn't always working with George Stevens."...

Alan would never work with a director who came even close to George Stevens, nor—with the exception of Jean Arthur or Olivia De Havilland—with a leading lady of Miss Fitzgerald's capability and perception.

Because he had neither script nor director approval under his revised contract with Paramount, he had no choice but to accept *Calcutta*, a contrived adventure yarn co-starring Gail Russell, which was to be dismissed by the *New York Times* as "the kind of melodrama which, while it may not ruin a star's reputation, certainly does not help to enhance same and causes audiences to mutter, 'We've seen this before and it seemed much better then.'"

At the time Alan was making *Calcutta*, though, he had far more important things on his mind than the movie he detested.

CHAPTER 15

In July 1946, Sue learned that she was pregnant again. She was at a dangerous age for child-bearing, but it was a now-or-never situation if she were to realize her ambition of giving her husband a son.

Although he seldom discussed Laddie on the set and made no reference at all to him in the hundreds of stories that flooded Sunday newspaper supplements and fan magazines, Alan was nonetheless deeply attached to his firstborn, despite the fact that Laddie's birthday, coming as it did just a month before Ina Beavers' suicide, always forced him to relive that tortuous month in 1937. Midge, who was coincidentally pregnant at this same time with her first child by Bill Farnsworth, permitted generous visitation rights and often took Laddie to see his father's movies. But for years she ignored Alan's subtle "feelers" about Laddie's remaining with him—although he was in a position to offer the boy far more materially than Farnsworth could.

So Sue's second pregnancy was a source of great rejoicing—for the Ladds and for the press, constantly on the lookout for a new story on Alan Ladd. The Ladds' apparently perfect marriage continued to intrigue reporters. Adela Rogers St. John wrote in Hearst Publications' *American Weekly*, "It's impossible to separate Sue and Alan Ladd in thought or fact anytime, anywhere, socially or professionally. Here is even more than that 'helpmate for man' of which we are told. These two people have taken their separate talents, characters and abilities as though they were different batches of clay and welded them together in one whole which we entitle the life work of Alan Ladd. This is the same deep, tender, spiritual oneness that existed in a different form between Mary Pickford and her mother.... Of course, this can only occur where there is a great love, a devotion on both sides big enough to set self aside, to have one mind, heart, aim...more extraordinary between husband and wife than mother and daughter. But just as without Charlotte Pickford there would have been no Mary Pickford as a cornerstone of the motion picture industry, without Sue there would have been no Alan Ladd." (A psychiatrist might suggest something less than ideal in a "mother-daughter" relationship describing a husband and wife.)

Alan would echo these sentiments and add to them. When asked what quality of Sue's he liked best, he replied, "Her self-control and her calm discipline. Nothing ruffles her and she's a great balance for my fidgets. She just knows everything is going to turn out all right, while I always imagine the worst will happen."

If the press gobbled all this up, so much the better. The public certainly did. Almost from the moment Louella Parsons broke the news about Sue's second pregnancy, hundreds of gifts began pouring in to the studio, to the Cromwell Avenue house, and to the ranch—together with suggested names for the expected heir or heiress. (Predictably, Alan, Jr., was the overwhelming choice, since Ladd's fans still weren't aware that an Alan Ladd, Jr., already existed.) As always, each letter received a personal reply. Each gift was acknowledged with a carefully written thank-you note.

Barring unexpected complications, the doctor assured both Ladds, Sue's pregnancy would go full term without incident. Despite this, Alan couldn't help being apprehensive, but whenever he voiced his concern he was teased for having fallen victim to "expectant-father jitters."

It was George Marshall who got Alan's mind off these worries by giving him a rather unusual assignment in still another of Paramount's star-studded soufflés called *Variety*

Girl. Marshall, having heard Alan singing for his own amusement during the filming of *The Blue Dahlia*, was impressed enough by his voice to team him with Dorothy Lamour for a rendition of "Tallahassee." Indeed, Alan's singing voice was something of a revelation—so much so that the studio announced it would pair him with Betty Hutton in *Sometimes I'm Happy* (it was never made), and there was talk of a record contract (which also never materialized).

"I'll confine my singing to lullabyes," Alan finally said. "Paramount already has a Crosby—the original."

As a gag he was given an unbilled walk-on as a private eye in Bob Hope and Dorothy Lamour's *My Favorite Brunette*. In January 1947 the studio told him he'd be co-starring with Lamour in a film with a rather inauspicious title *The Big Haircut*, a mediocre drama with alleged comic relief. Described by one wit as "a sort of cheerful person's version of *The Grapes of Wrath*," *The Big Haircut* (retitled and released, believe it or not, as *Wild Harvest*) dealt with the problems of a chummy gang of combine workers trucking from one wheat field to another. Bosley Crowther would call it as "a terrible movie," but Alan accepted the assignment without protest, as did Robert Preston, who also had little choice in the matter. The film went into production in mid-February and reunited Ladd with Preston for the first time since *This Gun for Hire*. Now, though, the situation was reversed: Robert Preston was the odd man out with third billing.

Preston, later a Tony Award-winner (for *The Music Man*) and one of Broadway's most respected actors, recalls his postwar years at Paramount in a perceptive fashion remarkably free of rancor: "I was away from the studio for four years—I left right after completing *This Gun for Hire*—and those were Laddie's biggest and best years. Now, if we were going to be in a picture together, I knew I was going to be the bad guy—the secondary role. That's what I was at Paramount anyway. When we went to work on *Wild Harvest* I never was conscious of his acting 'the star.' From the time I first met Laddie, he was a very straightforward little guy, and throughout the years I knew him that never changed. Of course, the studio's attitude toward him did. He was really a victim of the kind of paternalism that the studios had in those days. I guess we all would have liked it, but fortunately we didn't get it. Alan was so well protected that you couldn't use a stand-in when you were working in a scene with him because there would be so many cables and stands and reflectors you couldn't get in or out. And this is what sort of stultified Laddie. They were photographing a doll—and, poor guy, they wouldn't let him raise his head. That's why, when the mimics do him, they just move the eyes and the mouth a little. It's so sad, because he was an awfully good actor. So many people didn't realize this. It's said that the publicity department invented him, but they didn't really have to. He would have made it without that—and I think his life would have been happier.

"And because Laddie was a good actor and was not taken seriously, I think that's what hurt him so. I loved Laddie—we were good friends, but not intimate friends. We were never as close as I think we could have been, because he had that feeling of '*you're* an actor and they won't let me be one.' Yet we all knew he was better than the studio image. We never had the feeling that we were talking to one of those quote leading men unquote. The one thing Laddie wanted more than anything was good reviews, and one just had to admit that Sue opted for the other thing."

Dorothy Lamour had been recruited for the female lead to add a touch of sex and provide poster art of the two stars cuddling in a haystack. She was the only woman in a cast of thirteen, and the *Wild Harvest* company was a rowdy and happy one... "Hell," recalls Preston, "when you're working with a director like Tay Garnett, you have so much fun you forget that the picture is ever going to be released. In those days your circle of friends was within the studio. It was almost like dormitory life, and after a day's work we'd all get together and have a drink... Laddie was never a 'problem drinker' when I knew him."

The cast would have "movie" talk or "man-talk," and Preston has no recollection of Alan ever discussing his past or his personal life. In fact, until now Preston did not know that there had been a first Mrs. Ladd. "Crazy me," he says, "I always thought that Laddie, Jr., was Sue and Alan's. The young Laddie I knew wouldn't sit down and reminisce about those sorts of things...."

Although Ladd invited Preston to see the ranch, Preston doesn't remember "being around Sue that much. I don't think any of the leading actors could ever get close to Sue. She had only one thing on her mind—and that was Laddie. And that left her no time for other people."

In characteristic fashion, of all the men in the *Wild Harvest* cast, Alan was drawn most strongly to Lloyd Nolan, a powerful character actor nine years his senior. The Stanford-educated, gray-haired Nolan and his wife, Mell, served as two more surrogate parents, and the association that began with *Wild Harvest* turned into a long and lasting one.

Nolan would eventually learn almost all there was to know about Alan Ladd, but at the beginning of *Wild Harvest* even he was not aware of the severe personal crisis from which Alan had recently emerged....

The Ladds had been informed by Sue's doctor that their second child would be born in mid-December. Then the date was changed to "about January fifteenth." Because Alan himself had been born several weeks late, the Ladds weren't particularly concerned—at first.

By February 1, 1947, however, they very much were. At eight P.M. on the night of February 4 the doctor ordered an ambulance, and Sue was rushed to Cedars of Lebanon Hospital. The following afternoon the doctor asked to see Alan privately. Complications had developed and a choice had to be made.

"My father told me the story many times," David Ladd reminisces. "The doctor told him, 'We can save your baby or we can save your wife.' My father grabbed him by the shoulder and said, 'You bring them both back, hear, or so help me God, I'll kill you.'"

A few hours later Sue's nurse came into the waiting room where Alan and his friend Chet Root were nervously waiting. "You have an eight-pound, eleven-and-a-half-ounce son," she told Ladd.

"And my wife?"

"The doctor will speak to you," and then, seeing Alan's look of horror, the nurse, a regular Florence Nightingale, deigned to add, "She's alive."

But just barely.

It was very much touch-and-go for days. Only after many transfusions could Sue be pronounced out of danger. She remained in the hospital for almost two weeks, then Alan brought her home to a house decorated with signs reading:

WELCOME HOME, SUE AND DAVID; GOOD BOY, DOC; and GOSH! IT'S GOOD TO HAVE YOU HOME.

Their son was named David Alan, which moved one of the trade papers to suggest that Mr. Ladd must have a fetish for his own name, with daughter Alana, son David Alan, racehorse Alsuladd, and ranch Alsulana. (There was, naturally, no mention of an Alan Ladd, Jr.)

As soon as Sue had her strength back, she called the paper, which printed her statement: "If there's anything in the Ladd family named after Alan it's my own doing. I happen to be in love with the guy—and if I had six more children I'd like to name them all Alan. *He* has nothing to do with it." . . .

With his wife and new son David now both doing well, Alan returned to the studio, and on April 10, 1947, began work on *Whispering Smith*, a film touted by Paramount as Alan Ladd's first Western (the studio chose to ignore the "quickie" Westerns he had made as an unknown) and his first in "glorious" Technicolor. Once more he was pitted against Robert Preston,—with both men "vying for the favor of beautiful Brenda Marshall" (Mrs. William Holden).

In *Whispering Smith*, Alan played a railroad detective who discovers his best friend (Preston) is "in league with a bevy of bandits." The movie was a good action-filled adventure, to be enjoyed and forgotten. The color film would enhance Alan's attractiveness and keep the fan mail pouring in.

Just as *Saigon* had marked the end of the Ladd-Lake duo a few months earlier, *Whispering Smith* brought an end to the Preston-Ladd teaming. Grateful for the experience he had gained at Paramount but realizing he was getting nowhere there, Preston opted to leave the studio when his contract was up. After freelancing for a couple of years, he headed for Broadway, and although he would return to Hollywood from time to time, he did not cross paths with Alan Ladd again.

But he always remembered Alan with great affection. "You see," he says, "I only knew the happy Laddie. I only heard about the other much later on."

Alan Ladd had always been good at hiding things. And with the front of celebrityhood the deception—public and personal— became at once easier, and more dangerous. . . .

CHAPTER 16

The appearance of well-being was full-blown in September, 1947 as Alan stopped in New York to celebrate his thirty-fourth birthday—before heading for West Point, where *Beyond Glory* was to be filmed.

He and Sue were among the celebrities invited to attend the annual Harvest Moon Ball at Madison Square Garden. Introduced from the audience, he was asked to join master of ceremonies Ed Sullivan in the spotlight. He had no idea why. When he demurred, Sullivan insisted so he went up and just stood silently for a moment. Suddenly the audience rose and sang "Happy Birthday" as Ed Sullivan presented a small cake to him. "I cried like a baby," Alan later told friends. "That entire audience—thirty thousand people—was applauding for me."

And when he returned to Hollywood he got the good word that he had made the annual poll of circuit and independent exhibitors conducted by *Motion Picture Herald*, a leading trade journal, to determine the top box office stars of 1947. Although he only came in tenth (as opposed to his perpetual position in the top three in the fan-magazine popularity polls), he still felt honored. The *MPH* poll was, and still is, considered the most important in the industry. Preceding Alan on the list of stars whom audiences paid the most money to see were Bing Crosby, Betty Grable, Ingrid Bergman, Gary Cooper, Humphrey Bogart, Bob Hope, Clark Gable, Gregory Peck, and Claudette Colbert—in that order.

Delighted, Paramount informed him that they had set a March 8 date for the shooting of *The Great Gatsby*. Although still not completely confident that he could handle F. Scott Fitzgerald's complex character, Alan was far less hesitant about the role now than when he had discussed it with Geraldine Fitzgerald two years earlier.

As was their practice, Paramount cast a relatively weak leading lady opposite Alan, in the role of Daisy Buchanan—although Betty Field was a respected Broadway actress, she somehow had never clicked with the movie public. Newcomer Shelley Winters was selected to play Myrtle Wilson, Ruth Hussey played Jordan Baker; and the other major male roles went to three actors who were all considerably taller than Alan Ladd: Macdonald Carey (Nick Carraway), Barry Sullivan (Tom Buchanan), and Howard da Silva (George Wilson)—the last appearing with Alan for the fourth time.

"Because of this [the height disparity]," Paramount makeup man Hal Lierley recalls, "the studio built a raised platform, which was covered with carpet that sloped down to the regular floor of the sound stage. Alan was humiliated by this and said to me, 'No more; no *more* . . . from now on I'm going to demand approval of the other male actors I work with. . . .'"

In *Gatsby*, there actually was no problem with da Silva's height, since their pivotal scene placed Alan in a swimming pool. A different order of embarrassment, however, did occur. Da Silva describes it: "My confrontation with Jay Gatsby comes in the scene where I shoot him because I believe him responsible for the death of my wife Myrtle. At the exact moment the bullet hits him—and the special effects managed that superbly with a capsule underneath the skin from which the blood comes oozing out in the swimming pool—just before they said 'Cut,' the take was ruined by the sound of a child whimpering. There in a corner was Alana, who couldn't have been more than five, with Sue. It wasn't just the question of the wisdom in having her see the scene where her father was killed, nor *my* stupidity of going down on my knees and leaning up to her saying, 'Look, he's coming out of the water, it's just pretend,' because a child that age doesn't know pretend from not pretend. It was also the fact that when Ladd came out, they spoke to her as if she were silly. 'Aw come on, this is movies...' I don't think Ladd was nasty or anything like that. He was just embarrassed, and I remember feeling quite strange about that."... Thirty years later Alana was to speak for herself: "I remember that day vividly, vividly. The blood hit the water and I started to cry. It had taken them a whole day to set up and two hours to form the capsule on his back and I ruined the take."

But this was from the perspective of the adult Alana. Carol Lee, who heard what had happened that night, recalls: "Alana *was* frightened to death. They should have given her some warning...."

Appearance, reality...believe, make-believe. The distinctions were perhaps more the problem of the Ladds than their small child.

Gatsby was the last film in which da Silva would play the menace to Ladd. Soon afterward he left Paramount, and after a few films as a freelancer returned to New York, which he made his home.

He did, though, see Alan's films and often thought about him... "Over the years, when people would talk to me about Ladd as Gatsby, I'd say, 'Oh yes, Alan Ladd, that nice-looking man. He was very, very sweet.' And I'd hear myself saying, 'And he was not a bad Gatsby'—very easy, patronizing things. Then I'd say to myself, 'Whoa there, hold on now. There's somebody in there; there's somebody *important* in there.' The very fact that there was melancholy in him, that there was that air of sadness about him; the very fact that I can say I have a feeling that he gave up, long before he had to give up—symbolized by that early death—is itself an indication of that.

"One of the problems with someone like Alan is that when an actor is not encouraged to develop his craft as a performer, the anticipation of not always being the loving leading man must, I suppose, be a terrible kick in the ego... the thought, 'When I'm no longer a lover what good am I?' If anyone allows his wife, his agent, his studio to be his alter ego to a great degree, he's already given up his self-determination. You can't blame it on Sue, you can't blame it on anybody. A man still owns his own soul and can stand upright, no matter what he is.

"It takes a very exceptional person to maintain the drive and passion necessary for this profession. If you have been exploited by a studio or an agent, it's easy to lose that passion. I was once so naïve as to think that Alan's melancholy was because he had sold his soul. But nobody does that. You can't do that."

Twenty-five years later da Silva returned to Paramount to appear in its remake of *Gatsby*. "It was so curious," he says, "doing *Gatsby* again—with Redford this time. But as much as I admired Redford as an actor, I felt he could never play a man from the opposite side of the tracks. And Ladd could and did. In retrospect, I think his Gatsby was very underrated, unfortunately."

However *Gatsby*'s director, Elliot Nugent, had different feelings on the subject..."I felt very unhappy when I was making *Gatsby*. I thought I shouldn't be doing it and Alan Ladd shouldn't be playing in it. Ladd wasn't quite up to it, but he got away with it." *Time* magazine, in its July 25, 1949, review, agreed: "Ladd looks as comfortable as a gunman at a garden party." And Bosley Crowther of the *New York Times* (July 14, 1949): "Indeed, there are reasons for suspecting that Paramount selected this old tale primarily as a standard conveyance for the image of their charm boy, Alan Ladd. For most of the tragic implications and bitter ironies of Mr. Fitzgerald's work have gone by the boards in allowing for the generous exhibition of Mr. Ladd. Solemnly representing Gatsby, he gives us a long and lingering look at a patient and saturnine fellow who is plagued by a desperate love. . . . But somehow he does not present us with the picture of a strangely self-made man as the pitiful victim of the times and his own expansive greed. . . . Blame this in part on a weak script. . . ."

Basically, Alan's portrayal of Gatsby failed to generate box-office excitement, one suspects, for the simple reason that his fans could not accept their hero mouthing such expressions as "Look here, old sport"—who could blame them?—while Fitzgerald buffs turned their noses up and their thumbs down in advance at the casting of anyone as grossly "commercial" as Alan Ladd in the revered American classic. (Ironically, the release of *Gatsby* preceded the great Fitzgerald renaissance by one year and so did not profit from it.)

Paramount, aware that *Gatsby* was going to present a problem, had held up the release of the film for fourteen months after its completion and hurried to cast Alan Ladd in what was considered standard, safe Ladd fare. *Chicago Deadline* "reunited" Alan with Donna Reed, although the two had no scenes together in the story, which presented Alan as a dauntless reporter who beats the police to the solution in the murder of a girl of "dubious repute." Once again the solemn Mr. Crowther went after Ladd, this time for "ridiculous posturing." The audiences, however, seemed to love this rather poignant, unpretentious little mystery, which had the mood if not the magic of *Laura* of a few years earlier.

One suspects Alan privately agreed more with Mr. Crowther than the audiences.

Toward the latter part of 1948 Alan realized another longtime ambition—he now had his own production company, under which he packaged and syndicated a diverting half-hour of mystery called *Box 13*. By not being committed to a network schedule, he could tape the shows at his convenience and was still active in radio.

Indeed, in almost all respects, 1948 was a perfect *public* year. That fall he received an invitation to a Royal Command Performance in England and made his first trip abroad—by boat, of course—to be presented to Queen Elizabeth, wife of George IV.

Newly married Virginia Mayo, Warner Brothers' top-ranked female blond star at the time, and her actor husband Michael O'Shea were also among the Hollywood contingent headed for London. The Ladds and O'Sheas became acquainted aboard the *Mauretania* the first night out, and because they had adjoining suites, they soon became inseparable. . . . "My husband was so fond of Alan," Virginia Mayo recalls. "Whenever a photograph was taken of the whole group of us we were asked to stand together in a straight line and Mike would always give Alan a little shove forward so he would look taller in the pictures because that was such a big thing with Alan—he was shy about

his height. But he was *not* that short. I worked with James
Cagney, who was much shorter than I. Alan wasn't. Later when
we worked together I never had to step into a hole to be
photographed with him. I wore flat shoes, but that didn't matter
to me. I often wore flats in my movies. People are always saying
to me, 'Alan Ladd was so short,' and I tell them, 'he *wasn't* so
short.' I wouldn't say he was five nine—not *that* tall. I'm five five
and a half. Alan was about five six and a half. I wasn't conscious
of his height. I was conscious of his fabulous beauty. His eyes,
his nose, his entire face were just remarkably beautiful.... We
saw a great deal of one another on the ship. Every morning Sue
would bang on the wall and shout, 'Get up, wake up you two,
let's get going.' And I would feel so bad because I was seasick
most of the time and felt like an awful party pooper. Still, we had
a wonderful time—except for my being seasick. In England
Mike and I and Alan and Sue were put up at the Savoy, and Sue
was darling. She learned that I had a birthday coming up on
November 30—when we'd still be in London—and gave me a
birthday party. She really didn't know me that well yet.... We
were all so shook up at the time. Meeting the Queen is such a
ceremony, and we were very nervous about it. We had to learn
scenes for the live presentation, Alan was particularly nervous
and shy about that. My husband did a scene with Alan and
helped him out because Alan was a little unsteady on the stage.
He wasn't accustomed to it. It was a gangster sketch, and it
worked out very well. They were crazy about Alan in England.
After the actors did their bit on the stage we went back to our
seats to see the rest of the show. We had the box next to
Laurence Olivier, who had been knighted a year earlier, and
Vivien Leigh, and were very awed." Virginia Mayo laughs as she
says, "This is awful of me, but I'll tell you something very funny:
Lady Olivier fell asleep, and as she dozed on the side of the chair,
one of her little bosoms started to pop out. Alan noticed it and
nudged Mike. 'Hey look, Mike, she's falling out. Tell her, tell
her.' And Mike said, 'No, you tell her. Why should I tell her?'
Alan said, 'I can't tell her, *you* tell her.' I'll never forget that.
Both were transfixed, but neither could get up the nerve to say
anything..."

The O'Sheas and Ladds enjoyed being together so much in
London that they decided to go on to Paris together. Sue had

been there as a young girl, but the city had changed considerably since the 1920s. The foursome reacted like starry-eyed tourists. "We went to the Folies Bergère, all those kinds of places," Ms. Mayo says. "We had a wonderful, wonderful time..."

It was taken for granted that the friendship would continue back in California, and indeed on December 31 the O'Sheas drove to Hidden Valley to attend Sue's New Year's Eve party at the ranch. "I don't think Alan was drinking heavily," Virginia says. "We really didn't have much to drink. But suddenly Alan wanted to take a horseback ride in the dead of night, and he insisted Mike join him. Now Mike was a good rider—he loved horses—but it was very dangerous riding up there in the night. He thought Alan had lost his marbles, but he agreed. They took a ride up and down those hills outside the ranch and, Mike told me, Alan wanted to go really fast. He kept saying, 'Come on Mike, let's ride, let's *go*.' When they came back Mike thought the whole thing was a little strange... It was around this time, that Alan and Sue were building their house on North Mapleton Drive, and they took Mike and me to see the foundation. Alan was so excited about the house. He couldn't stop talking about it."

All the Ladds were full of anticipation and impatience, waiting for the day their home would be completed. By now, they required a staff of fifteen to help keep everything running smoothly. Their payroll included a cook, a maid, a nurse for David, a gardener, a houseman, a private secretary and two girls to handle the fan mail, a man who supervised the ranch, two couples at the ranch, and an accountant to take care of tax matters.

There were many tax matters to take care of. Alan Ladd was a very, very rich man. And he was close to becoming a great deal richer.

And riding for a fall...

CHAPTER 17

By early fall 1949 Alan Ladd had a house in town in which he could play host with a vengeance, literally, and where he would be happy—for a while, at least.

He proudly took all new arrivals at 323 North Mapleton Drive on the "grand tour," and his guest lists were four-star-studded. Such as Lucille Ball and Desi Arnaz, the Lloyd Nolans, Dinah Shore and George Montgomery, Paul Douglas and Jan Sterling all felt at home in the Ladds' magnificent new home....

The formal living room was mainly a showplace, its focal point an elegant marble fireplace over which paints of Laddie, Alana, David and Carol Lee were hung. Two large, tufted chintz-upholstered sofas stood on either side of the fireplace, separated by a marble-and-wood coffee table. Built-in bookshelves displaying beautifully bound—if rarely read—classics (not so out of character for Gatsby, after all) ran parallel to the fireplace.

Tastefully and expensively decorated though it was, not much living took place in the Ladd living room. Alan preferred the garden room, where he would conduct his interminable press interviews, hold informal business conferences and entertain friends who came by for a quick drink. Pine-paneled cabinets concealed a bar, radio and storage space. There were tricorn antique mirrored tables built by George Montgomery and raspberry-colored sofas.

The adjoining dining room was painted apple green—and the same soft gray-green extended through to the living room. Sue had brought over her French Provincial dining room set from the old house because it was in keeping with the decor, but the bedroom she shared with Alan was a break from the other rooms. Because it was done in a color scheme that combined dull green, lemon yellow, brown and red, Sue chose a print with a brown background and the other colors in it for her bedspread and headboard, the fireside chair and also covered one wall with it.

On the red shelves in their bedroom were Dresden and Royal Copenhagen figurines symbolizing the eight years of Alan and Sue's marriage: four small Dresden figures of the muses—Painting, Music, Sculpture and Dance—had been bought in Chicago during a personal appearance tour for *This Gun for Hire*. A Royal Copenhagen miniature of a mother and baby commemorated Alana's birth and a little boy the arrival of David.

Each of the children had his or her own room. (Carol Lee was now at U.C.L.A. and Alana was enrolled at Westlake School for Girls, but both girls lived at home.)

Although Sue personally supervised every detail of the interior decoration, Alan was almost obsessive about the pool and patio areas. Since there were two young children running about, he had the far side of the patio enclosed by a small flagstone fence topped by a wrought-iron rail. A gate of matching wrought iron led to the swimming pool and was always kept locked. The top of the fence, however, was planted in red geraniums. The pool was built to be functional and had none of the exotic flourishes *de rigueur* with most other stars of the time. With access from five rooms, the patio itself was decorated with meticulous care. Its furniture was of wrought iron, the tabletops glass. The raspberry cushions of the chairs reversed to a dark green with a pink cabbage-rose print that was carried over to the lining of the parasols shading the two lounges. Under a *porte-cochère* leading from the garden, sectional chairs surrounded a large coffee table. Beach chairs and lounges were spread over the grass by the pool. On each side of the patio doors grew two camellia bushes which Sue had transplanted from their former home. Two olive trees were planted in flagstone tree wells, and a profusion of flowers grew alongside the gray-painted redwood picket fence that marked the end of the property.

Alan's office doubled as an entertainment center, with a large screen, hidden in a ceiling recess, that came down to turn the room into a theater whenever the Ladds chose to end a dinner party by screening a new film provided by Paramount. Chocolate brown and coral were the dominant colors. Two dark brown sofas had horsehead appliqués cut from the polished cotton drapery material. These, the horsehead lamps and several wall prints provided an equine theme for the room. . . .

The cost of building, furnishing, decorating and maintaining this worldly Shangri-la was astronomical, but perhaps for the first time in his life Alan was unconcerned about cash flow. The lot on Mapleton Drive had cost him $13,000, but even before construction of the house had begun he had been offered $125,000 for it. With the house, the property was worth a half-million dollars. Unless there was a natural disaster, he could not lose money on it.

In terms of publicity, too, the house was a considerable asset. Magazine editors and news photo services seemed forever on the hunt for "something new on the Ladds" to keep the momentum going. The house provided it. *Photoplay* went on about the big red bow Alan had nailed to the door of the house the day the Ladds moved in, with an accompanying card that read, "To Sue with Love from Alan." *Motion Picture* covered the solid-gold keys which opened the front door—keys inscribed with the words "Our World." *Modern Screen* dispatched photographer Bob Beerman up in a small plane to get an exclusive aerial view of the estate . . . Sue, happily besieged with requests for the first photo layout of the new house, would reply sweetly; "Just as soon as it's completed and Alan has a few free days." She lived up to her word but avoided promising "exclusives" that would mean the enmity of any of the rival publications. It was come one, come all. And all came. Larry Barbier and Don Ornitz of Globe Photos, Beerman of *Modern Screen*, Hymie Fink of *Photoplay*—the best of the fan-press photographers.

Sue carefully kept track of what she and Alan and the children wore at each sitting, how they posed and in which rooms. If there were to be no "exclusives," there were to be no duplications either.

David, considering the layouts a wonderful new game, was something of a little ham. Alana, by now a veteran at this kind of thing, was blasé but tried not to appear bored or restless. Alan and the children stripped down to swim trunks and splashed about in the pool as the cameras clicked. The family dogs got more photo coverage than Lassie. Sue would appear in the layouts but avoided swimsuits and poolside activities. The photographers did not insist, nor did they protest when she asked to see contacts in order to "kill" any unflattering shots before publication. The Hollywood publicity game still had its rules, and in this way the press insured the kind of cooperation that was becoming a rarity among the major stars.

With this kind of exposure to the public the Ladd domain was rather more like a well-groomed stage setting than a real home. No area was sacrosanct or off limits except, perhaps, Laddie's room. Most of the photo layouts were scheduled during school hours, but on rare occasions Laddie, who had come to live part time with Alan and Sue, was seen wandering around the house. When it was suggested that he do some posing, Sue would sweetly discourage the idea. "Oh, let's not bother Laddie," Albert Delacorte recalls her telling his photographer. "Why remind the public of what was such a painful episode in Alan's life?" She was referring, of course, to his first marriage to Midge.

Nor was Carol Lee, who was now seventeen, ever part of those family layouts... "I was grateful I was left out of those layouts because the kids had to stay home and have their hair done and spend their Saturdays posing for pictures, and Laddie and I got to go out and fool around and do just what we wanted. If anything, David and Lonnie (Alana) resented our leaving. You know, people think the kids were made to feel important, but they would much rather have been out fooling around the way we were. However, there was never any petty jealousy in our family, and I thank my parents for that. They made us all feel so worthy we didn't need to feel jealousy."

And editors, columnists, writers and photographers all

deferred to Sue's wishes. Why jeopardize the Ladds' cooperation and goodwill for the sake of a picture or two? By now Alan
would often talk about his first son, but Midge's name would
continue to be omitted. Of the thousands of photographs taken
in the house on North Mapleton Drive, young Laddie was
conspicuous by his absence. If he accidentally appeared in a shot
during this period, he was either cropped out of the finished
print or the negative was destroyed. Occasionally a novice
freelance photographer would notice a chubby boy with a crew
cut on an outing with the Ladds, but even then Alan, Jr., was
never identified by name. As one cynic remarked at the time, "It
was almost as though Alan had a 'closet' son." Never actually
hidden, Laddie just was never put on public display. His father
loved him, wanted him in his home, but this child was a "living
reminder" of the old days, and of Midge, and that was a story the
press was not to have....

The now celebrated Ladd Jr., reflecting upon the days he was
shoved in the background harbors no ill-feelings. "It was
explained to us that the studio wanted it that way. I might have
been a raging neurotic if I'd been in the limelight. Who knows?"

However, both the radio public and Louella Parsons were
"officially" introduced to Alan's eldest son when Louella did a
broadcast at the Ladds' new home for her Christmas show in
1949.

"Laddie, it's so nice to meet you," she gushed. "You're always
away at school when I come to visit." So much for that. The rest
of the show was devoted to the joy of Christmas at the Ladds.

Because of the children, Christmas on North Mapleton Drive
was a lavish and merry occasion. Cards were strung on ribbons
crisscrossing the ceiling of the garden room. Colored lights
twined around green bushes in front of the door. Mistletoe hung
in strategic places throughout the house, and there was a
spectacular tree surrounded by dozens of presents for everyone
in the household, including the three dogs. The Christmas table
groaned with a thirty-pound turkey brought down from
Alsulana Ranch, together with enough side dishes, mince and
cherry pies, fruitcakes, and eggnog to feed the family ten times
over. Everyone ate and ate.

Everyone but Alan.

In an interview for the holiday season he said, "If only

Mother could be here ... If only she could have lived to enjoy a real Christmas like this." As always, he made no mention of how Ina Beavers had died.

His was a rich man's Christmas, a successful man's Christmas. But he was still unable to shake the unhappy ghosts of Christmases past, or to stop worrying about the looming ghosts of Christmases to come. . . .

Ladd

A HOLLYWOOD TRAGEDY

THE STORY IN PHOTOS...

Ina Ladd was 27 years old when she posed for this studio photograph with 2-year-old Alan Walbridge Ladd, Jr. in Hot Springs, Arkansas. No pictures exist of the senior Alan Ladd.

Alan and Midge and 2-year-old son Laddie (Alan Ladd, Jr.) in front of $20-a-month bungalow-court apartment, shortly before Alan met Sue Carol. No other photos remain of the three together.

Signed to Paramount in October, 1941, Alan showed off for a studio photographer. This photo was used to show Americans how to save gasoline as the country entered World War II.

Brian Donlevy, left, had star billing with Veronica Lake in *The Glass Key*, but Alan, cast in the film before *This Gun for Hire* was released, stole the picture and the girl. (Photo: Paramount)

Anxious to get as much footage as possible of their newest star, the studio rushed Alan into *Lucky Jordan* with Helen Walker, a few weeks after *This Gun for Hire* was released. (Photo: Paramount)

Alan Ladd, Dorothy Lamour and Robert Preston co-starred in *Wild Harvest.* Originally titled *The Big Haircut,* the film underwent a title change because, according to Preston, a Ladd vehicle with that name "sounded like a gangster movie," instead of a story about migrant farm workers. (Photo: Paramount)

Alan and Sue at a gala premier of the British film *Black Narcissus*. That's Sonja Henie directly behind Alan. Alan would co-star with *Narcissus* star Deborah Kerr a few years later in *Thunder in the East*.

The title role in *The Great Gatsby* (filmed in 1948, released in 1949) was the biggest challenge of Alan's career. Here he's with Elisha Cook, Jr. and Ed Begley.

Paramount's ads for *Shane*, with Jean Arthur, center, and Van Heflin, right, proclaimed, "There never was a motion picture like *Shane*." There never was for Alan, who reached the peak of his career with this classic Western, and formed a deep and abiding friendship with Heflin. (Photo: Paramount)

Laddie, now 20, dropped by the studio when Alan and David returned from location shooting for *The Proud Rebel*. (Photo: Formosa Productions Inc.)

Alan Ladd and Marilyn Monroe won the coveted Photoplay Gold
Medal Awards as the most popular performers of 1953, presented
March 9, 1954, the night after Alan's return from Europe. He won
for *Shane*, she for *How to Marry a Millionaire*. (Photo: UPI)

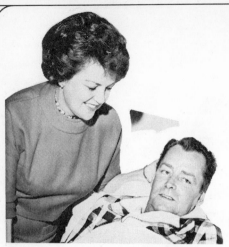

Alan recovers in the Woodland Park Community Hospital from a gunshot wound in his chest in November, 1962. He told police that he had stumbled and shot himself accidentally while investigating noises he believed to be made by a prowler at the Hidden Valley ranch. Sue rushed up from Los Angeles, where she had been at the time of the mishap.

On January 29, 1964, Alan Ladd succumbed to a lethal combination of alcohol and pills. The Palm Springs coroner decreed "accidental death." A grief-stricken Sue Ladd, accompanied by Alana and David, is seen leaving the Church of the Recessional in Forest Lawn after funeral services on February 1. Three thousand fans showed up to view Alan's body. (Photo: UPI)

CHAPTER 18

The 1950s had begun, and Alan Ladd greeted the new decade with his by then characteristic apprehension.

"I'm the most insecure guy in Hollywood," he told a friend. "If you had it good all your life, you figure it can't ever get bad, but when you had it bad, you wonder how long a thing like this will last."

It was useless to point out that even if he abruptly decided to retire, the appreciation on the ranch, the Holmby Hills estate, and other astute investments made by Sue would make him financially independent for life.

He had barely had time to enjoy the comforts of his new home when he was given the script for a Western temporarily entitled *Montana Rides* and later to be released as *Branded*, Paramount being eager to cash in on the box-office popularity of *Whispering Smith*. Once again Alan Ladd was to be presented in "glorious Technicolor" against the "glorious" natural settings of Salt River. Without protest he went along with a hackneyed story and a director inexperienced in the techniques of filming a Western. Rudy Mate was no John Ford. His previous credits were black-and-white dramas which included *No Sad Songs for Me, The Dark Past, D.O.A.*, and *Union Station*. His assignment to this film was mystifying.

The "plot" of *Branded*: Alan Ladd portrays Cheya, a penniless drifter, convinced by ne'er-do-well Robert Keith to impersonate the long-lost son of a wealthy rancher and his wife (Charles Bickford and Selena Royale). The clue to the boy's identity is a birthmark on his shoulder. Cheya eventually convinces the family but comes to regret this "cruel deception"—out of both a guilty conscience and a not-too-brotherly attraction to the daughter of the family. *So* . . . he sets out to find the *real* son (Peter Hansen) and risks his life in battle against bandits to return him home, etc.

Mona Freeman was an ideal choice for Alan Ladd's leading lady. Just five feet, three and a half inches tall, with the same coloring as Ladd, she was twenty-three years old to his thirty-six, so their relationship either as brother and sister or potential lovers was credible—considerably more credible in either case than the plot. The wife of Pat Nearney and mother of a two-year-old daughter, Mona Freeman, despite her Dresden-china beauty, presented no challenge to Sue. She had been a teenage model when Paramount was dazzled by her photo on a Miss Subways-of-the-Month poster. She had arrived at the studio just as Alan was returning from the service, but, she says, "He was already a big star. We were worlds apart socially and professionally. I heard wonderful things about him. I saw him on the sets and around the studio but we were never introduced. Eventually it was a case of nodding to each other as we passed. I had him sized up as a very shy and reserved person, though I never really knew him. When I got the part in *Branded*, I had no idea what Alan would be like as a leading man. Frankly, I didn't expect too much because I'd never thought of him as an actor. Instead he seemed to me to be a personality with a beautiful voice who underplayed everything. But since I underplayed too, we got along fine. I certainly had no chance to find out what he was like as a screen lover. Since he played a man posing as my brother until the end of the movie, we had little chance to be romantic in front of the cameras. I imagined that he'd be good in his love scenes because there was a tender quality in his work. . . ."

Perhaps it was the influence of the part he was playing, but in any case, by the time the company moved on to Arizona and New Mexico locations Alan was taking a very brotherly interest in his new leading lady... "On this picture," Ms. Freeman recalled, "we had a ball. Alan just relaxed and had fun. Where once I thought he'd crawl into his shell on a production, he was actually full of gags and kidding most of the time on the set."... However, the thing she remembers most about *Branded* was Alan's deferential attitude toward veteran actor Charles Bickford, who played the pivotal father role: "On location, early in the picture, there was a scene in which he was to fight Mr. Bickford. Alan didn't like the setup at all and flatly refused to hit the older man even though he didn't mind if Mr. Bickford hit him. So at Alan's insistence the scene was shot the way *he* saw it. When the scene was shown back at Paramount, it was nixed. Without the fight, the studio insisted, it lacked meaning. It was reshot. Later Alan was the first to admit he was wrong, although he was still uncomfortable about having to fight with a man twenty-four years his senior."... Mona Freeman was too young to understand why Alan Ladd could not strike back at a father-figure.

Branded opened at the New York Paramount on January 10, 1951, and consistent Bosley Crowther of the *New York Times* commented the following day: "Let us not try to deceive you. There is no particular brilliance in this film. As a matter of fact, for our money it is a pretty dull lot of stuff. Neither is Mr. Ladd outstanding as a Western wrong-righter on this swing. He does his job with professional trumpery just as all the other actors do.... But there is something about the silken smoothness with which Mr. Ladd plays a poke that is vaguely idly amusing. He is so ultra indifferent, so wearily suave. When he perspires it is even incongruous."

Alan pretended to be—and wasn't—amused by the review. In fact, he was at the point at which critical shots couldn't hurt him with either the studio, the public, or even the less highbrow members of the press. The end of 1950 found him at the top of his popularity. For the third year in a row he had topped the *Modern Screen* poll. As proof of his now international appeal, the Foreign Press Association's ballots, coming in from every country—from Scotland (where he shared honors with Greer Garson) to the Union of South Africa (where Esther Williams was his female counterpart)—made him the leading contender for "World's Favorite Star." At home, the ladies of the

Hollywood Women's Press Club gave him (and Loretta Young)
the prized Golden Apple award for being the most cooperative
personality in filmland, and he continued to receive the largest
amount of fan mail of any player on the Paramount lot. Even
Darryl Zanuck of competitor Twentieth-Century-Fox noted,
"There aren't any box-office stars anymore except John Wayne
and Alan Ladd."

He was literally everyone's favorite nice guy.... The Los
Angeles Police Department got five hours of his time recording
fifty radio spot announcements urging weekend drivers to "take
it easy." He said yes to the Air Force when asked to spend several
days at the Travis Air Base in Fairfield, California, talking to
G.I.'s as they returned home from Korea. Colonel Kelly, in
charge of the operation there, later said that Alan Ladd did more
for the men's morale than medicine could possibly do. When he
learned at Travis that thirty percent of the wounded men in
veterans' hospitals had no family ties and therefore received no
mail, he sponsored an "Adopt a G.I. Pen Pal" campaign and
went about urging the public to get names from the Armed
Forces Information Service. Louella Parsons, Hedda Hopper,
and Sheilah Graham dutifully publicized the program, and
within a month Alan had received some twelve hundred
thank-you notes from grateful G.I.'s....

That first year of the new decade, it seemed that everyone in
the world loved Alan Ladd.

Except Alan Ladd.

He was an angry man—and a bitterly disappointed one.

Though unwilling to admit it, he desperately wanted a
prestige film. No one at Paramount was interested. Alan Ladd,
presented in "typical Alan-Ladd fashion," was "money in the
bank." Why rock the boat?

Summing up Alan's career, Adela Rogers St. John pointed
out in *American Weekly:*

> ...from *This Gun for Hire* until now [1950] Alan Ladd
> never had made a great picture or even a very good one; he
> never had a big supporting cast, an important leading
> woman or co-star; he'd never been nominated for an
> Academy or New York Film Critics Award, nor been in a
> picture so nominated.

Nevertheless, today Alan Ladd has more of the thing upon which the movies were built—without which they will not continue as the world's favorite form of entertainment—than anyone else on the screen today. Millions of fans rush to the theaters to see Alan Ladd. We know this because there is nothing else in his movies to see. Actually, since *This Gun for Hire*, Alan Ladd has never given a great performance. Whether he plays sailor, soldier, doctor, gangster or cowboy, he remains Alan Ladd. Which must be what the folks want, for not one of his pictures has ever lost a dime. They grossed $55,000,000 in the last decade.

At all times the test of true movie stardom has been the star's personal appeal over and above his studio's margin for error. A real Movie Star must have a following that survives bad pictures. Alan Ladd has survived so much that Darryl F. Zanuck, the brilliant, iconoclastic head of Twentieth-Century-Fox, once called him in print, "the indestructable man."

He's even survived, let's face it, some pretty bad acting of his own.

He survived. He did whatever the studio wanted him to do. He shrugged off the bad parts, the bad stories, and—what he was painfully aware of at times—the bad acting.

Because his own self-image was so deeply impaired, he stoically accepted whatever "Big Daddy"—for which, read Paramount—decided. Always his acceptance of the way things were prevented even a minor rebellion (with the exception of that one Sue-and-Alan brief sit-out and suspension). But although he kept a cool exterior, inside he was being eaten up—and was eating himself up...

He may have made jokes about playing Hamlet but in truth he had no desire to attempt any Shakespearean role, and was terrified at the prospect of appearing in the theater (although his early radio shows had been done in a theater before a live audience). Yet there was one part he desired with a passion.

For years he had carried around a dog-eared copy of T. E. Lawrence's classic *The Seven Pillars of Wisdom*, and even admitted to surprised interviewers that he wanted to play Lawrence of Arabia. (Those who associate the role with Peter

O'Toole in the 1962 Oscar-winning film may find the idea incongruous, but it wasn't as ridiculous as it seems. Especially not to Alan or Sue.)

In writing about his friend in his 1924 account *With Lawrence in Arabia* (Century Publishers) Lowell Thomas, the noted journalist and world traveler, described Lawrence as "carrying his five feet three with dignity, marking him every inch a king, perhaps a caliph in disguise who stepped out of the pages of *The Arabian Nights* . . . as blond as a Scandinavian in whose veins flow Viking blood and the cool tradition of fjords and sagas. This youth walked rapidly . . . his blue eye oblivious to his surroundings. . . ."

Physically, at least, Alan was perfect for the role. His English heritage gave some validity to his playing the legendary British hero, and with a director as powerful as David Lean or, closer to home, Fred Zinnemann or George Stevens, perhaps Alan could have been altogether up to the role. All pure speculation, of course. Paramount had neither the intention nor the need to build an expensive epic around a property they could put into anything and end up making a fortune. Besides, Paramount wasn't particularly epic-oriented; Cecil B. DeMille's spectaculars were the only exception to this policy, and that bold, crusty director had his own ideas about the nature of the epics he wanted to make and the stars he wanted to see in them.

Alan Ladd was not one of them.

Despite a fondness displayed for Alan during their "Lux Radio Theater" days and a warm greeting when they met on the Paramount lot, DeMille acted as though Alan didn't exist when he was assembling his casts.

Neither Alan nor Sue ever knew the reason for this boycott, but Robert Preston readily understood it. "DeMille hated short people. He would get the tallest actors in the world and then build up their shoes. I remember wearing lifts, Preston Foster wearing lifts. Gary Cooper didn't have to wear lifts because he had cowboy boots on. And we were all over six feet tall."

The big excitement at Paramount at the time was the newest DeMille epic, *The Greatest Show on Earth*. On June 20, 1949, the studio had paid $250,000 for the rights to make the picture. After spending a summer traveling with Ringling Brothers and cramming notebooks with circus data, DeMille and writer

Frederic M. Frank began to develop the story on which the screenplay would be based.

For Paramount's king of the epics, nothing but an all-star cast would do. He chose Betty Hutton, Cornel Wilde, Jimmy Stewart, and Gloria Grahame. For the part of Brad, the circus manager, he picked a young Broadway actor named Charlton Heston whose work he had admired in an obscure film version of *Julius Caesar*. Heston's role was described in standard studioese as "a man who has sawdust for blood and puts the circus and its welfare above all else." It seemed a perfect part for Alan Ladd, but not once during the long months of preproduction and casting was he even casually considered. Nor did Alan try to sell himself to DeMille, as did Paulette Goddard, who had set her large eyes on the role of the elephant girl (!) and was rejected, or Betty Hutton, who had sent DeMille a thousand-dollar floral arrangement with a tiny replica of herself swinging on a trapeze on top of it—a gimmick that got her the part.

If Alan was bitter about the DeMille snub, he kept his feeling—as usual—to himself. But within a year he was to receive another ego-shattering blow which he couldn't handle with his typical apparent indifference... *Detective Story* had been one of the unqualified hits of the 1948–49 Broadway season. Written by Pulitzer Prize-winner Sidney Kingsley, it had provided Ralph Bellamy one of the most powerful roles of his career. The lead character was "the detective who has a bitterness toward the world that drives him to go after criminals with a relentlessness and overpowering zeal—a man whose fixation on convictions brooks no pity or compromise." Every studio in Hollywood was bidding for the rights. Every rugged male star had his sights set on the top role, since there was little chance that Ralph Bellamy would get a chance at it; at forty-five he was a star in the theater, but at best a featured actor in films.

Picking up the *Hollywood Reporter* one morning, Alan was startled to see an item with a New York dateline headlined: DETECTIVE STORY BOUGHT BY PARAMOUNT. ALAN LADD SET FOR STARRING ROLE.

He read it twice. It was detailed, sounded valid, conclusive. Not since he was named for *This Gun for Hire* had he felt this kind of excitement.

At the studio he cornered an executive, waving the trade paper: "Hey, is it true that I'm doing *Detective Story?*"

"We haven't closed the deal yet. Expect to finalize it over the weekend."

During the weekend Alan could think of nothing else and he read the play carefully, savoring its lines. Here was the kind of property that could get him respect as an actor. The role of Detective James McLeod, under the right direction, could almost guarantee an Oscar nomination.

The next week it was officially announced that Paramount had secured the screen rights to the play. William Wyler, one of the best, was set to produce and direct. Lee Grant, Joseph Wiseman, Michael Strong, and Horace McMahon would be brought in from New York to recreate their original stage roles, and Bill Bendix would return to the studio for the first time in two years to play McLeod's close friend, Detective Lou Brody.

Bellamy was definitely out, as was Meg Mundy who played his wife on Broadway. But there was no further indication that Ladd was in, and the studio avoided mentioning *Detective Story* to him again.

Direct inquiries from Sue or Alan's agents were met with evasions. They took for granted that Wyler would have final approval in casting the two leads, and he was a man who had no interest or patience with what he considered "manufactured" movie stars. Even with proven actors he was a taskmaster, known to shoot fifty takes or more until he got what he considered perfection. It was only too clear he did not want Alan Ladd. Eventually Kirk Douglas, who had started his career at Paramount under the direction of Hal Wallis five years earlier, was set for the role.

Presumably contrite, Paramount came up with another detective role for Alan: a postal inspector who stymies a million-dollar mail haul and brings to book the murderers of one of his colleagues. Released as *Appointment with Danger*, it was a nice melodrama that put Alan back into his natural element, but a *Detective Story* it was not. The studio planned to follow this with *Quantrill's Raiders*, another formula Western. With each assignment Alan was more certain that no one from Adolph Zukor down wanted to tinker with brand success.

Alan *finally* complained.

"Why worry?" he was told. "Your pictures make money."

"Nobody's strong enough to stand up under a flood of weak material," Alan argued back. No one was listening.

Although his contract was about to expire, none of the executives felt that he would be either foolhardy or disloyal enough to bolt. Paramount was, after all, more than his home. It was his roots, his security, his benevolent father. The studio was prepared to offer him a substantial raise to stay, plus irresistible fringe benefits. Alan, however, felt that time was closing in on him.

Sue; Herman Citron, Alan's agent at Music Corporation of America, which now owned his entire contract; and Lew Wasserman, the agency's powerful head, discreetly let it be known that Alan Ladd was not irrevocably bound to Paramount Pictures. To the contrary, he was on the auction block.

Hollywood began its hottest bidding in thirty years. Darryl Zanuck said openly that of all the stars not already under contract to him he'd rather have Alan Ladd than anyone else in the movies. But even Zanuck couldn't compete with Jack Warner's offer—a deal that many felt was to set a dangerous precedent in Hollywood. Warner Brothers would guarantee $150,000 per picture and ten percent of the *gross* for one picture a year over a period of ten years. In addition, Alan would have (a) his freedom to make outside pictures; (b) story approval; and, most important of all, (c) the residual rights he wanted for his children.

It was both an emotional and financial triumph for Alan to be returning as a prince to the kingdom where he had once been a pauper. Contracts would not be signed nor an official announcement made until the following spring. But after he completed *Quantrill's Raiders* with Lizabeth Scott (released as *The Red Mountain*), he felt an unfamiliar sense of exhilaration. This first year of the new decade had brought with it a real promise of security.

Which, after a near-fulfillment, would be broken before the decade was half over.

CHAPTER 19

Shane was hardly a man at all but something like the spirit of the West, beautiful in fringed buckskins. He emerges beautifully from the plains, breathing sweetness and a melancholy which is no longer simply the Westerner's natural response to experience but has taken on spirituality: and when he has accomplished his mission, meeting and destroying in the black figure of Jack Palance a Spirit of Evil just as metaphysical as his own embodiment of virtue, he fades away again into the more distant West, a man whose "day is over," leaving behind the wondering little boy who might have imagined the whole story.

—Robert Warshow
Essay on "The Westerner"

Alan Ladd, Van Heflin, Jean Arthur, Jack Palance, and director George Stevens all knew they had something good going for them when they left Hollywood for the Jackson Hole, Wyoming, location of *Shane*. But surely none of them was aware that they were involved in a classic, a movie that would be considered the finest Western ever made.

Alan's most constant critic, Bosley Crowther, said in his April 24, 1953, review of the picture for *The New York Times:*

> ... Shane contains something more than the beauty and the grandeur of the mountains and plains, drenched by the brilliant Western sunshine and the violent, torrential, black-browed rains. It contains a tremendous comprehension of the bitterness and passion of the feuds that existed between the new homesteaders and the cattlemen on the open range. It contains a disturbing revelation of the savagery that prevailed in the hearts of the old gun-fighters, who were simply legal killers under the frontier code. And it also contains a very wonderful understanding of the spirit of a little boy amid all the tensions and excitements and adventures of a frontier home.
>
> As a matter of fact, it is the concept and the presence of this little boy as an innocent and fascinated observer of the brutal struggle his elders wage that permits a refreshing viewpoint on material that's not exactly new....
>
> The story Mr. Stevens is telling is simply that of the bold and stubborn urge of a group of modest homesteaders to hold on to their land and their homes against the threats and harassments of a cattle baron who implements his purpose with paid thugs. And it is brought to its ultimate climax when the stranger, who seeks peace on one of the farms, tackles an ugly gun-fighter imported from Cheyenne to do a job on the leader of the homesteaders, the father of the boy.
>
> This ultimate gun-fight, incidentally, makes a beautiful, almost classic scene as Mr. Stevens has staged it in the dismal and dimly lit saloon, with characters slinking in the background as the antagonists, Alan Ladd and Jack Palance, face off in frigid silence before the fatal words fly and the guns blaze. It is a scene which, added to the many that Mr. Stevens has composed in this film, gives the whole thing the quality of a fine album of paintings of the frontier.

From that summer morning in 1951 when *Shane* began shooting in the shadows of the Grand Tetons until George

Stevens called it a wrap in mid-October, Alan Ladd experienced feelings unlike any he had known during his ten years as a Paramount star. He responded to Stevens' direction like a kid absorbing wisdom and knowledge for the first time, and he obediently, sensitively, followed the master's instruction. He did his work well. The *New York Times* noted—in Ladd's obituary—that his performance in *Shane* was "generally regarded as one of the best performances ever given in a Western movie."

Alana, David, and Laddie accompanied Alan and Sue to Jackson Hole, Laddie with Midge's blessings even though it meant not seeing her son for the entire summer. But Laddie was movie-mad, and she wouldn't stand in the way of the opportunity of seeing George Stevens at work. Her own daughter, Cynthia (Cindy), was four now, and Midge was thinking of adding to the family, since Laddie's absence created a large void in her life.

Shane required a number of children for "atmosphere." Laddie and Alana were asked to join the company for a salary of six dollars a day. Although Alana's role called for her to lug a ten-pound sack of potatoes back and forth throughout a long afternoon, she remembers her film debut with pleasure. "I was constantly surrounded by my family and friends and I remember the experience as a very happy time of life. I can recall going to a preview of *Shane* with my mother and crying like a baby afterward. The picture still gets to me."

Stevens didn't require Laddie's services after all, so the boy earned his pay by just sitting around and watching.

Carol Lee remembers coming to the *Shane* location: "I had the drawing room on the train next to Fran Heflin," she recalls, "and by that time Dad and Van had become close friends. I don't think either said, 'We're in the process of making a classic,' but when you're working with a man like George Stevens you know you have something good going. And Stevens had infinite patience, particularly with the little boy Brandon De Wilde, who drove all the actors a little crazy because his idea of fun was jumping up and down in the mud—splashing mud all over everyone. But George Stevens knew how to work with him." And with Alan Ladd. The Stevens-Ladd mutual admiration society would continue for many years after the filming.

"You know," said Stevens, "it's against the formula, but Ladd seemed to have a decency on the screen even in violent roles like this one. He always seemed to have a large measure of reserve and dignity." When reminded of the long-standing Hollywood rap about Alan being "an actor with only one expression," Stevens countered, "You show me an actor with one *good* expression and I'll be happy. I can recollect only one good expression from Gary Cooper, but I've seen great pictures built around it."

And Alan in turn said about Stevens, "I learned more about acting from that man in a few months than I had in my entire life up until then. Stevens is the best in the business. He knows exactly how to handle actors, how to relax them and win their confidence."

But it was even more than Stevens' direction that made the *Shane* location such a happy one for Alan. During the summer months he established what would turn out to be a lifelong friendship with Van Heflin, who played Mr. Starrett, the farmer who befriends Shane.

Heflin, just three years Ladd's senior, was perhaps closer in age to Alan than any of his friends, and the fact that he was a native Oklahoman also helped establish a bond. In addition, Heflin possessed most of the other qualities Alan had always been drawn to. He was a quiet man but of above-average intelligence, a college graduate, and a respected stage and screen performer. And although he had never prompted mass hysteria from the public or made any fan magazine polls or attracted large amounts of fan mail, he *had* won an Oscar as Best Supporting Actor for 1942's *Johnny Eager,* and always received splendid reviews—whether he was appearing in a dud like *Kid Glove Killer* or in a classic like *Madame Bovary.* Before signing for *Shane,* Heflin had startled the Hollywood establishment by asking MGM to relieve him of a contract that had two and a half years to run so he could explore Broadway and television for far less money than he had been earning at the time.

Heflin's life-style and career were, in short, the opposite side of the coin from Alan's, but in spite of—or perhaps because of—the differences, the two men became, according to Heflin, as "close as brothers."

Echoing the sentiments of the majority of Alan's co-stars,

Heflin would later say, "Alan was a far better actor than he would ever believe himself to be. As with most of us, he needed a director who could bring out the best in him. With George [Stevens] he had it. [Alan] was a very sensitive person and he had a terrific inferiority complex. He got excellent reviews for *Shane,* but because of studio politics he was passed over for an Oscar nomination. So, for that matter, was I. But I had already won an Oscar, and because I was a character actor I felt there was always another great role in the future. Alan later said that he thought *Shane* was a fluke. . . . One of the sadnesses in my life is that Alan and I never had the opportunity to work together again after *Shane.* . . . But we talked about it a lot. And although actors usually go their separate ways after a movie is completed, Alan and I remained very close. God, how I loved that man!"

On October 16, when *Shane* wound up, Alan, Sue and Jean Arthur gave a party for three hundred—cast, crew and spouses—to celebrate, Alan attending with his arm in a sling as the result of a barroom brawl scene (another accident). Even Jean Arthur, who was extremely shy when not in front of the camera, was jubilant that afternoon. "We all felt," remembers makeup man Hal Lierley, "that we had a pretty good movie in the can."

Better than they knew . . .

One suspects that Paramount was unaware of *Shane*'s potential impact. It seemed an accepted if rather self-defeating practice of certain major studios in the Forties and early Fifties to "kiss off" a defecting or fading star with a property that seemed likely to damage his or her reputation. At MGM, Lana Turner would barely survive *The Prodigal* and *Diane* or Clark Gable, *Betrayed;* Joan Crawford would be carelessly cast in *Above Suspicion,* and even Greta Garbo was humiliated by a horror called *Two-Faced Woman.* It was the same at Warner Brothers, where Bette Davis was punished with the awful *Winter Meeting* and made a near-laughingstock by *Beyond the Forest.* Errol Flynn's expendability was demonstrated when he was assigned *The Master of Ballantrae.* All these great stars suffered before leaving the studios that had made them famous—and for which they had made fortunes.

Paramount seemed of the cast of mind that said, "If *we* can't have them, let's make sure no one else will want them." Since

Warners had already proved just how much they had wanted
Ladd with their record-making deal, a few more mediocrities
like *Thunder in the East* with Charles Boyer and Deborah Kerr
(which had been made well before *Shane* but shelved for nearly
three years) hardly mattered for the long run and a Ladd movie,
no matter how bad, still continued to produce some profits.

So it seems unlikely that the powers at Paramount would
have generously given Ladd a solid-gold epic as a farewell
present had they been blessed with a gift of prophecy. And if
Ladd had had a gift of prophecy, it seems just as unlikely that he
would have ever considered another studio's offer, no matter
how lucrative....

Because of Paramount's practice of allowing a long interval
to elapse between the shooting of a film and its release to
theaters, the *Shane* impact was still nearly two years in the
future. But well before then, Alan Ladd was painfully aware of
the very bad mistake he had made by shutting the DeMille Gate
behind him.

CHAPTER 20

After the completion of *Shane,* Alan was left with a let-down feeling he couldn't seem to shake, or in fact totally explain.

He had one picture left under his old contract—*Botany Bay,* a fanciful sea adventure co-starring James Mason and pretty Patricia Medina. Alan told Van Heflin that he "wished it was over and done with so I can pack my gear and get out." Then he backtracked, admitting, "It's going to be hard to say good-bye. I'm still not sure I've done the right thing."

He had lost ten pounds on the Wyoming location of *Shane* and his energy level was sagging, but his spirits got a boost when *Modern Screen* sent word that once again he was near the top of their readers' poll—second only to the indestructible John Wayne.

Which was still not enough to quiet his perennial fear that his luck could run out overnight. He wanted another tangible guarantee of security.

Bing Crosby had spoken often about his ranch near San Diego—how land could literally, in his case anyway, be picked up for a song in that growing area. Although Alan still had not overcome all the problems of the Hidden Valley operation, he and Sue drove south to scout promising real estate. He was attracted to a fifteen-hundred-acre spread of choice cattle-breeding land, but at the last moment changed his mind. Instead, his urge to buy was diverted into a twelve-carat ruby ring in a diamond setting as his birthday present to Sue....

Laddie had just turned fourteen, and his exposure to the filming of *Shane* had intensified an already strong interest in motion-picture making. Although he had the advantage of a projection room at home, Laddie would spend hours at the Westwood Village or Bruin theaters, completely absorbed in the images on the screen.

Alan sounded amused—still with remarkably bad fore-sight—when he told a reporter that his older son had informed him he wanted to be a producer. He was, he added, taking great pains to impress upon the boy that no one could say "I guess I want to be a producer" and turn into one just like that. "I told Laddie that he'd have to work at almost every other possible job on a movie lot first and *learn* it, because a producer has to know all about everything from set-building to costumes to acting. Laddie said he was willing. We'll see."

Alan and Sue now talked frequently to the press about Laddie and Carol Lee, acting as though things had never been otherwise. Reporters, eager to get a new slant on the family, latched onto every word and *still* tactfully refrained from asking why the two children had never been mentioned during the 1940s. They wrote about Laddie and Carol Lee but still found it impossible to get photographs of the four children together. One shot of Laddie taken at the cast party of *Shane* was printed without any accompanying identification. Paradoxically, the Ladds had no objection to posing before their home fireplace, where the portraits of all four children were mounted. This was the only chance Alan's public had to see what the son of his first marriage looked like.

Stella Roach, a Paramount publicity department woman assigned to coordinate Alan's interviews, today says that as far as she remembers, "No one asked about a previous marriage."

Possibly. More to the point, few dared. The ladies of the Hollywood Women's Press Club who had presented Alan with his Golden Apple the previous year couldn't risk having him or

Sue turn sour on them for the sake of one story. They concluded that whoever Alan's first wife was, she was probably being paid off to maintain her silence. Not one of them, it seems, took the trouble to check this out—or in fact find out if Laddie's mother were living or dead. As for Nick Stuart, still active in Hollywood and to remain so for years, he was known and liked by most of the press but his name also was rarely mentioned in connection with the Ladds. . . .

As usual, Alan dreaded the approach of the holiday season. This year of 1951 would be even more difficult than most, since the gifts he chose for the people he had worked with for a decade would be serving as both Christmas and farewell presents. In mid-November he was hit by the flu and confined to his bed for nearly ten days. Depressed and weak, he decided to spend the Thanksgiving weekend in the warm Palm Springs sun, hoping to get himself back in shape before starting work on *Botany Bay*.

The film was anything but a distinguished follow-up to *Shane,* although Paramount was said to be trying for a "class" production. Based on a novel by Charles Nordhoff and James Hall (of *Mutiny on the Bounty* fame) and directed by John Farrow, who was responsible for the box-office success of *Two Years Before the Mast,* the story dealt with a shipload of convicts being hauled from England to Australia in the late eighteenth century. The screenplay lacked dramatic punch, but with James Mason portraying a Captain Bligh-style villain with powerful malevolence, Alan had a strong foil to play against and the two men worked well together.

Alan's role, that of a young American who turned highwayman in order to get back his rightful inheritance, was colorless in comparison to Mason's, so the studio wrote in enough extra floggings, fights, keel-haulings and mutinous intrigues to strike a balance. And almost masochistically, Alan insisted on doing much of his own stunt work, to prove to himself that at thirty-eight he was in the same physical shape as in his prime. The way the cameras saw him he was, but still not completely over the effects of the flu, he tired easily.

On December 28, he suffered a relapse and was rushed home from the set with a high fever. The shooting schedule was adjusted to allow him to shake the bug. After spending a dismal New Year's Eve and Day on his back, he felt well enough to be driven to the ranch to convalesce for a few more days. But he would have little rest. On January 3 a horse got stuck in a trough, and he insisted on staying up most of the night attending to it. At one point on the verge of strangling itself to death, the animal lunged forward and took a severe bite out of Alan's right hand, an injury which would cause him recurring pain for months. . . .

And so it began in earnest—a seemingly never-ending chain of minor illnesses and freak accidents that was to afflict him for the rest of his life.

Why?

Was it more than coincidence that this unhappy sequence began with his departure from Paramount? His professional father-surrogate? His former studio had picked his scripts and directors; polished his image—shaped him into a star. His career at "home" at Paramount was earthquake-proof—as long as he followed orders like a good little Ladd. New freedom at a new studio, Warners, meant difficult decisions on his own, which could revive the old bugaboo of insecurity, of feeling like an orphan. Were these maladies symptomatic of that revival? Or were they, like Job's boils, some sort of a psychic rebellion against the constraints of authority? Either way, a self-destructive pattern was emerging that would one day end with the ultimate disaster. . . .

The final weeks of shooting on *Botany Bay* passed without incident, and on the last day, most of Alan's decade-long friends on the lot came by his dressing room to say good-bye . . . Pauline Kessinger, head of the Paramount commissary; her husband Coley, who had been a grip on the lot when Alan first arrived; Stella Roach and Bill Cunningham from the publicity department. Although he wasn't as close with his crews as the magazine stories led fans to believe, he was always affable, considerate, and generous. He had handed out several complete wardrobes to technicians and publicity men who were having tough times, and a seven-hundred-dollar camera went to one man who had been kind to him in the early years and had happened to admire the camera.

At Paramount, Alan Ladd was loved. No doubt about that. Stella Roach, now retired and able to speak freely, says, "He was a publicity person's dream—one of the most cooperative stars on the lot. He was always on time for interviews and layouts, always one-hundred-percent prepared. He told me once that when he was nervous he always whistled or hummed. And he certainly seemed to do a lot of both. He had trouble relaxing around adults, but with the children in his films he was completely at ease and outgoing."

He was also a favorite with the top company executives. When he told Y. Frank Freeman he wanted to buy his dressing-room furniture and take it with him to Warners, his boss shook his head: "Sorry, not for sale. We want to give it to you as a gift."

But once he'd said his final farewells, Alan couldn't bring himself to return to the studio to tie up the loose ends. Instead he sent his secretary, Bella Rachoff, to supervise the removal of his possessions and the shipment of most of them to Warners' Burbank lot.

Alan's furniture and other belongings were all in place and waiting for him when he reported to Warners for preproduction conferences on March 17. His new bosses made much of the fact that the last time he was on the lot it was as a common laborer. Studio publicity departments loved the sort of rags-to-riches story that perpetuated the myth that Hollywood was indeed a magic land where miracles were the rule. Now Alan Ladd was driving through the front gate of a studio where he had once lugged a lunch box. Terrific. One of the best tables in the executive section of the Green Room, Warners' intimate commissary, would always be reserved for him. And a poster-sized photograph of him would be hung on the walls alongside those of Doris Day, Gordon MacRae, Virginia Mayo, Will Rogers, Jr., Steve Cochran, James Cagney—Cagney being the only star from the old days still on the lot; Bogart, Davis, Flynn, and Robinson—all had left Warners for other pastures.

His welcome couldn't have been more solicitous. And Alan couldn't have felt more uncomfortable. "I wish," he said, "I wish I were the type who could walk into a place and have everybody love me. But I'm not, and there's no use wishing. Strangers still leave me self-conscious." . . . Shades of the little boy with a second father—a stranger. And to him, Warners was still a house of strangers; compared to Paramount, an alien land. Only the barren sound stages were familiar.

Sue and Alan promptly took off for a week in Palm Springs so that he could relax before officially starting work. Although now the owner of the Hidden Valley ranch, he was drawn to the small desert spa. It seemed to be the only place he could really relax, enjoy some peace of mind, and he began to think of looking for a home there.

That idea, however, had to be temporarily shelved. *The Iron Mistress*, in which he was to portray Jim Bowie, went into production in early April under the direction of Gordon Douglas. The title was a romantic euphemism for the lethal knife bearing the legendary designer's name. The story was an even more romanticized, if not totally distorted, version of the man's life. History depicts Bowie as something of a rascal around New Orleans in the days of buccaneer Jean Lafitte. He was, it seems, a man who achieved heroic recognition mostly by dying at the Alamo.

Screenwriter James R. Webb added gloss to historical fact by idealizing Bowie as a hick from the bayou who elevates himself in the world for the sole purpose of winning the love of a beautiful, high-born lady. He gambles, speculates in land, plays the horses and eventually designs the famous knife for self-protection—only to learn that the lady wasn't worth the effort. So he goes to Texas to settle for the sweet and loving daughter of the governor, and eventually to fight and die for the Lone Star State.

All this, on paper, sounded like the kind of vehicle Ladd fans would storm theaters to see. Since the studios had been forced to give up their theater chains, Warners planned to premiere *The Iron Mistress* at the New York Paramount, the familiar showcase of previous Ladd films. As further box-office insurance, they scheduled the release for November in order to beat Paramount's releases—*Thunder in the East, Shane,* and *Botany Bay*—to the nation's screens. Which turned out to be one of Warners' less shrewd decisions. Had *Mistress* been released *after Shane*, it might have been a blockbuster.

Alan, however, was enthusiastic about the film, and any anxiety he may have felt about working with strangers at Warners was relieved when Virginia Mayo, who had just completed *Captain Horatio Hornblower* opposite Gregory Peck, was cast as the femme fatale.... "Alan usually didn't have much to do with his leading ladies," she says, "but because we were friends outside the studio, it made for a happy experience.... I think I fell in love with Alan. I really do, because of the love scenes—so tender, so really sweet and touching. He really made me feel the part very easily. In *Iron Mistress* we were always hugging and kissing, it had its effect on me. I was married, though, and couldn't have asked for a better mate than Mike [O'Shea]. We had a great understanding and loved each other dearly, but I was very attracted to Alan during the course of the picture. Very much so. And that was good, because we were supposed to be lovers in the movie. I played a flirty kind of a woman—a real bitch—and gave him the dirty end of it and made him so unhappy. I had to keep putting him down. I kept marrying other people and disappointing him. In one scene I remember very distinctly I had to tell him I was married, and the look on his face was so unusual, so expressive—beautiful but sad. All the emotions played across his face. I had never seen that look on any man's face in acting.

"Alan was such a wonderful person. I really loved him more than anyone else I ever worked with. I had some leading men I disliked intensely. But Alan was really very, very sensitive, even more than Gregory Peck. I think that was unfortunate, because nobody was that sensitive to Alan in return... The whole problem with Alan's psyche was his inability to remember that he was a big star. And he was the *biggest*. His picture was always on the magazine covers, but he couldn't accept the fact that he was a good actor. The lack of artistic recognition affected him, affected him tragically—the fact that he was not recognized by all those artistic geniuses. The critics actually crucified him. It's just a shame that these people, who are so cruel that they can't wait to stick a knife in someone, have such power... During *Iron Mistress* I never noticed anything melancholy about Alan. Oh, he didn't make jokes, but he was full of them. I really hated to see that picture end. It was such a joy. It was one of my favorites. Alan and I talked about working together again and because he was now at Warners, we were sure we would. And we did—in *The Big Land*, which Alan produced himself, but that was five years later..."

There was more to *The Iron Mistress* than love scenes, however.

Anxious to maintain the strong macho Ladd image Paramount had so carefully developed over the years, writer James Webb and director Gordon Douglas had filled the story with ferocious action sequences. In addition to the mandatory fight scenes, they included several vicious knife duels. As in *Botany Bay,* Alan chose to forego the services of a professional stunt man, which he would regret. On April 25, he suffered a serious knee injury that left black-and-blue marks for weeks. On May 27 he broke a bone in his right hand when he missed a punch and slammed his hand against a concrete floor. With the injured hand in a carefully camouflaged cast, he completed the last few days of shooting in great pain but at least without further mishaps.

Typically, Alan accepted the injuries without any rancor. "Wounded in action," he wryly told a friend. "I'm a helluva hero in this picture. I kill nine guys and duel and talk and talk and talk and make love all over the place. Don't miss me. I'm very big."

But even after the cast was removed, his injured right hand continued to cause considerable pain whenever he moved his fingers. Additional X rays revealed that the broken bones were not healing properly, and his doctor told him that he could expect his hand to be partially incapacitated for a year, and he was advised to avoid any pressure in the sensitive areas or any activity that would aggravate the condition.

Nevertheless, he refused to cop out of his next assignment, *Desert Legion,* which was being produced by Universal. In the film he had to chase traditionally evil Arabs across the Sahara and rescue gossamer princesses, among them five-foot-seven Arlene Dahl. *Desert Legion* was later described in the *New York Times* as an "impossibly dull type of ephemera designed expressly for little boys who wear pistols to the theater on a Saturday afternoon and those desolate souls who find some escape in films of lost cities and marbled seraglios."

One obvious reason Alan accepted the lead in the film was money. "Just as Jimmy Stewart and Tyrone Power get fifty percent of the profits—so do I," he told Louella Parsons on an obligatory visit to her home in July. "It's being paid over a period of years, which is a real safeguard for my family."

Also for financial reasons, Alan had already committed himself to the newly formed British company, Warwick

Productions (which released its films through Columbia), to make his first picture abroad—in England. In addition to a flat $200,000 salary for *The Red Beret*, Warwick had agreed to pay him another $50,000 in expenses and provide suitable housing so he could take his whole family along while shooting.

Louella Parsons, in one of her more motherly humors, told Alan, "The only thing I don't like about your freelance idea is that you'll probably work yourself to death. I know how you like to work." He dutifully promised that as soon as filming on *The Red Beret* was completed, he would take a vacation with Sue and the kids and "see the places I've dreamed of all my life."

Louella, in approval, wrote: "Something tells me the Ladds won't be gone too long. They love their home in town. They love their ranch, and their family life is one that might be held up as an example to others." This time it seemed the fearsome Louella was the one being had.

To Sue now came the responsibility of preparing the family for the trip abroad. In mid-August, Sidney Skolsky noted in his column in the *New York Post*, that "Alan Ladd would like to sell his fabulous new house. Too high an upkeep on the showplace, which has a living room the size of the Waldorf-Astoria main lobby." Two weeks later, Skolsky, still acting as an unpaid real estate broker, amended the initial item with, "While Alan Ladd and his family are in England, you can lease his home and have his servants wait on you for a year for only $40,000. The price is $2,500 a month—first come first served." The house was rented without any difficulty.

Alan spent his last few days in Hollywood on an eighteen-hour schedule of fan-magazine layouts and interviews. A photographer was even sent to ride the Super Chief from Los Angeles to Pasadena for a sentimental last good-bye. The Ladds arrived in New York on a Tuesday. They spent most of the three days before their Friday departure for England either giving interviews to the local papers or entertaining and being entertained by the fan-magazine publishers Sue had so skillfully cultivated—particularly, Irving Mannheimer of *Photoplay*, who was still flattered by the Ladds' friendship and hospitality. Invitations were casually extended to "be our houseguest if you can make it to London"—an invitation Ruth Mannheimer accepted within two months.

Indeed, the lion's share of Sue's attention was now directed to *Photoplay*. Although *Photoplay* was seesawing with *Modern Screen* for number one spot among the fan magazines, *Modern Screen*'s interest in Alan Ladd had diminished, despite his position on its polls. Under the editorship of Charles Saxon, an aspiring and later highly successful cartoonist, the magazine was concentrating on a more glamorous approach. Elizabeth Taylor, Lana Turner, and Esther Williams competed for cover space; male stars were considered poison. Saxon was bored with the repetitious "Susie loves Alan—Alan loves Susie" copy. And annoyed by the constant evasions of his requests for pictures of Laddie to accompany stories in which the young man was mentioned, he rarely gave Alan more than one story a year. Mannheimer, on the other hand, pushed his editors into using Alan on their covers. He rationalized the resultant drop in circulation during those months, taking comfort in the triumphant "scooping" of his archrival and overlooking the fact that he too was being conned when it came to pictures of the older Ladd children.

On September 5, the Ladds boarded the *Ile de France* and Alan patiently explained to ship reporters that he was taking his four children to Europe with him because, "My parents were so poor when I was a kid I never went anywhere. I take our youngsters with us because I don't know anything that teaches them so much. Besides, we love them, and they're a lot of fun."

In truth, the five days at sea were an adventure for the children, with Laddie happily mingling with other teenagers in exploring the wonders of one of the last of the great ocean queens. Carol Lee, now twenty and a beauty, was pursued by handsome young French officers, and Alana and David were occupied with activities for youngsters their age.

For Alan, five days afloat provided a much-needed rest. His hand was still bothering him. He was made uncomfortable by the stares and aggressive attempts at friendliness of his fellow travelers, and was in no mood to socialize. Unable to work up much enthusiasm for the script of *The Red Beret,* he was apprehensive about the months ahead.

He had reason to be. He was on the first stage of a journey out to nowhere.

Part Four

1952-1958

Alan was never really happy after he left Paramount. He loved that studio. To him that was his home.... He was always frightened at the other studios because he didn't know the people he was working with.

—SUE CAROL LADD

One wonders if she did not, consciously or unconsciously, reinforce this feeling in him, thereby presumably reinforcing his dependency on herself.

—MARTY RACKIN

CHAPTER 21

The *Ile de France* approached the English seacoast just after dawn on the morning of September 10, 1952.

Alan made certain that the children were up, dressed and finished with breakfast before the big liner was ready to drop anchor. He didn't want them to miss seeing the original Plymouth Rock emerge from the fog, as he'd seen it three years earlier while in England for the Command Performance. He had expected a warm welcome in England. His following there was as extensive as it was back home, and for a decade he'd always been among the top five on both audience popularity polls and box-office charts.

Suddenly, though, the English wanted no part of him, at least not in the picture he had crossed the Atlantic to make. A Columbia Pictures/Warwick Productions public relations man came aboard to tell him bluntly that there might be problems with the photographers and reporters once he disembarked. "In fact," the man warned glumly, "those waiting outside customs would just as soon you stayed aboard and sailed back with the ship."

For Alan the reason behind this sudden hostility didn't need spelling out. Before sailing he'd been very aware that his casting

in *The Red Beret* had provoked a controversy in England, where
feeling about their heroic World War II parachute troops was
still high—though the war had been over for more than seven
years. And the English were also still piqued about the re-release
of an old Errol Flynn film, *Objective Burma,* in which Flynn and
the Yanks were totally responsible for winning the battle and the
war for England. Alan's assignment added injury to an already
well-insulted public.

He and his producers nonetheless hoped that once they
emphasized that although he was half-English (on his mother's
side) he wouldn't be playing an Englishman but an American-
born Canadian, and the trouble would go away.

It aggravated the situation. A leading Manchester newspaper
editorialized: "We've nothing against Alan Ladd personally, but
why not our own Richard Todd, who, like Trevor Howard and
Anthony Steele, actually wore the Red Beret and parachuted for
England's glory?" Columnist Leonard Mosley erupted with:
"Why can't we make films about *our* war with *our* players just as
America does with hers? Once upon a time there was a British
war film in which the principal role was not played by an
American pretending to be a Canadian soldier, sailor, airman,
nurse or WAAF. Alan Ladd is proposing to play not in an
ordinary film but the story of one of Britain's greatest and most
glorious efforts in World War II. I'm sick and tired of having
Hollywood types lurking around every turret, cockpit and
machine gun post where the Union Jack waved during the war."

Only the fan-oriented *Sunday Graphic* and the fans
themselves ran counter to the press's opinion. Headlined the
Graphic: WELCOME TO MR. LADD, AND SHUT UP TO HIS CRITICS!

The public also wrote letters to the more high-toned papers:
"Entertainment is the aim," one writer pointed out. "Who cares
if Alan Ladd wins the war in a red beret or Errol Flynn won it in
Burma? If it's a documentary film you want—apply to the
Minister of Information!" And a theater owner in Birmingham
came to the Yank's defense by insisting that he, for one, was
delighted Ladd was going to star in the picture because "that
way I know I'll be able to fill the house at every performance.
With a British star, that's rare." Finally the editor of a small
conservative Derby paper called on the English sense of fair
play: "Let's silence these petty outcries. Let's consider how

amazed Alan Ladd must be at the bitterness and cold shoulder reception. Frankly, we haven't a he-man star left in England even to offer as a replacement. May that settle that." (Such was the innocent state of Anglo-American relations.)

Alan told them at a press conference, "Look, I didn't come over to conquer anything or anybody. All I'm going to do is play the part of a guy who comes to England to learn to fight. Got that? I said *learn* to fight. Not to *teach*." . . .

As the boat train from Plymouth to London rolled through England's lush countryside, Alan's apprehensions about his forthcoming self-imposed eighteen-month exile increased. He was aware that the press knew why he had chosen to appear in *The Red Beret*. London, together with the major European cities with motion-picture facilities, was being overrun with Hollywood film stars wanting to take advantage of a tax loophole their government had offered Americans working abroad. The law had been passed originally to lure abroad industrial technicians who were badly needed to rebuild a war-torn Europe. But lacking an exclusion clause, it applied to any American willing and able to work and live outside the United States for a minimum of eighteen months. A few smart Hollywood tax lawyers had fastened onto this, and a major exodus began as the stars realized they'd be able to keep the majority of their earnings.

So, in the summer and fall of 1952, Clark Gable was filming *Never Let Me Go* and Gene Kelly *Invitation to the Dance* at MGM's Elstree Studios. Jose Ferrer and Zsa Zsa Gabor were at work on *Moulin Rouge* at Shepperton. Other stars such as Gregory Peck and Kirk Douglas were moving from country to country, though other American actors chose to return home before the eighteen-month requirement. But by the time Alan Ladd arrived, London had already been dubbed Hollywood-on-the-Thames. Once again, by English lights, the Yanks were "over-paid, over-sexed and over here. . . ."

Warwick Productions had carefully publicized the time of Alan's arrival, and when the train pulled into Paddington Station, hundreds of fans formed a central reception committee. They didn't care about either his tax advantages or the press controversy over national pride versus *The Red Beret*. The fact that their hero was in London was what counted, not the why of it. Hundreds of grasping hands competed for a touch. Screams for autographs almost drowned out the normal cacophony of the crowded station.

Planning to drive directly to the house the studio had rented for them, the Ladds paused to note that they were being trailed by a taxi filled with hysterical fans who, unable to get Alan's autograph at the station, had pooled their money for the fare to follow him to his secret destination. He asked his chauffeur to pull over to the side of the road, signed the autographs, and drove on. At least he had comforting proof that the following he had developed during the past decade had not turned altogether fickle.

The house chosen for them was a rambling, unpretentious country cottage, located in the town of Wentworth, Surrey, twenty-five miles from London. It was only a few minutes away from Shepperton Studios, where interior scenes were to be shot, and close to the local golf course, where he could indulge in his newest passion. A spare room was converted into a schoolroom, and Jean Martin, one of Alana's teachers at Westlake hired by the Ladds, conducted regular daily classes for Alana, Laddie and David from nine-thirty to two-thirty. A chauffeur, gardener, and cook were also on hand.

Alan's shooting schedule called for three weeks of location work along the rugged North Wales coast. The family was given temporary lodgings in the town of Penrhyndeudraeth, and while their father was at work the children tried to amuse themselves with visits to Carnarvon Castle, the fourteenth-century home of King Edward II. The weather in Wales, damp and gloomy, made for endless delays in filming, and Alan became friendly with co-star Leo Genn, who would later say, "He was an affable chap—untemperamental and a better actor than one was led to believe. But he didn't seem to appreciate our British sense of humour. The weather was enough to get anyone down, but I don't recall his *ever* smiling. In fact, what I remembered most about Ladd was an indefinable aura of sadness. But he was always very generous to the company—with American smokes and the like. They were still very expensive and difficult to obtain even though the war had been over for seven years."

Sue made several visits to the beach despite the weather, looking rather dowdy in slacks and bulky jacket. Her matronly appearance brought raised eyebrows from the cast, and even

Genn dropped his typically British reserve to comment: "She did seem a rather pushy type. Not what one expected from the wife of Alan Ladd. But then one never knows, does one...?"

During his stay in Penrhyndeudraeth, Alan could not get his mother out of his mind. Her birthplace, Chester, was located on the northern border of England and Wales, no more than a few hours away. It would have taken little effort on the days production stopped because of weather to drive down, investigate old court records, wander through nearby country graveyards, and seek some clue to his origins.

He was tempted to do so on several occasions, "but," he confessed, "I got cold feet." He was, in fact, persuaded that if his investigations aroused the curiosity of reporters, he would be risking the danger of the details of Ina Beavers' death coming to light. There was little chance of maternal relatives finding him. In his early publicity, Ina's maiden name was spelled "Rawley." Only on her death certificate was it listed as "Raleigh." His roots would remain buried in the sod of the English countryside....

When Sue wasn't visiting the location site, Alan would spend most of his spare time with Hal Lierley, his makeup man. After leaving Paramount, he had taken Lierley along with him to Warners and insisted on his services for *The Red Beret,* a request both the English government and the unions found impossible—under no circumstances would a foreigner be hired for a job that could be done just as well by an Englishman. The impasse lasted for weeks, until it was suggested that Lierley go on payroll as Ladd's personal valet and secretary with two local makeup men hired for the film. If Alan wanted to put on his own makeup with the "help" of his valet, neither the government nor the unions could object. Diplomacy triumphed....

After what seemed from here to eternity to Alan, the company left Wales and began two weeks of filming at the Royal Air Force Base at Abingdon, a few miles outside of Oxford. Because the base was off limits to civilians, Alan and Sue sent the family back to Surrey, where they were secure under the watchful eye of Jean Martin. Besides, "We had no need to worry about them," Alan said. "They were trained to take care of each other. Carol Lee looks after Laddie, Laddie after Lonnie, Lonnie after David, and David has his own charge in the person of Beret, his dachshund puppy."

The children did seem to adjust well to their foreign

surroundings. Carol Lee and Laddie were inseparable companions for going to the movies or taking walks to the neighboring villages. As in America, they were conveniently off somewhere when either studio or newspaper and magazine people were at the house. Alana and David shared most of their time away from the schoolroom taking joint riding lessons or going sightseeing with their mother—with a photographer usually alerted.

In a story published under her by-line (but actually ghost-written by one of *Modern Screen*'s regular writers, as was customary) Sue noted: "It's been a wonderful aid to their education. We saw the changing of the guard at Buckingham Palace and David spotted little Prince Charles at one of the windows. We went to Madame Tussaud's where Laddie was deeply impressed by the wax image of Sleeping Beauty, mostly, I suppose, because of the mechanism inside the figure which made the chest rise and fall with a breathing motion. David was home with a cold that day and afterwards listened glumly to our glowing accounts of the wax museum. He brightened only when he learned we hadn't seen the Chamber of Horrors without him."

The fans—their loyalty, goodwill, and satisfaction—were topside in Sue's mind. Even six thousand miles from Hollywood she made sure all letters were answered, the pictures—autographed before Alan's departure—sent.

Marjorie Harrold Farnsworth would see the magazines and search without success for a picture of her son among those of Alana and David—with their father, on their horses, with their teacher, at Trafalgar Square feeding the pigeons. Laddie wrote and sent cards, but his mother and half-sister missed him. Still, Midge was convinced she'd done the right thing by allowing him to go. Looking after Cynthia, now five, and the new baby Darrick, a cerebral palsy victim, occupied most of Midge's time. Always in delicate health, she was enervated by the intense smog that frequently blanketed the San Fernando Valley, and during the hay-fever season she was in particular agony. And Darrick's birth did little to help her by now tension-filled marriage to Farnsworth. She was certain that Laddie, now at the sensitive age of fifteen, was happier and better off with his father. Nothing she could offer, she felt, could compete with the cultural opportunities he was being exposed to. And pushing aside her own feelings about her successor, she reassured herself by their phone contacts over the years that Sue seemed fond of the boy.

"In fact," recalls Hal Lierley, "it seemed to me that it was Alan who was somewhat harsh with the boy sometimes. Laddie really had to toe the mark more than the others did. I really thought Sue took better care of Laddie than Alan did; at least for my money she did. She was more compassionate. But still, Laddie and Carol Lee *were* always kept in the background. I was always very fond of Laddie and I think he liked me. We spent a lot of time together on the ship and in England. He was a sensitive boy and a good boy, but he didn't have it easy."

Alan never talked about Laddie's mother, and Hal Lierley didn't ask questions. "I think that's one of the things Alan liked about me," he says. "I never pried. I never asked anything."

As shooting progressed on *The Red Beret* at Shepperton Studios, Alan's regrets about becoming involved in the picture continued to grow. "I never saw Alan get angry at anyone besides himself," Lierley says, "but I had been around him long enough to know he was very unhappy about the whole deal."

Although Alan wanted to pack it all in and head back home the day his final scene was shot, Sue reminded him of that eighteen-month tax break that they'd enjoy from Warwick's proposed films *Hell Below Zero* and *The Black Knight,* as well as Universal's *Saskatchewan,* which required a foreign—Canadian—location.

And certainly he didn't lack for companions in exile. One of his few social pleasures was attending the regular gatherings hosted by his friend and *Wild Harvest* director, Tay Garnett. The Ladds hobnobbed with the elite of Hollywood's homesick exiles: Ava Gardner, Robert Taylor, John Huston, and Lana Turner. One night they watched Ava Gardner, the sleeves of a three-thousand-dollar ball gown rolled up, fry up a mess of chicken. Throughout most of that "memorable" evening, Clark Gable sprawled on the floor "crooning," as one of the guests recalled it, "to a fifth of cognac."

"I don't recall its being publicized," says Lierley, "but Alan and Gable's friendship went back a great many years. I think they knew each other back when Carole [Lombard] was still alive."

Although their life-styles were totally different, with Gable a freelance bachelor at this time, Ladd and Gable's interest in ranching created a bond. Alan, however, could never quite forget that he was a bit player in *They Met in Bombay* when Gable was king of the MGM lot. For years now he had topped Gable both at the box office and on popularity polls, but he still considered Gable more of an idol than an equal.

Sue meanwhile kept busy sightseeing with the family, visiting the set, shopping or writing chatty letters to Louella Parsons and Hedda Hopper to keep them up to date on Alan's activities. When she gave a party for the members of Alan's earliest British fan clubs, more than four hundred fans arrived.

But Alan's battered psyche wasn't assuaged. He was convinced that he could not redeem himself with the anti-Ladd factions in England. He was sorry he'd listened to Sue, who had encouraged him to sign with Warwick, then felt guilty for his disloyal feelings. He endured the last few weeks of shooting as she made plans for a "merry" Christmas in Paris and New Year's week in Switzerland.

Still, once he was free of the grip of the chilly, damp English winter, his spirits picked up. He continued to have no illusions about either *The Red Beret* or the quality of his performance under the direction of Terence Young, but he could at least hope neither would be damaging to his career or his box-office pull at home. He had, he tried to remind himself, survived considerably worse films than this, and there was *Shane,* still waiting for release. . . .

In mid-January 1953, the Ladds motored through the south of France with their friends Dennis O'Keefe and his wife Steffi Duna. The children, accompanied by Hal Lierley and Jean Martin, joined them on the Riviera, and they spent a lazy month sunning and swimming until Alan was called back to London to begin work on *Hell Below Zero.*

A whaling drama based on the Hammond Innes novel *The White South, Hell* was garden-variety adventure fare. With the exception of a grisly fight between Alan and Stanley Baker on treacherous ice floes, it was a movie in search of excitement. Alan was a former naval officer who signs on as first mate on the whaler to pursue his leading lady, Joan Tetzel, to frozen Antarctica.

Reminiscing about the film shortly before his sudden death

of a heart attack in the summer of 1978, director Mark Robson said, "We all knew we were working on a stinker...A second-unit team provided the Antarctica footage, so for the most part we were using both back projection and superimposed film—which helped some. But audiences were becoming far too sophisticated by then to be fooled by process shots. Alan did the best he could—under the circumstances. None of us was very happy being trapped in this one, but Alan frequently remarked that he was fed up with Europe, that he had made a mistake in tying himself up for so long and felt he was serving a prison term. He was a very, very unhappy man. But I couldn't fault his performance before the cameras. Even when he smashed his hand playing football, and was in absolute agony, he refused to hold up production. Frankly, I don't know how he stood the pain."

This was the third freak accident relating to Alan's hands in just over fourteen months.

It would almost cost him his arm. It could have cost him his life....

CHAPTER 22

Alan was incapable of spending his only day of rest (Sunday) just resting. He always had to do *something*, anything... it was better than letting unacceptable feelings in....

In mid-April 1953, the weather was still frigid but the smells and sounds of the English countryside were an invitation, and Alan decided to join Laddie in some casual football practice. Carelessly he smashed his left hand against some concrete, scraping the skin and crushing the nails of two fingers so badly that a local doctor had to be called in.

Hal Lierley, who had been invited to lunch, recalls the afternoon. "One of those socialized-medicine doctors came over and he pulled the nails right off Alan's fingers. I was watching when he dressed the fingers—and this doctor had the dirtiest kit I had ever seen in my entire life. He just put his things under tap water, not boiling water. That's how Alan got the terrible infection. It was so bad that he finally ended up in the hospital. And it stayed bad for a long time."

To compound Alan's problems, David became ill and required an immediate tonsillectomy. Both father and son were released from the hospital at the same time. David, with the resilience of a six-year-old, considered his stay "in hospital" an exciting adventure. Alan's hand was protected from further injury by a heavy cast, but the infection began to spread and, despite medicinal drugs, the pain often became agonizing. Nevertheless he returned to work, anxious to finish up as quickly as possible.

"I'm going to get back to America and have this looked at by the Mayo Clinic," he told a friend. "What good will a tax break do me if I'm crippled for life?"

But he didn't go back. Instead he and Sue rented a suite at the Dorchester Hotel to be in the midst of things for Queen Elizabeth's Coronation. He was assured that although his hand was taking longer to heal than anyone had anticipated, he just had to be patient. So he'd live with the pain, he didn't want the children to miss the Coronation.

By now the English press had softened in its earlier hostile stand. One paper even gushed, "The Ladds are the most popular people ever to visit from Hollywood."

Lierley agrees. "Alan got an awful lot of good press while working on the pictures we did over there, and the people got to know him and like him."

They liked him enough, in fact, to make him the third most popular box-office attraction in England that year. And Sue, forgetting briefly about the Coronation, wrote Hedda Hopper that "Alan's fan mail is at an all-time high."

And for good reason. On April 23, while Alan fought the threat of gangrene of the hand in London, *Shane* was premiered at New York's Radio City Music Hall. The first of his movies to play in that prestigious cinema temple, it was also his last...

Shane received outstanding critical acclaim, with even the toughest reviewers extravagant in their praise for both Alan Ladd and the film. "Magnificent." "A classic." "A great Western." Those words appeared in all the reviews along with the prediction that the film would be the year's strongest Oscar contender. Had he been in America at the time, he could have tasted his triumph firsthand. Finally, he was getting the kind of professional approval and respect he had wanted so badly all his life. Even his severest critics conceded that perhaps they had been wrong in kidding his talent.

But while *Shane* was still drawing crowds at the Music Hall,

Desert Legion opened four blocks to the southwest at the Palace—on a bill with eight acts of third-rate vaudeville. And three thousand miles away, Alan Ladd was back at square one—involved in yet another insult to the intelligence of critics and audiences alike. Paramount's ad campaign proclaimed, "There never was a film like *Shane*." For Alan Ladd there never would be one like it again.

On July 9, 1953, the Ladds boarded the *Queen Elizabeth* for their trip back to North America. They had magnificent weather—sunny skies during the day, calm seas at night. Alan did not confine himself to his cabin as much as he had on the trip over, though he still remained aloof from the other passengers. His mood was distinctly not that of a man who had just scored his greatest triumph....

A few hours after the liner docked in New York, the family was on a train bound for Banff, Canada, where Alan was due to start *Saskatchewan* opposite Universal's "blond bombshell," Shelley Winters. The studio had rented the Royal Suite (usually occupied by England's sovereigns) of Spring's Hotel for the Ladds. But fans hoping to catch a glimpse of Alan Ladd either at the entrance or in the lobby were disappointed. Uncharacteristically, he avoided his public by entering and leaving through the basement garage door—no doubt an indication of the way he felt about the movie he was making.

Saskatchewan was typical Royal-Mountie-gets-his-man-and-girl, cowboy-and-Indians nonsense. The only redeeming feature was the breathtaking views of Canadian rivers and forests. Although Raoul Walsh did bring some excitement to the action scenes, Alan and Shelley Winters emerged as little more than stock characters.

The two leads, who had first met during the filming of *Gatsby*, had little in common. And because nothing was sacred to the irrepressible Ms. Winters, she made fun of the fact that she, too (at five feet four), had to be planted in a ditch to make the famous Alan Ladd appear taller. "I tripped over some rocks or something one day and was lucky I didn't break my neck," she later said.

Columnist Erskine Johnson of the *World Telegram-Sun* blind-itemed that "a movie doll who had seen the Ladds in Canada said: 'Sue and I didn't get along. Sue hates any woman under the age of fifty when Alan is around.'" Though Johnson insisted he wasn't referring to Shelley Winters, she was the only woman featured in an all-male cast.

Aside from the social activities in and around the hotel, which Alan continued to avoid, there was little to do in Banff. Anxious to know what all the commotion was about back home, he sent for a print of *Shane*. While still shrugging off the possibility of an Oscar nomination for himself, he was pleased with his work, which he continued to credit entirely to George Stevens' genius. Whatever exhilaration he might have felt about the film was tempered by more intense regrets about (a) leaving Paramount at the wrong time; (b) getting tied up in Europe; and (c) making four movies that he felt would offset any prestige he had finally gotten from *Shane*.

Ironically—while Alan was still in Banff—the United States Government, aware that the tax-incentive law was being misused, rescinded it with slight warning. There was, however, no way that Alan could back out of returning to Europe to make *The Black Knight*. Work on the sets in Spain had already begun. Other contracts had been signed and commitments made. He was angry at himself, angry at Sue, angry at the world. And he kept it all inside. . . .

He became seriously ill again, this time with a virus infection. Though the studio doctor insisted he return to the hotel and stay in bed for two weeks, he rested for less than two days over a weekend, then rejoined the company. He was up early every morning, riding his horse into icy waters, insisting on finishing the picture despite a high fever, a hacking cough, the doctor's warnings, and Sue's obvious concern. Well, he told them, at least a warm Spanish climate would be a good remedy for what ailed him.

On the way to Madrid the Ladds had to stop in London, where once again Alan represented Hollywood at a Royal Command Performance. Winston Churchill had sent him a note commending his performance in *The Red Beret* (released as *Paratrooper*). The English no longer seemed to resent him: he would, in fact, capture first place in a British poll of the world's most popular actors.

Laddie had celebrated his sixteenth birthday a few days before the Command Performance, and Alan felt the year abroad had been particularly beneficial to him, as well as to Carol Lee. But he sensed that both were anxious to return home to their friends. Laddie had a quiet, gentle nature—like his mother—and not surprisingly there were times when Alan looked at him that he was disturbed by memories of the teenaged Midge...

Alan was also troubled by Laddie being overweight, and wondered if it was caused by psychological problems he himself might have been responsible for. Ironically, Laddie's chubbiness and dark coloring made many of the Ladds' acquaintances think he was Sue's son. According to Hal Lierley, the confusion was compounded because "Carol Lee was as blond as Alan and David and Alana, and everyone took it for granted that she was Alan's natural daughter."

Lierley and his wife Bea planned to join the Ladds in Spain, but just as Alan was preparing to leave England, he had still another accident—he tripped and fractured an ankle. Moreover, a typhoid epidemic spread through Spain, delaying the start of the film indefinitely. These two grim events seemed to insure that *The Black Knight* was going to be a black experience all around.

Actually nothing could have saved this film, which had disaster built-in. Warwick was trying to cash in on the sudden and short-lived popularity of medieval epic tales of knights and their ladies, initiated by MGM with *Ivanhoe* and follow-ups such as *Knights of the Round Table*. Unfortunately they came up with a concoction that was more reminiscent of Hopalong Cassidy than of Camelot.

Then too—despite his agility on a horse or with lance, sword, or dirk—Alan Ladd was no Robert Taylor, who, if nothing else, looked as if he belonged in the mythical land of King Arthur. Nor was Alan's fair lady in the film, the beautiful Patricia Medina, any match for Elizabeth Taylor or Ava Gardner in box-office appeal. As usual, on Ladd's slim shoulders alone rested the success of the film. And in armor, with mannerisms that were strictly American-modern, he was more than a little incongruous in the role. He knew it, too.

After two weeks of filming in Spain the company returned to England for the climactic sequences at Stonehenge. The

December weather was, as usual, gloomy and dispiriting: the cast froze in medieval costumes more suited to warmer climes. Even director Tay Garnett's fine sense of humor could provide little cheer for the company. Everyone wanted the thing over as soon as possible. But no one more than Alan, for whom the final shot would bring an end to his eighteen-month exile.

During the Christmas holidays, which the Ladds spent in London, Alan received word from Irving Mannheimer that the readers of *Photoplay* had chosen his performance in *Shane* the year's favorite and that he would be awarded the *Photoplay* Gold Medal at the magazine's annual banquet at the Beverly Hills Hotel. It wasn't a setup. Mannheimer could coerce his editors into using Alan Ladd on their covers, but he wasn't foolhardy enough to risk either the prestige of an award considered by the public second only to the Oscar at the time, or the respect of the studios whose cooperation was essential to his survival as a publisher, no matter how fond he was of the Ladds. Alan Ladd *was* the people's choice—fair and square.

The winners for the most popular performance of the year had been chosen by the public through the combined results of a magazine ballot and an extensive Gallup Poll. Alan Ladd (for *Shane*) and Marilyn Monroe (for *Gentlemen Prefer Blondes* and *How to Marry a Millionaire*) won by wide margins.

The Gold Medal banquet was traditionally held sometime during the first two weeks of February in an attempt to steal the thunder from the Oscar hoopla, but since there was no way Alan could be back in Hollywood then, Mannheimer moved the event back to March 9. Sue promised to be home by that date no matter what, and made the reservations for the return trip accordingly.

As he stood on the rail of the *S.S. United States* on a misty March day and watched the English coastline fade, Alan felt like a man released from a long prison sentence.

Earlier fears about being forgotten were dispelled by the Gold Medal tribute. His public—the readers of fan magazines, the moviegoers—had given him their vote of confidence. And that was all that mattered. Wasn't it?

CHAPTER 23

The *United States,* after four and one-half days, made it safely into port on March 4. After being rushed through customs despite "enough souvenirs to fill a playhouse for the children," the Ladds hurried down to the train station to catch the streamliner to Chicago, where they'd make the final connection to Los Angeles.

Had he flown Alan would have had eight additional days to relax before the *Photoplay* whoop-de-doo, but whenever air travel had been suggested he'd turned it down. Terrified of flying, he neither could nor would offer a reason for his fear. Hypnosis was suggested, but he wanted no part of that either. Some felt that his aversion to planes was at least precipitated by the horror of the crash that killed Carole Lombard. As a former diving champion, he certainly had no fear of heights and his insistence on doing his own stunts whenever possible indicated physical courage—when *he* was in control. However, given the choice, he apparently would not and could not put his life in the hands of a male stranger. "If I get on a plane, it will go down," he said, still, perhaps, reacting to his mother's "crash" after her second warning....

The Ladds' train arrived in Los Angeles at eight o'clock on

179

the morning of March 7, 1954. As Sue recalled: "At least thirty friends met us at the station. Alan invited them all home for breakfast and about a hundred people dropped in to say hello throughout the day."

However, it was the *Photoplay* banquet that would serve as Alan's official welcome-home party. He and Marilyn Monroe, sitting on either side of editor Fred Sammis, had little to say to one another. Monroe, wearing a clinging white dress that focused all eyes on her braless bosom, concentrated her charms on the magazine executive—to the exclusion of everyone else present. Fox-Movietone News filmed the ceremony and, showing partiality toward their parent company's contract player, edited the footage so that only Marilyn Monroe was seen on local theater screens. In short, so to speak, Alan Ladd was upstaged throughout the evening. Sue may have been a master at manipulating the press to advance her husband's career, but she wasn't in the same league with Marilyn Monroe.

Nonetheless Alan did receive a warm welcome from his peers. His acceptance speech was grateful and brief, ending with a genuine, "Thank God." The congratulations and "welcome backs" he received were in some instances rather tactlessly accompanied by regrets about his being ignored by the New York Film Critics, who had chosen Burt Lancaster as Best Actor of the Year for *From Here to Eternity,* over James Mason and John Gielgud for *Julius Caesar,* Spencer Tracy for *The Actress,* and William Holden for *Stalag 17.* The Academy of Motion Picture Arts and Sciences members had also bypassed Ladd in nominating Lancaster and Holden, together with Montgomery Clift *(From Here to Eternity),* Richard Burton *(The Robe),* and Marlon Brando *(Julius Caesar)* for their Best Actor Award.

Sue, who had been talking Oscar for six months, was angry, but Alan took the disappointment philosophically. In effect, it was a familiar story: approval from the public, thumbs-down from his fellow actors and the New York critics.

He really didn't have a prayer, through no fault of his own or of his performance in *Shane.* Studio politics, it was felt, prevailed in the Oscar sweepstakes.

Shane was nominated for Best Picture, although *From Here to Eternity* was favored to win. George Stevens got a nod from the Oscar nominating committee for Best Director. (He lost to

Eternity's Fred Zinnemann, but was honored with the Irving G. Thalberg Award—for special achievement—instead.) *Shane*'s Brandon De Wilde and Jack Palance canceled each other out in the Best Supporting Actor category; neither stood a chance against *Eternity*'s Frank Sinatra. *Shane*'s sole Oscar winner was Loyal Griggs, for color cinematography. Van Heflin and Jean Arthur failed even to be nominated, an oversight perhaps even more glaring than Ladd's rejection.

An explanation: Since neither Heflin, nor Arthur, nor Ladd were now under contract, Paramount had put all its clout behind William Holden *(Stalag 17)* and newcomer Audrey Hepburn *(Roman Holiday)*, who were contract players, and they won. *Shane* and *Holiday* split the movie vote—adding to *Eternity*'s strength and assuring its win.

The reviews of *Saskatchewan,* which opened at Oscar time, were hardly balm for Alan's considerably bruised ego. Critics raved about the gorgeous scenery and the Indians' gymnastics, and mocked Alan Ladd's "infallible cool."

In spite of this, Alan still insisted on launching his own company, Jaguar Productions, with another Indian-versus-Homesteaders epic called *Drum Beat*. Marisa Pavan and Audrey Dalton were set for the female leads, but, today at least, the strongest name in the film belongs to a then little-known actor signed to play the mean-spirited redskin, Captain Black: Charles Bronson. Delmer Daves, an old hand at action-adventure, was to direct.

Now past forty, Alan was very aware of the telltale signs of approaching middle age, but back in familiar surroundings he was caught up in the excitement of being his own boss. Although he had no illusions that *Drum Beat* could be turned into another *Shane,* it had, at least, all the ingredients of a big moneymaker, a good launching for Jaguar Productions.

And at 323 North Mapleton Drive, things were running smoothly. David and Alana were romping through the house as though they had never been away. David, at seven, was particularly happy about attending a public school for the first time in his young life. Laddie, who had missed companions of his own age during private tutoring sessions, was enrolled at University High and qualified easily for positions on both its football and baseball teams. Sue, a full partner in Jaguar, was kept busy reading scripts and deciding how to redecorate the house. Carol Lee, twenty-one, was thinking about marriage to a young MGM contract player named Richard Anderson.

And Alan Ladd and Bill Bendix had resumed their friendship. Tess Bendix remembers: "Alan called Bill and said how silly it was that they weren't talking, and he couldn't remember what the whole thing was all about. And Bill said he couldn't either. Alan invited us to the house for dinner, and it was as though there had never been an estrangement."

Perhaps things were going too well. . . .

In April, Alan had another accident. While taking a quick shower he slipped in the tub, injuring his back and cracking a rib. Once again he would be forced to endure months of agony that would be relieved only by pain-killing drugs, a stiff drink—or both. Louella Parsons, first to hear and tell the news, remarked with a double edge, "Never heard of anyone having as many accidents as Alan Ladd."

While being treated for his latest injury, Alan was dismayed to learn that he was suffering from high blood pressure. His doctors recommended "shots" to bring it back to normal and warned him to take it easy. He refused, however, to delay production of *Drum Beat* or to cast another actor in his role. He did promise to relax for a few days at Hidden Valley before leaving for location in Arizona.

The Ladds found the house and the ranch in good condition, much as they had left it. Hollywood itself, however, was beginning to fall apart, and although in familiar surroundings, Alan suddenly felt like a stranger in a foreign land. (At Warners, all but a handful of the old contract stars were now gone, and most of those who remained were just marking time. But Alan wasn't too affected by the atmosphere of gloom there. He had spent only a few months at Warners during the filming of *The Iron Mistress*, and didn't have the strong ties he had formed at Paramount.)

In the early fifties television had overwhelmingly captured the imagination of the public. Movie attendance had fallen off alarmingly, and there was a desperate attempt to reclaim the old audiences. Warners, as well as MGM, was experimenting with three-dimensional movies. Twentieth-Century-Fox was testing a new process called CinemaScope. Every major studio went into battle against the exploding new medium with its strongest weapons—big outdoor films and new gimmicks.

Only Warner Brothers decided that if you couldn't lick an enemy, join it. To the dismay of his movie colleagues, Jack Warner started searching for properties in the studio library that could be adapted for TV series. By the time Alan returned from Arizona, three such properties—*Cheyenne, Kings Row,* and *Casablanca*—had been selected.

After the phenomenal success of *Shane,* George Stevens was eager to work with Alan again. According to Sue, Alan in turn "thought Stevens was the greatest man who ever walked in Hollywood" and was anxious to perform again under Stevens' direction. It was simply a matter of finding the right property at the right time, at the right studio. The property, already owned by Warners, was there—Edna Ferber's *Giant,* a sprawling saga of Texas family life and the conflict between cattlemen and oil tycoons.

This epic, budgeted at the then-astronomical sum of $5,000,000, was scheduled to start shooting in the spring of 1955. From the start, it was planned as "the big one of the year," the one to beat at Oscar time.

Before any cast was set, Stevens approached Ladd about accepting a lead in the film. Alan read the book and was eager for the role of Bick Benedict, raw-boned owner of the great Renata cattle ranch. There was only one hitch. Stevens had him firmly down for Jett Rink, the surly ranch hand who later becomes the most vulgar of the new crop of millionaires—a role some said was patterned after the career of Glen McCarthy, the flamboyant Houston oil man and builder of the Shamrock Hotel.

When Alan refused, Stevens begged him to reconsider. The Rink role, he said, was by far the stronger and more memorable of the two. For weeks Alan wavered between a desire to work with Stevens in a class production and a reluctance to accept anything but the starring role. Pressed for a decision, he finally turned Stevens down.

He would regret that decision the rest of his life.

Even some twenty years later, Sue felt compelled to

acknowledge in an interview with the *Hollywood Reporter:* "It was my fault as much as Alan's. I was used to his being top banana, and we both felt the Jimmy Dean role was a secondary part. It didn't turn out that way. But no matter."

But, of course, it did matter, and it's difficult to resist speculating on how things might have turned out if Alan had accepted the part. Stevens and Dean feuded throughout the production, with Stevens complaining, "Dean was not my choice for the role. He had the ability to take a scene and break it down...into so many bits and pieces that I couldn't see the scene from the trees, so to speak. From a director's point of view that isn't the most delightful sort of fellow. All in all, it was a hell of a headache working with him." By the time the picture was completed, the hostility between the two was so intense that Stevens publicly stated that "Dean will never appear in another film I do."

Meeting Alan in the studio commissary one lunch hour, Stevens was overheard saying, "You know, you could have spared me all this aggravation if you had taken the role." Under Stevens' direction, many felt, Alan could have been brilliant in the part. At forty-one, he still looked young enough to get through the early sequences with careful photography. And his maturity could have given the final sequences the conviction that Jimmy Dean, encumbered by excess "aging" makeup, didn't have the resources to project.

Dean, who died days after completing his last scene in *Giant*, was to receive a posthumous Best Actor Oscar nomination. Other nominations went to the film itself, to Rock Hudson as Best Actor and to Mercedes McCambridge as Best Supporting Actress. Stevens, who won as Best Director, would always argue privately that Dean's nomination was a sentimental gesture on the Academy's part, that it split the Hudson vote. And Alan Ladd, he was certain, would have been a nominee had he accepted the part.

One tends to speculate, too, about the fate of Jimmy Dean—and whether he would have been in the same place, at the same time, and in the same mood if he had not been seeking relief from the tensions of the film, on September 30, 1955....

So many "ifs."

If, for example, Alan had said yes to Stevens when he first was asked, would he have been as restless, and vulnerable, as he was when he started *The McConnell Story* in the late fall of 1954? ... For the first time in fifteen years, Alan was definitely attracted by another woman. And in one of those it-only-happens-in-the-movies coincidences, she was a woman with whom he had shared top honors on all the magazine popularity polls. She was also probably the last woman in the world the gossip peddlers would ever have linked him with in the Forties, even if both had been free. Because, although they both flourished during the same period as products of the same star system, they were *not* from the same studio. Which made romance nearly impossible.

But petite, blond June Allyson bore a haunting resemblance to the first Mrs. Alan Ladd.

CHAPTER 24

June Allyson and Alan Ladd met for the first time at a preproduction meeting at Warners in December 1954. "It's usually assumed that everyone in the movies knows everyone else, but that's not so," June Allyson says now. "I came to MGM in 1943—when Gable was king—and we were both there for over a decade but I never met him. Not even a casual introduction...It's weird. But of course people like me just didn't walk over to the King and say, 'Hi there.'"

Alan Ladd had similar reservations about June Allyson. The wife of actor-producer Dick Powell, she was Hollywood's crown princess and certainly the biggest box-office draw he had worked with in a decade. Alan was reserved that first afternoon at the studio, and somewhat awed about working with her, but he was pleased that he had a leading lady who could look *up* to him while wearing high heels. And everyone in the cast agreed that they looked just fine together.

Actually, apart from her size, June Allyson was an ideal choice for "Butch" McConnell, Alan Ladd's screen wife. Cast opposite Jimmy Stewart in *The Stratton Story* in 1949, she had made an easy transition from Van Johnson's romanticized "girl-next-door" to what the *New York Times* would call the "perfect all-American young-wife." She had played this role in *The Glenn Miller Story* (again with Stewart), *Executive Suite* (opposite William Holden), *A Woman's World* (opposite Cornel Wilde), and *Strategic Air Command* (her third teaming with Stewart). Before *The McConnell Story,* she had completed a grueling exercise as the less-than-perfect wife in *The Shrike*—a lapse her public apparently deplored.

She recalls little about her first meeting with Alan Ladd at Warners except that "he didn't seem to be feeling very well that afternoon and I noticed that he had a large gash on his forehead—he attributed it to a recent accident. He was very quiet and seemed sad, but he was anxious for the picture to start shooting."

Alan, in fact, was feeling awful when he began *The McConnell Story.* In early November he had been rushed to the hospital with a virus infection that developed into pneumonia. He was still shaky after returning home, and even the news that he and Barbara Stanwyck shared top honors for *Modern Screen*'s Star of Stars Awards (the most popular players over a period of ten years) did little for his morale. Then in early December, forced to bring his car to a sudden stop to avoid a crash, he had hit his forehead against the windshield and had to return to the hospital for eight stitches. The makeup department at Warners had assured him that they could conceal the wound, but he hated the thought of starting a film in such a condition. By now he was beginning to feel grateful if he got through a week without some illness or accident.

Life at home was also less than tranquil. Carol Lee and Richard Anderson had become engaged during the summer, and Sue was intent on giving her daughter a wedding that would put to shame Jack Benny's for his daughter Joan. The nuptials had been set for January 22, and throughout December Sue was absorbed in her plans as she managed carpenters, caterers, dressmakers, and florists. Alan, though, couldn't muster up much real enthusiasm for the role of stepfather-of-the-bride. He still detested big parties. He was uncomfortable in formal clothes, and he had little energy—physical or emotional—for getting involved in the elaborate preparations. Privately he held a secret wish that Carol Lee and Richard would just run off somewhere and get married quietly. But Carol Lee, on the surface at least, seemed just as excited as her mother, and Alan was grateful that he had *The McConnell Story* as an excuse to avoid the prenuptial frenzy.

During the first few days of shooting on the film he was withdrawn, somber. But *The McConnell Story* was a happy set. June Allyson's exuberance was contagious. Everyone was having a wonderful time, and Alan found himself caught up in the mood. June was "a joy to work with," and he was relieved that he didn't have to endure the humiliation of standing on a box or a co-star standing in a ditch.

June Allyson recalls, "Alan was so totally professional. When he came onto the set he was always prepared for the scene, and he was a wonderful actor. We never had any problems with our scenes together. Never. But when I'd tell him how good he was, he wouldn't believe me. He simply couldn't accept that truth, and it *is* the truth."

Years later, Ms. Allyson would hear the stories of Alan's drinking problem and find them hard to believe ... "Alan never had a hangover when we were working together, and he certainly didn't drink on the picture. I would have noticed it—or smelled it on his breath. But I never did. If those stories about his drinking were true, I have no idea when it all started." (How could she? ... it had all "started" a very long time ago. ...)

She continued, though, to sense an underlying sadness in Alan, even though his mood changed for the better as the picture progressed ... "We began having a wonderful time," she recalls. "He could be a very funny man. Oh, I don't mean he was a stand-up comic, but he had a very wry sense of humor and we always found something to laugh about."

Alan was particularly amused that he was portraying the late Captain Joseph McConnell, a restless, intrepid airman who became America's first triple jet "ace" during the Korean War, when he, himself, was plain terrified of flying. Every time he got into the cockpit of the mock-up the studio had installed before a rear-projection screen, he'd have a pointed comment to make about his simulated heroics.

In the past he had preferred scenes with male cast members and had often said that he felt uncomfortable in love scenes and kissing sequences—he didn't object to playing those scenes with June Allyson. If they disturbed him, it was for a different reason.

He was impatient to get to work in the morning, and let down when shooting stopped for the day. He was invariably disappointed on the days she was not "on call," and he found excuses to spend as much time as possible with her between "setups."

She remembers: "We'd talk about everything—our families, the way the film was going, acting . . . But nonetheless I felt that Alan was a very private person. He never discussed the past. I never knew he had been married before Sue, and whenever Laddie's name came up in the conversation, I naturally assumed he was Alan's son by Sue . . . Alan and I drove everybody on the set out of their minds, though. We were both crazy about music, and whenever the cameras weren't rolling we had the music just blasting away. But when Sue came onto the set—it was turned right off."

Sue was seemingly friendly with June Allyson the first few weeks of shooting, though June would notice that "she was really only interested in things that directly pertained to Alan—the way he was photographed, things like that. . . ."

When Sue wasn't on the set Alan couldn't take his eyes off his leading lady, and his infatuation didn't escape the notice of cast and crew. Rumors of a hot romance began to spread throughout the studios and then show up as "blind items" in several of the lesser Hollywood columns. Alone, they meant nothing; collectively, they were explosive:

Which happily married couple of many years (their names will surprise you) are straining at the leash? Followed by, "It's very cool between the Alan Ladds and the Dick Powells.

Aware of the gossip, yet not wanting to dignify it with denials, June and Alan talked about the situation in her dressing room one day. "I suggested," recalls Allyson, "that maybe it would be better if we didn't talk to each other when we were not on camera. And then we decided that was silly. We'd just keep our friendship intact, let anybody say what he wanted to and ignore the whole thing."

Sue, of course, also knew about the gossip, but throughout

the early weeks of January she said and did nothing about the situation when she was on the lot. Cast and crew would hold their breath as she walked onto the sound stage, but there were no fireworks—not yet.

Alan continued to be disturbed about his feelings for June and had difficulty falling asleep at night, but he noted, to his astonishment, that while working on *The McConnell Story* he was never ill; nor did he break so much as a fingernail. He even began looking forward to Carol Lee's wedding, to which June and Dick Powell were invited guests and had accepted a few weeks earlier. Their presence at his home, Alan thought, would help silence the gossip. He was wrong. . . .

Carol Lee's wedding to Richard Anderson on Saturday evening, January 22, was one of the most lavish nuptial spectaculars staged in Hollywood since the prewar years. Sue had thought of everything. The entire back garden of the house was topped by a billowing green-and-white canopy with walls of cellophane attached. Immediately after the ceremony waiters converted the church setting of the garden into a nightclub scene.

Local photographers were out in force, and Louella Parsons, writing in full purple, was on hand to report the details to her readers the following Monday morning:

Believe me, there was a sentimental tear in every eye of the five hundred assembled guests when the music struck up "Here Comes the Bride." First came Carol Lee's lovely bridesmaids all in white, carrying white bouquets, then eleven-year-old Alana Ladd, the maid of honor. And back of Alana was David Ladd (a picture of sartorial splendor in white tie and tails—and himself just seven years old!).

. . . What a picture Carol Lee was when she appeared in the doorway on the arm of Alan Ladd. He was so proud of her, he was all but busting his buttons. The lovely blonde bride wore a gown of white Italian raw silk with mandarin collar and cuffs trimmed with tiny seed pearls and a huge veil of white tulle . . . (I found my eyes going back time and time again to Sue Carol Ladd, the lovely mother of Carol Lee. Never in years have I seen Sue look so lovely. She had lost twenty pounds (she later told me) and she was a vision of dark-eyed loveliness in her soft champagne lace dress.

I wish I had the words to paint for you the scene of unbelievable beauty that greeted the guests stepping over the threshold of the Alan Ladd home in Holmby Hills....

Louella, protective of her special pets, failed to mention either Laddie's participation as an usher in the festivities or the existence of Nick Stuart, the real father of the bride.

The guest list was democratic: Eighty-year-old Adolph Zukor, bearing Alan Ladd no malice for his defection from Paramount, was the hit of the party, mixing with such lesser-known employees and Alan's friends as the Hal Lierleys, Paramount commissary supervisor Pauline Kessinger, and her husband Coley, a studio grip. Hollywood's younger set, the bridegroom's friends, were represented by Jane Powell and her new husband Pat Nearney; Pat's former wife, Mona Freeman, with her new man, Dr. Al Meitus; and Robert Wagner. Mary and Jack Benny, Gracie Allen and George Burns, Jack Warner, the Van Heflins, and Cary Grant—a friend of Richard Anderson who served as an usher—helped make the evening a photographer's field day.

Alan couldn't take his eyes off Mrs. June Allyson Powell the entire evening, although he did his best not to be obvious. Sue, of course, noticed. She and June smiled graciously at each other, and Sue resisted the obvious temptation to shove her rival into the swimming pool. (Later, according to *Saturday Evening Post* writer Richard Havler, she admitted to a friend, "I'd like to drown her in a teaspoon of water.")

Sue realized that if she had rescinded the invitation it would have been as good as a for-real admission that there was truth to the rumors. She decided to wait until the Andersons were happily off on their honeymoon before arranging an open confrontation with June.

A few days after the wedding, just before *The McConnell Story* was completed, she cornered June at Warners. It was an incident June still remembers vividly... "She came up to my dressing room. In essence, she accused me of enticing her husband. And I said to her, 'Sue, you know that can't possibly be true. You've been on the lot every day and you've driven to and from the set with Alan all the time. And if you think about it, there couldn't possibly be anything going on. I'm married to Richard [Dick Powell]. You don't think for one minute he would stand by and accept anything like that. I think you had better talk to Richard.' So she called Richard and she said, 'Well, I suppose you know that my husband is madly in love with your wife.' And you know what Richard's answer was? 'Isn't everyone?' And I later told Richard I thought he was rude to say even that."

Although Powell kept his cool at the time he later told friends that he was offended by Sue's behavior, but to June he merely said, "Sue had had several husbands before she married Alan and she was the one who always walked out on them. I guess she thinks every woman behaves the same way."

In this instance, however, Alan was the one to do the walking. Learning of Sue's call to Powell and controlling his rage for the children's sake, he packed his bags and moved out of the Holmby Hills house.

In less than a day the news that "Hollywood's most perfect couple" had separated swept through the town. Alan couldn't be located. The phone at North Mapleton Drive rang incessantly, but only Louella was able to get through to talk to Sue. She may have seemed overly sentimental about her friends, but Louella was nobody's fool. Though fed rumors about June and Alan for weeks, she had refused to use them, even as a blind item. At Carol Lee's wedding, she had kept an eye on the two, trying to judge for herself if the gossip was true. She had just about managed to convince herself that it wasn't when she heard the news of the separation.

After speaking to Sue, she filed the following story for her January 28, 1955, column:

The Alan Ladd separation rumors were denied in no uncertain terms to me today by Sue Carol Ladd. "I've never heard such nonsense," said Mrs. Ladd. "Alan always goes out to the ranch when he finishes a picture, but he doesn't happen to be there now. He's on his way to Rancho Santa Fe to play golf and to rest after finishing

The McConnell Story. I had planned to go to Las Vegas with some friends, but now I'll join Alan as soon as possible at Rancho Santa Fe."

Six days later Louella was writing to a different tune:

I'd be willing to bet that Sue and Alan Ladd will be happier than ever now that they are over this bad time in their lives. Sue just isn't going to let anything jeopardize her marriage. Alan is very happy to have her back, too. Sue's whole life has been wrapped up in Alan's career and in their children.

Louella, as she so often did, had the scoop, but the following day Sheilah Graham noted that "Mrs. Alan Ladd called from Rancho Santa Fe. She's back with Alan and everything will work out OK. The parting of this couple was a great shock." Hedda Hopper disdained the entire affair. Offended that Louella had scored a beat on her, she did not mention Alan in her column for the next year and a half, literally keeping the whole story under her hat.

These three powerful ladies of the press had little to fear from either the Ladds, the Powells, or the studios, but there was good reason for choosing to ignore what obviously was a "hot" story. Hollywood and its leading stars were under assault at the time from *Confidential* magazine, which was depicting the motion-picture capital as Sodom and Gomorrah. Frank Sinatra, Ava Gardner, Lana Turner, Robert Mitchum, and Maureen O'Hara, among many other stars, were all objects of attacks. For years the Ladds and the Powells had been held up to the rest of the country as proof that happy marriages and well-adjusted children could exist in Hollywood. That image had to be maintained. In the past, one way the columnists helped maintain it was by ignoring the existence of Sue's three earlier marriages and Alan's first wife. With Alan still soaring on all the popularity polls, they had no intention of doing an about-face.

Eager to assure her readers that the Ladds were back on cloud nine again, Louella wrote, "They have weathered the storm and are closer than ever"; "they have a new and stronger sense of what their marriage of fourteen years had built"; and "they love each other with even deeper devotion." She planned, she told readers, to travel south to visit Alan and Sue at their "reconciliation house" at Rancho Santa Fe, where they were enjoying a second honeymoon.

Both second honeymoon and Louella's plans were blitzed when Alan—predictably—came down with the chicken pox. He phoned the columnist and said he and Sue would grant a joint telephone interview as soon as he was feeling better. By the time Louella called back, Alan and Sue had agreed upon and rehearsed the official version of the separation. As usual, Sue did most of the talking, and Louella dutifully printed her words:

> "Everything is all right, believe me, Louella. There isn't a chance of our marriage, which has been so perfect for fourteen years, coming to an end. I love Alan and he loves me. What was a temporary and personal problem between us—and will remain that—could have easily been solved in privacy and would have been forgotten by both of us now, if it had come at a different time. We had a quarrel when both of us were nervous wrecks.
>
> Alan had been working too hard. He made too many pictures in too short a time. When he should have taken a rest because he was tired, he signed to do the physically and emotionally difficult *The McConnell Story*. His nerves were on the jagged edge and so were mine. I was the mother of a bride-to-be ... The comfortable home I've tried to make for Alan and the children all these years was completely disrupted. So we blew up. Right after the wedding, we had a quarrel, a serious one about something that is still our private affair and we both acted impulsively, each of us guilty of feeding the gossips.

Sue went on to assure Louella that there had never been any talk of divorce, just a trial separation; that after a couple of days apart she had come down to Rancho Santa Fe at Alan's request, which really did happen, and all their misunderstandings were a thing of the past [which remained to be seen]. June Allyson's name was never mentioned. Like Midge, June was swept under the rug.

A couple of days after the completion of *The McConnell Story* June Allyson and Dick Powell went on a skiing vacation in Sun Valley, Idaho. "Months later," June recalls, "we were invited to a party for Grace Kelly. Alan and Sue noticed us the moment they came into the room. They immediately turned around and walked out the door. I never saw Alan again after that... I've always regretted that Alan and I couldn't have maintained a friendship over the years or at least worked together again. But nasty gossip prevented that. I can't say Alan was in love with me. I don't really think so. But if there had been no Richard and if there had been no Sue, who knows how things might have turned out...? I'll always remember Alan as one of the kindest, gentlest, and sweetest men I've ever known. And I promise there was none of that nonsense we were accused of."

There is no reason to doubt that. David Ladd doesn't.

Although David Ladd was only seven at the time and of course unaware of the gossip, he heard the story years later... "I don't believe that there was anything between my father and June Allyson, and I don't think my mother does either. I think it was a period of male menopause. You know, a man worries about not feeling attractive and all of a sudden he thinks someone finds him attractive and he's attracted to the attraction—and that's what it was."

Whatever it was, Alan played the role of the repentant husband admirably. All the magazines went on publishing glowing stories about the Ladds' "rediscovered love," complete with intimate home layouts. But Alan's smile appeared forced in the photographs, and the light, as they say, was gone from his eyes. That once-expressive, vulnerable face was now more a waxen mask. Alan Ladd would never quite look—or be—the same again....

Sue's appearance was altered too—for the better. Slimmed down, she adopted a youthful hairdo and acquired a wardrobe of girlish, fashionable clothes. For the first time she looked as young as, if not younger than, her husband, perhaps because Alan had aged so quickly—almost overnight, it seemed. He and Sue stayed in seclusion at Rancho Santa Fe for more than a month, with Alan postponing the start of his next film, *The Darkest Hour* (to be released as *Hell on Frisco Bay*), until April. He needed time to regain his health. Chicken pox had left him weak, and he had to forego most activities, especially sexual or athletic....

On the weekend of March 27 the Ladds drove to Palm Springs to houseguest with their friends Bob and Andrea Howard. Howard, who had recently built some desert resort homes on speculation, persuaded Alan to look at a piece of land at 323 Camino Norte. "It's a steal," said Howard. "I can let you have it for $49,000 cash. I guarantee it will double in value in a few years." Howard underestimated. The property was eventually worth more than a half-million dollars.

The house itself was typical desert-modern—a sprawling pink-and-charcoal structure with glass walls and mandatory swimming pool. Alan was amused by the fact that it had the same street number—323—as the mansion on North Mapleton Drive. A frequent visitor to the Springs, he had often thought of buying his own place and was convinced that fate, with an assist from Howard, had directed him to this house. He thought of it not as a good investment or a third residence, but as a sanctuary where he could retreat whenever he wanted to leave the outside world behind. Before the weekend with the Howards was over, Alan had clinched the deal and made arrangements to build special quarters for the children on the property.

A few days later he left for the San Francisco location of *Hell on Frisco Bay,* together with co-stars Edward G. Robinson and Joanne Dru, and his long-time friend, director Frank Tuttle, the man who had given him his big chance in *This Gun for Hire.* Although Tuttle had directed only five pictures—most of them flops—since leaving Paramount in 1943, Alan had signed him to a two-picture deal with Jaguar Productions: *Hell on Frisco Bay* and *Cry in the Night,* in which he would not appear. (The latter, starring Natalie Wood and Raymond Burr, would be Tuttle's swan song.)

On the surface, the signing of Frank Tuttle appeared a shining example of Alan Ladd's gratitude to the man responsible for his stardom. But it went deeper than that. As his own producer, Alan persisted in using people who had been associated with him during his Paramount years, trying to recreate the atmosphere in which he had once thrived. Clinging to the past, he had also put aging cameraman John F. Seitz (who was behind the lens of *This Gun for Hire* and ten of Alan's other Paramount films) under contract to Jaguar. For *Frisco Bay* he engaged other Paramount alumni such as Paul Stewart, William Demarest, and Anthony Caruso, the last a fixture in nearly all his more recent films.

The plot of *Frisco Bay* was also a relic of the early Forties: an ex-con's efforts to track down and get even with the man responsible for sending him to prison. Robinson, in the role of a ruthless ruler of the San Francisco wharfs, repeated a characterization that had made him famous in the Thirties, but he played the part with verve and style, while Alan wandered through his scenes like a, so to speak, spiritless ghost. Television was giving audiences this kind of fare for free, with no fewer than twenty shows of the genre divided among the three major networks. Alan, however, seemed unable to accept the fact that in order to survive he would have to change with the times and take chances. Few stars, directors, or producers from the Forties could make the transition; it would take Mike Todd with *Around the World in Eighty Days* and Federico Fellini with *La Strada* to show the industry where it should be heading.

In mid-May, a few days before completing *Frisco Bay,* Alan caught his foot in the cable of a boat about to leave its mooring. Only a warning shout from Eddie Robinson prevented another serious accident, and Alan managed to get away with a slight bruise.

But they were beginning again—the freak accidents, the illnesses, the enervating chain of self-destructive "mishaps." . . .

CHAPTER 25

It was October 1956 and Sophia Loren was totally bewildered by Alan Ladd's attitude.

All summer she had been looking forward to her trip to Athens and to the Greek islands of Hydra, Delos, Rhodes, and Mykonos for her first American film, *Boy on a Dolphin,* and was excited about working with Alan Ladd. She had seen many of his early films when they started making their way into Italy years after World War II had ended and considered him "*un uomo molto seducente.*" But when director Jean Negulesco introduced him, Sophia's Neapolitan ebullience evoked a distant response, and throughout the entire shooting her attempts at establishing at least a friendly working relationship were discouraged. When Sue—apparently reassured by Alan's seeming indifference to Sophia—suggested that some romantic photographs be shot for publicity purposes, Sophia was more than willing, hoping that this bit of intimacy might break the ice, but Alan managed to make even that contact with Italy's sensuous beauty coolly businesslike.

When shooting began on *Boy on a Dolphin,* Sophia was in love with Carlo Ponti. She was frantic to become his wife, and, facing nearly insurmountable difficulties because of the Italian divorce laws (Ponti was separated from his first wife at the time), she had no romantic designs, she said, on her co-star. But she simply could not understand why he remained so aloof.... Talking about the experience twenty years later, she would recall, "Alan Ladd was my only leading man with whom I could not make friends. Cary Grant, Clark Gable, Frank Sinatra—all would later become good friends, but not Alan. We spent hours together on a small boat. There was a political upheaval nearby. All this should have made us close. But no. He was always polite but never seemed to want to have any social contact. I liked Alan, but he didn't seem to like me. I couldn't understand it."

There was something else about working with Alan that puzzled Sophia: She had to do their more intimate "two shots" in a freshly dug ditch. Granted, she was tall—five feet eight inches—but she had worked in Italian films with leading men who were as short as or shorter than Alan Ladd without anyone's caring about the height difference. She towered above Carlo Ponti, and that clearly did not affect her feeling for him. So the fuss over height struck her as ridiculous, and she talked about it to the international press with considerable amusement.

The Greek dockhands and studio crew—an irreverent lot—were also filled with merriment both by Sophia's descent into the ditches and Alan's rather dazed, indifferent air. They wondered among themselves whether Señor Ladd was perhaps indulging in too much *ouzo* once the sun went down. The language may have literally been Greek to Alan, but the looks he received, combined with the word *ouzo,* were understandable in any tongue. Still, like June Allyson, no one on this film ever claimed to have seen Alan Ladd under the influence of alcohol when the cameras were rolling. His mysterious desire to keep a distance from Sophia Loren may have been a result of the fiasco with June Allyson, but his moodiness was more likely caused by a growing regret that he had ever returned to Europe to begin with. He disliked the script of *Dolphin*—a story about a hunt for buried treasure in the Aegean Sea. His role as a dedicated archeologist was hardly one likely to offset some of the poor reviews he had recently received. His latest Jaguar production, *The Big Land,* was being readied for release and needed his time and attention. But he had been susceptible to the $275,000

Twentieth-Century-Fox was willing to pay him for *Dolphin*—a sum that raised his freelance picture fee to a new plateau.

To add to his unease, for the first time during an extended location trip none of his children were with him; because shooting was scheduled in the middle of the school term it had seemed impractical to uproot them for a few short months. Alan had insisted, however, upon a clause in his contract guaranteeing that if the picture were delayed beyond December 10, 1956, the studio would pay to fly his family to Greece for the Christmas holidays.

Carol Lee, now twenty-four and back home since her divorce from Richard Anderson the previous April, was looking after the house, Alana (now in the ninth grade), and young David. Laddie, about to turn nineteen, was quite self-sufficient. And Edmond O'Brien—who had become fast friends with Alan when he had costarred with him and Virginia Mayo in *The Big Land*—joined Bill Demarest and Bill Bendix in an informal pact to have the children to dinner frequently. And the ranch was in good hands. The Palm Springs house was being cared for, and Bill Higgins had the hardware store Alan had opened on an impulse in mid-1955 running smoothly. Despite all this, Alan continued to feel uneasy about being away and wanted to get *Dolphin* finished as quickly as possible.

It was in this mood that he and Sue had boarded the legendary Orient Express in Paris enroute to Athens. It had been a tedious trip, but as usual his fear of flying had prevented him from going by plane. While the train was passing through Yugoslavia, a thief had ransacked the Ladds' compartment, making off with some of Sue's jewelry, Alan's dinner clothes and other valuable items. (Later they discovered that their insurance wouldn't cover the losses, since no policies were in effect in Communist-controlled countries.) The robbery had added to Alan's discomfort, although the staff at Twentieth-Century-Fox had gone out of their way to make the Ladds' stay in Greece comfortable and pleasurable.

Most of the difficult location work on *Dolphin* was to take place on the Aegean Sea, off Hydra, a rocky little island located four miles by boat from Athens. A picture-postcard community with cobblestone streets and pastel-colored houses, Hydra was judged to lack appropriate housing facilities for a Hollywood crew. So the studio had rented luxury cabin cruisers to serve cast and crew as floating hotels. Clifton Webb and his mother Maybelle were assigned the *S.S. Neraida,* owned in prewar years by Mussolini's son-in-law Count Ciano. Alan and Sue were sole occupants of *The Daphne,* a one-hundred-twelve-foot yacht with a large bedroom, den, gray marble bathroom, dining room, card room, and galley. Below decks were six double bunk beds and an extra bedroom. All this opulence lost its charm, however, in bad weather, when the yacht would roll like a matchbox, furniture would dance around and tables would go smashing from one side of the craft to the other, sending china, silver, food and water flying in all directions.

The Ladds were assigned a Chinese cook whose idea of a perfect dinner was fried mashed potatoes for an appetizer and there was no toaster, no broiler, no oven aboard nor even a ship-to-shore telephone. Ten years earlier Alan had taken location inconveniences in his stride. Now, at forty-three, inappropriately outfitted yachts were a distinct irritant. Perhaps if he hadn't thought he was being misused in *Dolphin* he'd have been less inclined to fret, but there were times he obviously felt he was merely a prop to help in the making of a new sex symbol—"full-lipped, almond-eyed" Sophia Loren.

He wasn't altogether wrong...Jean Negulesco's camera angles consistently favored Sophia Loren. Later Alan was to tell New York *Herald Tribune* columnist Hy Gardner: "Negulesco fell in 'love' with her, so she got all good close-ups. All you ever saw of me in most scenes was the back of my neck. I got fed up with it."

Virginia Mayo adds: "That was a bad picture for Alan to do because Sophia Loren was exceptionally tall and big and the director, Jean Negulesco, was stuck on the girl. Alan liked to be photographed from the right side, and the director kept photographing him from his bad side, from bad angles. And Negulesco had him do walking scenes with Sophia Loren that made Alan look bad. It was a mess. I saw the picture when it came out, and I was very unhappy about it."

By early November it was obvious to everyone else as well that Sophia was getting the star buildup at Alan's expense. Her costumes were designed to focus attention on her figure, and photos taken of her in a clinging black wet suit would be used on posters advertising the film. Given little or no help from Negulesco, Alan sleepwalked his way through the shooting.

Even if Negulesco had not adored Sophia, he would have favored her out of a desperate need to enliven the film. Clifton Webb, as a rich, suave esthete dedicated to snagging a priceless gold-and-bronze statue of a boy on a dolphin, handled his role in the same detached manner he had long since made his trademark. And Alan's appearance had been a shock to Negulesco. The actor's once-chiseled face was now bloated, his body misshapen by excess weight. The cameras picked up these flaws and magnified them—so much so that when Negulesco saw the daily rushes he was forced to order several scenes cut.

After what seemed like an interminable stay in the Islands, the company went to Athens. Alan picked at his Thanksgiving dinner with Sue in their luxurious hotel suite, put through a long-distance call to his family in California and, because rain had extended the shooting schedule, brooded over whether he'd make it home by Christmas.

It seemed, though, that things had gone smoothly in his absence, with a few exceptions: Laddie's convertible had caught fire on the Hollywood Freeway when a passing motorist flipped a lit cigarette into the back seat but quick thinking on the young man's part had prevented any serious injuries. *The Big Land* had been previewed at Warners and had received a cool reception. These, however, were only minor distractions compared to the current political crisis in Greece. There was rioting in nearby Cyprus, and the Suez Canal had been seized by Egypt from the British, the French and the Israelis. Talk of an impending revolution or a major Middle East war was everywhere, and the State Department was evacuating American personnel from the area as swiftly as possible. Under this kind of pressure the studio rushed to bring *Dolphin* to a conclusion, and the Ladds took off for Le Havre to catch the *Mauretania* back to New York.

An Atlantic crossing in mid-December is seldom a pleasant experience. In this instance, it was a nightmare. Buffeted by storms, the *Mauretania* beat its way through dense fogs, barely missing a collision with a passing freighter. Alan was furious with himself for being so terrified of flying. Once again, he swore he'd avoid working in Europe and cursed the weather conditions which would delay the arrival in New York for at least a day, which in turn meant missing all connections back to California.

His parting with the cast and crew of *Boy on a Dolphin,* including Sophia Loren, had been superficially pleasant. But in a five-page interview with *Photoplay*—a glorified version of those awful months in Greece—he never once mentioned his lovely co-star's name.

Alan—and Sue—had mistakenly turned down a secondary role in *Giant.* Now it seemed he was going to *have* to get used to playing second fiddle, or else.

Or else . . .

CHAPTER 26

The Ladds made it home in time for Christmas.

Alan was exhausted, angry with himself because of the weight he had put on in Greece, anxious about his work in *Dolphin* . . . defensive, and defiant, about his drinking. For the children's sake, though, he went through the motions of enjoying the holidays—and in their presence, at least, he stayed away from the bar.

On December 28 he received an alarming call telling him that a fire raging in the Malibu Canyon mountains was heading toward the Valley and that Alsulana was in danger. He rushed north to help save his property, which he was able to do thanks to a fortunate shift in the wind.

Faced with a crisis like this, he was sorry he had become so involved with the ranch. But he would not give it up. He had a near-fetish—an illness?—about owning and keeping. And unlike the cool, impassive image he projected on screen, he was now increasingly restless—afraid to be still for more than a few seconds at a time, afraid to allow his mind the luxury—or pain—of introspection.

When Richard Hevler visited North Mapleton Drive to interview Alan for the *Saturday Evening Post,* he noted: "He rarely sat down. He'd do anything to keep busy—from emptying ashtrays and taking the cook's telephone calls to diving into a pool to escape conversation. He'd finger his favorite dagger—a finely etched gold-inlaid job supposed to be a personal weapon of Hermann Goering's—or turn on blasting hi-fi music. He was forever speculating about new deals for himself or his friends."

When asked by Hevler why all the feverish activity, Alan shrugged and said, "I'm working myself to death so that the guy Sue marries afterward won't be in financial want." No longer was it "my Susie," no longer the all-encompassing "we." He tersely admitted, "We have quite a few beefs," and "God only knows what we talk about most of the time."

Sue, too, grew careless about trying to keep up a squeaky-clean, candy-coated marital façade: "People like to make me the heavy with Alan—but I don't make his decisions for him. I contribute my judgment and he goes ahead and does what he wants anyway." She even conceded that her judgment *could* be wrong. "He's always inventing household gimmicks in his head. I pooh-pooh them, and a little later someone else puts them on the market. I've had 'I told you so' said to me so many times it almost sounds like 'howdy.'"

Still, despite what seemed widening cracks in Hollywood's allegedly most idyllic union, Sue continued to try to protect Alan. She rationalized the June Allyson interlude by explaining, "Alan felt abused and he should have. I hadn't been giving him the attention he needs." She tried to keep bad reviews and articles away from him by cutting them out of the papers, unwilling or unable to face the fact that shielding a forty-three-year-old man from the unpleasantries of life could be more destructive than the realities.

Among the grimmer of those realities was the continuing decline of motion-picture grosses throughout the country. The major studios were indeed drowning in a sea of red ink. Most independent producers were seeking other employment unless they could come up with a blockbuster like *Around the World in Eighty Days* or *The Bridge on the River Kwai*.

Under an iron-clad agreement, Warners was committed to financing two of Alan Ladd's Jaguar films a year, in addition to paying him $150,000 per picture plus a percentage of the gross, but it became an agreement Jack Warner regretted. One wag at the studio suggested that Jaguar be renamed "Alley Cat" because of the inferior quality of its product.

Although Alan was elated to get *The Big Land* booked into New York's Paramount Theater on March 1, *Times* critic Bosley Crowther damned the picture the next day in every area, unable to find a single virtue in the production, including the scenery, which he called "downright synthetic." "Synthetic too is the story (about a cattle drive), and even more so is Mr. Ladd, who herewith presents a pasteboard cut-out of the performance he gave in *Shane*."

Nor did Alan do much better with *Boy on a Dolphin,* released in April. Reviewed by second-line critic A.H. Weiler for the *New York Times* on April 20, 1957, Sophia Loren and the Grecian scenery received raves, Alan Ladd was dismissed as "merely a moody scientist who doesn't give the impression that he is really her type."

Alan tried to be philosophical about the reviews by reminding himself of the money he had pocketed from *Dolphin* and telling friends that, in truth, he didn't like the movie any more than the critics. But he was wounded when Sheilah Graham asked rhetorically, "Won't Alan Ladd have to go on a diet if he wants to continue playing lover-boy roles?" He had considered her a friend. Her remark hit him right in his undeniable spare tire.

Having nothing scheduled for release for the remainder of the year, Alan plunged into plans for his next film, *The Deep Six,* which was to go into production in mid-May. The title was a nautical term referring to burial at sea, and in it he was to play a World War II naval lieutenant—a Quaker who loses the respect of his men, then regains it through an act of heroism. The script was overlong and tedious, but Alan planned to surround himself with a strong male cast—Keenan Wynn, Efrem Zimbalist, Jr., and James Whitmore. Once again turning back the clock to his Paramount days, he signed Bill Bendix to play his doomed good old buddy. Janet Leigh was announced for the female lead, but the part went to a rather bland starlet named Dianne Foster—Alan was interested in building up a select roster of promising young contract players.

Meanwhile Alan's seeming compulsion to accumulate intensified. Expanding his stable of horses, he bought a three-year-old, Dava, named for son David. Adding to his property holdings, in mid-April of 1957 he acquired an office building at 9250 Wilshire Boulevard (still known today as the Alan Ladd Building) and one hundred more acres in Palm Springs, which he planned to subdivide. Alan may have grown up poor, but he was hell-bent—perhaps *not* so to speak—on making certain that he would not die poor . . .

Laddie was now a sophomore at the University of Southern California, majoring in business administration. He had not inherited his father's looks but had his prowess at sports. He was far more interested, however, in film. He haunted movie houses on weekends and holidays, seeing nearly every movie that was released—the private screenings on North Mapleton Drive didn't satisfy his appetite. He had no desire to emulate his father by becoming an actor, but his ambition to be a producer kept burning. "When you were Alan Ladd's son, you knew that there would always be comparisons, as a personality or an actor," he says.

Throughout the years Laddie had maintained close contact with Midge. Today he says, "Never once did I hear my mother say an unkind word against my dad, nor did he ever have anything unkind to say about her."

Life, though, hadn't been easy for Midge. During the war years she had been happy with husband Bill Farnsworth, but according to her sister Barbara, "After the war, the man changed a great deal. Midge didn't have an easy time of it but she tried her best to keep the marriage together." Her efforts failed. Shortly after the birth of Darrick in 1953, Midge and Bill Farnsworth were divorced.

Midge's health had also been failing for years. Stricken with diabetes, she was in constant pain. At forty-one, she was still a shy, sweet-looking woman known only as Mrs. Farnsworth to her friends in Newport Beach, where she had moved in 1956 and was working in a dress shop. A private person, Midge maintained a discreet silence about her girlhood connection with a man who had become a Hollywood superstar. She was grateful that she and Laddie had never been subjected to the interrogation of an inquisitive press. She was proud of the way Laddie was developing, delighted that he was doing well in college. No amount of money could have persuaded her to sell her story, though growing medical bills strained her finances.

On Tuesday, April 30, 1957, she awoke with knife-sharp pains in her stomach and back, muscle spasms more severe than she had ever experienced. As the day progressed so did her agony, and against her wishes a friend summoned an ambulance. She was taken to Orange County General Hospital, arriving there at 7:45 P.M. Doctors tried to save her, but it was no use. She was placed in the crowded "dying room." Just as she was unable to fight for her life when it still lay ahead of her, so she was unable to fight as it slowly slipped away.

At three forty-five on the afternoon of May 1, Midge was pronounced dead. To brother Robert Harrold, Jr., who was at her side when the end came, fell the duty of informing the family—including Laddie—and transporting the body back to North Hollywood for burial in a single gravesite at Valhalla Memorial Park Cemetery. A local columnist, George Putnam, noted Midge's passing—and her association with Alan—but none of the more illustrious writers picked up on it. Midge had been "buried" long before she was buried....

Laddie was devastated, and Alan too was shaken when he learned of his first wife's death. Although she belonged in a chapter of his life that had ended a long time before, her passing revived memories of those dark months in 1937 and reactivated the guilt feelings he had never actually rid himself of. He became increasingly moody and uncommunicative, and threw himself into work on *The Deep Six*. All business on the set, he wore two hats as both star and producer, but out of habit he deferred to Rudy Mate's direction, and working with Bill Bendix again after eleven years seemed to help make him feel something of his old self again....

Now more than ever before, in the summer of 1957 his thoughts were turning to television, though he had declined numerous offers to appear on TV as an actor. What he really wanted was to get in on the production end of the medium and was considering producing a series with Bill Bendix in the leading role.

Many of the old radio shows—*Gunsmoke, Our Miss Brooks, Father Knows Best, Life of Riley* and *Dragnet*—had made a successful transition to television; even *I Love Lucy* was a slightly revamped version of Lucille Ball's *My Favorite Husband*. So Alan decided to adapt his *Box 13* show for television, with a new young actor in the lead. It obviously never occurred to him that *he* might have been the main reason for the show's original success.

But anything to keep busy, anything to prevent his thinking too much about himself...about the past...about the future...lights, camera, *action*—that was the ticket for numbing unacceptable feelings...

He agonized over having no definite property for his next Jaguar production. "It's so damn hard to find good properties," he complained to Bill Bendix. But just as he had wondered why he had gotten so involved in real estate and then gone out and bought more property, so now he was questioning the wisdom of his commitment to Jaguar while starting to blueprint his own movie/TV studio, to be built on his new Palm Springs land.

This was his state of mind when he received a phone call from Samuel Goldwyn, Jr., who was attempting to follow in his famous father's footsteps by running an independent production company of his own. Goldwyn was preparing a script for *The Proud Rebel*, a sentimental post-Civil War father-and-son drama with a mood not unlike *Shane*'s.

Would Alan be available? And would he consider allowing his young son David to be considered for the role of the boy? The film was scheduled to roll in Utah in mid-August and would not interfere with David's education....

Neither Goldwyn, Jr., nor Alan, nor anyone else could know that *The Proud Rebel* would be the last "class" movie Alan Ladd would make.

Or rather, just possibly Alan Ladd was the only one who *did* know, or at least had a strong presentiment of it. And, with all the rest he was carrying locked inside, it would simply be too damn much to bear....

CHAPTER 27

Alan's entire demeanor would change when his son David was with him. His voice was softer, his eyes were filled with tenderness, the defeated aura replaced by a quiet authority and a gentle protectiveness.

It was as though in David he saw a miniature replica of himself, and wanted to shield the boy from the hurts and rejections he had known at David's age. David was not ill-fed, ill-clothed, and sickly, as his father had been, but Alan was aware of the psychological wounds that could result from being undersized and was constantly reassuring David that he could shoot up overnight.

He kept his son on a fifty-cent-a-week allowance, with an extra twenty-five cents a day when he had worked in *The Big Land.* He also told friends proudly that "David saves his allowance to buy presents for us—Father's Day, Mother's Day, birthdays, Christmas." He had been disappointed when Laddie had shown no interest in an acting career, so it was with considerable pride that he noted David's apparent talent for "make-believe." "When he was smaller, he was always putting on puppet shows for us," Alan said. "All his life he's been accustomed to being photographed. He always wanted to be an actor." Alan strongly denied that David got the *Rebel* part because of nepotism... "Sam was going to use David even if I refused the picture. He tested a hundred boys and couldn't find the right one for the part. Then he remembered the bit [David] did for me in *The Big Land* and asked me if he could interview him. After the interview, he just wasn't interested in anyone else."

It was a mutual admiration society. When David was asked if his father was the same at home as he was on the set, the boy, seemingly amazed by the question, answered, "Oh, yes, he's always nice." Even Sue, impressed by this unusual devotion, had to admit, "I've never seen a boy to have such a crush on his father as David has on Alan."

Michael Curtiz, a fiery Hungarian whose talent was exceeded only by his lack of tact in dealing with actors, was set to direct *The Proud Rebel*. Curtiz had been under contract to Warners from 1927 to 1953, where he had directed some eighty-five films, including *Life with Father, Night and Day, Mildred Pierce,* the Oscar-winning *Casablanca* and a dozen of Errol Flynn's most successful epics. Loved, hated—sometimes both—by the actors with whom he worked, Curtiz could be vitriolic. Protesting young Bette Davis's casting as a siren in a 1932 film called *Cabin in the Cotton,* Curtiz had said, "Are you kidding? Who'd want to go to bed with that!" (Ms. Davis, one hears, still talks about that.)

Known in Hollywood as a realist with a penchant for blood and guts, Curtiz was particularly rough on what he called "sissified actors" who faked difficult scenes with stunt men. Flynn, Bogart, Cagney, Garfield—they were the macho types he liked. After leaving Warners at about the same time Alan had left Paramount, he directed the ill-fated *The Egyptian,* for Zanuck, a disastrous remake of *The Vagabond King,* and a few moderately successful films. He needed a major hit as badly as Alan Ladd—and although lacking George Stevens' gentle patience, Curtiz was an accomplished director.

The Proud Rebel was a tearjerker of great charm, centering on the efforts of a Southern Civil War veteran to find a doctor capable of curing his mute son. The part of John Chandler, a father whose anxiety and devotion to the boy prove more powerful than his pride, was a plum. For the role of the farm woman who temporarily hires the two, Goldwyn enticed Olivia de Havilland back from Paris, where she had resettled. De Havilland, who had worked with Curtiz in seven of the Flynn epics—from 1935's *Captain Blood* to 1940's *Santa Fe*—was a favorite of the volatile director and unaffected by his volatile temperament. She had never met Alan Ladd, although she had done several pictures at Paramount after leaving Warners, including *To Each His One* and *The Heiress*.

Although Alan had apprehensions about Curtiz from the stories he had heard, he was genuinely pleased to be co-starring with a woman who had won two Academy Awards—his first time opposite an actress so honored. From their first introduction Olivia de Havilland—perhaps the finest actress he'd ever worked with—seemed warm, friendly, and, more important, genuinely fond of David.

Ms. de Havilland remembers... "I liked Alan. I think he liked me too, and we certainly worked very harmoniously together. I thought he was a proud and a sensitive man. *Very* sensitive. And throughout the picture he was very concerned about the boy. Because Mike Curtiz could be quite harsh with people, Alan was afraid that Mike would be rough on David... Alan wanted very much to be a good actor—and he was. But he needed the assurance of somebody who had faith in him as a performer. He was the kind of man who would wilt, I felt, if he didn't get it, but still would not show it. His confidence would be destroyed if he was handled without great tact by a director, and I suppose this kind of approval is very often a substitute for parental support and approval."... When Alan was not preoccupied with David, Olivia de Havilland—who seemed to understand him better than any of his other colleagues—would also sense a distinct if undefinable aura of melancholy about him. "One day—I can't remember exactly why, but I felt he needed reassurance—I said something that had been on my mind since we began working together. 'Alan,' I said, 'I don't know why they didn't choose you for Ashley Wilkes in *Gone with the Wind*. You would have been marvelous in the part.' You have no idea what that did for him. It was wonderful. He brightened so. He really did, and it seemed to make a difference in his work that day. He put himself into it with far more strength."

After that afternoon, Alan went out of his way to seek Olivia's company. So did Sue. In contrast to the coolness she had shown Veronica Lake, June Allyson, Sophia Loren, Geraldine Fitzgerald and others of his leading ladies, Sue extended herself with Olivia de Havilland. Obviously, since Olivia was very happily married to *Paris Match* editor Pierre Galante and had two children, she could hardly be considered a threat. Sue was won over completely.

"Sue was really very darling," Ms. de Havilland says. "She was very hospitable. Alan loved being a host too. While we were on location Sue would always work something out so she could have Mike Curtiz and me and a couple of others over for dinner. Whether she fixed it herself or had it catered, I've forgotten. But on that remote location it couldn't have been easy. It was so nice of her, and really not necessary, but she did it." Olivia de Havilland remembers that everyone was pleased at the way the film was progressing, that David's performance seemed outstanding, and the consensus was that he'd be a major child star when *The Proud Rebel* was released.

In early fall the cast returned to the Goldwyn Studios to film interior scenes, and the picture was completed on schedule. "Often actors do not become very close when they're working," says Olivia. "To begin with, they're working too hard to become intimate friends, and they don't set up a close relationship, usually because they know it has to be a temporary thing that comes to an end when the film does. After that, another film takes all our time and energy and attention. But it wasn't that way with Alan. After *Rebel* the Ladds always kept in touch with me—even David. When I was in Los Angeles, Sue always invited me to parties and that kind of thing. They entertained me straight through the years and we exchanged Christmas cards every single year without exception."

David's affection for Olivia never diminished, and she remembers with delight that "when he was on his honeymoon with his Cheryl, he brought her to Paris to call on me and to take me to dinner." Yet despite her warm friendship with the Ladds, Olivia de Havilland, like so many of Alan's co-stars, wasn't even casually informed of Laddie's heritage. She, too, thought Laddie was Sue's son because he looked so much like his stepmother, and she didn't ask questions.

When *The Proud Rebel* was completed, Olivia returned to Paris, certain she had added another hit to her credits. "It was really a delightful movie," she says, "quite perfect in its way—all of a piece. We all loved it." Goldwyn, agreeing, opted to hold up its national release until the following summer when school was out, hoping to get a Radio City Music Hall booking. Because of that theater's reputation for family films and the successful showcasing of *Shane* there, *Rebel* seemed a natural.

David, whose performance had been outstanding, went back to school. Alan, with his now chronic restlessness, wanted, needed another film as quickly as possible. It was announced variously that he'd be starring in Columbia's *The Chiselers* for Rudy Mate, who directed *The Deep Six;* that he'd be making his television debut in General Electric Theater's *The Deadly Hush;* that together with Doris Day he was buying screen rights to *Wings of Life,* the autobiography of aviatrix Ruth Nichols. Louella Parsons, aware of his declining popularity, happily reported that "Alan Ladd is making a switch from his strong rugged heroes back to the gangster type that hoisted him to stardom in *This Gun for Hire.* He bought *Thunder in the Rain* and the character Alan will play is that of a racketeer quick on the draw."

None of these projects materialized, and when Alan returned to work after the first of the year in 1958, it was for MGM in another stereotyped role in still another hackneyed Western. *The Badlanders* was no more than a rehash of MGM's earlier hit, *The Asphalt Jungle,* with the story transferred to a different time and place. In the film Alan and Ernest Borgnine set out to rob a gold mine. The mine actually had belonged to Alan but he had been cheated out of it. A pretty starlet named Claire Kelly provided romantic interest.

Once again, filming involved a long, arduous location junket that took Alan to Arizona and Mexico. It was beginning to appear that he would do anything to get away from his home, or homes. Why? His actions seemed unrelated to his reality. He was drowning in money and property. He had every opportunity to relax in luxury, and yet he kept exposing himself to the rigors of location work. One could understand this if the film had the potential of becoming a big moneymaker or a classic, or if the role were an irresistible challenge. But this was the kind of predictable potboiler Alan could have done with his eyes shut—and many critics insisted he did. The movie didn't make much money, but Alan Ladd did—he received a six-figure salary, although like all his other income, most of it eventually went to the government.

Alan continued to seem obsessive about earning money, acquiring property. Now it even irked him that he was co-owner of the Palm Springs hardware store with Bill Higgins, and he made plans to buy Higgins out. The old litany "This can all go up in a puff of smoke" was on his lips more frequently than ever. And one grievous professional error after another made it seem like a self-fulfilling prophecy.

At home Carol Lee, now twenty-five, had fallen in love again—this time with thirty-seven-year-old film executive John Veitch. Alan and Sue had met him in a veterans' hospital when they were on tour after World War II and had invited him to visit them in Holmby Hills. When Veitch first met Carol Lee she was fourteen, but he didn't forget her. On February 8, 1958, they were quietly married at the Little Brown Church of the Valley with just a few close friends in attendance—a far cry from Carol Lee's first star-studded wedding spectacle. She told her stepfather that she planned to forget about an acting career and, because of her age, start a family of her own as soon as possible.

Alana, on the other hand, envying her baby brother David's new career, could talk of nothing but acting. Now a slim blond beauty of fifteen, she had her father's blessings—with some reservations. "If Alana is going to be an actress," Alan told a friend, "then I want her to study at a good drama school in New York. There'd be no point in her going to college." . . . Sue wasn't at all enthusiastic about that. "I wouldn't want her to go far away." But, she added, "Alan is definitely the boss at home, and what he says goes." What Alan said didn't go too far. Alana remained at home.

Laddie, still on fire with his dreams of becoming a producer but wanting to be self-supporting and independent, started a small telephone answering service in Beverly Hills with Helen Hayes' young son, James MacArthur. Laddie was not, however, adverse to seeking business from the Ladds' friends and acquaintances. A year had passed now since his mother's death, and whatever feelings Laddie had, he kept to himself. . . .

Although Alan tried not to show any partiality in his treatment of his children, it seemed obvious that his son David was his favorite. He'd tell friends with mock solemnity, "This thing about having a son who's a star has its drawbacks. Now when I walk down the street, the neighborhood kids yell, 'Hey, there's David Ladd's pop.'" But he didn't bother to hide his parental pride when *Parents Magazine* bestowed its "Pin and Nipple Award" on him because of his trouping with David in *The Proud Rebel.*

The film opened throughout the country in June to extremely favorable reviews. Alan received his best notices since *Shane,* but there was unanimous agreement that David had stolen the show. Radio City Music Hall, though, did not opt to present *Rebel;* instead it chose the sophisticated Ingrid Bergman–Cary Grant comedy *Indiscreet* for its summer attraction. The Ladd name, it seemed, was no longer considered powerful enough to fill the six-thousand-seat house.

The Proud Rebel was booked instead into the Guild, a four-hundred-fifty-seat mini-theater in the Rockefeller Center complex located a few yards away from the Music Hall, in an attempt to catch the spillover of parents nervous about exposing their children to *Indiscreet,* which, for 1958, was pretty risqué stuff. In spite of the lesser booking, *Rebel* received the same enthusiastic reviews in New York as it did in the hinterlands. *Times* critic A. H. Weiler called it a "a genuinely sentimental . . . often moving . . . honestly heartwarming drama," praised Curtiz's direction, commented that "Alan Ladd, not known for explosive portrayals, is restrained but exceptionally expressive as the father," and obviously lost his critical heart in noting: "Although he has but one or two lines of dialogue, Mr. Ladd's eleven-year-old son David contributes an astonishingly professional and sympathetic stint as his son. The tow-headed youngster . . . is not only extremely likable but also projects movingly and with surprising naturalness and fidelity the helplessness of the mute."

Delighted by the reception David had received, Alan was determined to be cautious about his son's future. Sheilah Graham, who had been close to the Ladds from the time Alan played the lead in Scott Fitzgerald's *The Great Gatsby* (she was living with Fitzgerald at the time of his death in 1940), visited the house on North Mapleton Drive shortly after *Rebel*'s release. She noticed that David seemed totally unimpressed by the excitement he had caused, and Alan assured her that the film had made no difference in his son's life: "When he saw himself on the screen, he couldn't realize the boy was him, and he enjoyed the picture. He has always seen me sign autographs, so it seems perfectly natural to him when people ask for his. We've had dozens of offers for him for movies and TV series, but I refused everything. . . . I want him to have a normal life. School comes first, but we have no objection to allowing him to work during his summer vacations if an exceptional part comes along." . . . As for himself, Alan continued taking any part that came along—if the *money* was exceptional. His own Jaguar production of *Guns of the Timberland* was postponed from July 1958 to January 1959, and there were problems within the company. Martin Rackin, who wrote and produced *Santiago* for Jaguar and worked on the screenplays of *Hell on Frisco Bay, The Proud Land,* and *The Deep Six,* had recently defected to Paramount. He explained: "By then I had written several dozen pictures and produced a fair share of them too. I had confidence. I knew how to handle stars and directors, and after working for Alan I had gradually taken over Jaguar, bailing Alan out when he was in trouble. I got his pictures made on budget. He made a lot of money with me. I felt I was not being properly compensated because his wife Sue wouldn't let anybody get near anything. I couldn't quite figure out Alan's personal relationship with Sue at the time. I felt he was champing at the bit. Maybe there was some monetary bond, but their private life was their business—as long as it didn't affect my professional life. The film business was undergoing some revolutionary changes, but Alan and Sue were still living in the 1940s."

While looking for a replacement for Rackin, Alan accepted the Mirisch Brothers' offer to appear in their production of *Man in the Net,* with Mike Curtiz again directing. In it Alan was cast as an artist suspected of murdering his erring alcoholic wife. The role of the wife went to Carolyn Jones, whom Alan had rejected for the lead in *The Deep Six* because he felt "she was too tall."

Once again he had agreed to a film involving location shooting—a summer in picturesque New England. It would turn out to be another summer of discontent, and from the most unlikely source he would receive a new blow to his increasingly fragile ego. . . .

Robert Mitchum is not a cruel man, but he has always been notorious for saying and doing outrageous things—more for laughs than from any urge to hurt. Certainly he had no reason to attack Alan Ladd, whom he scarcely knew. In fact, the only connection between the two men dated back to 1949. When Alan had been handed his "Golden Apple" by the Hollywood Women's Press Corps, Mitchum had received a "Sour Apple" for being the most uncooperative of movie stars. Rather than show up for the presentation, he had sent the ladies a funny telegram expressing his thanks.

In 1958 Mitchum was in Athens shooting *The Angry Hills,* a picture he considered of little importance. In typical "Mitchum-ese" he explained to the London *Sunday Express*'s Roderick Mann just how he had gotten roped into this uninspiring role: "Originally," he rumbled, his face strictly deadpan, "they wanted Alan Ladd. But when they got to his desert home to see him, he'd just crawled out of his swimming pool and he was all shrunken up like a dishwasher's hand. You know what a little guy he is. Well, when he got out of the pool he was so small they could hardly see him and they decided he wouldn't do for the big war correspondent. So what happened? Some idiot said, 'Ask Mitchum to play it instead. That bum will do anything if he's got five minutes free.' Well I had five minutes free. So I did it."

Another idiot sent Alan the clipping and he was devastated. If, at the time, he had had anything remotely resembling a sense of humor, he would have cabled an appropriately funny reply. But Alan had lost his ability to laugh at himself. He descended into a frenzy of quiet rage. And once again, unable to express his anger, he turned it inward.

At forty-five Alan Ladd was a rich man, and still a superstar, but he couldn't seem to escape the same kind of humiliating insults he had received some three decades earlier. Mitchum was considered a womanizer, always his own man, and possessed the humor Alan lacked. As an actor, Alan felt, Mitchum could easily have taken over every part he, Alan, ever played—*Shane* included—without the reverse being true because of Mitchum's powerful build. Coming from Mitchum, then, the attack was especially pointed.

"Tiny" Ladd he had been. In the eyes of his peers, "Tiny" Ladd he was still. Now middle-aged, Alan felt he hadn't "grown" an inch.

None of the Hollywood papers picked up Mitchum's statements. Alan was still being protected by Louella and Hedda and by photographers who continued to "kill" revealing candids. And there were kindly editors who refused to print Alan Ladd photos that exposed the deterioration caused by too much alcohol, too much pain.

In England, though, where the Mitchum bombshell exploded, Alan felt his image had been seriously damaged. The *Sunday Express* had a huge circulation, and he agonized that the entire country could be thinking of him as a man "all shrunken up like a dishwasher's hand." Only the time spent with David now brought him any real pleasure. When David was romping through the house, Alan stayed away from alcohol. It was only after the youngster was tucked in for the night that he headed for the bar.

Shortly after the Mitchum interview appeared, Alan came down with a painful case of shingles that simply would not go away. (Coincidence?) "Overwork, nervous exhaustion," his doctor told him, and prescribed a long rest after he wound up *Man in the Net.*

Contritely Alan told friends that he and Sue were planning to spend three months on their Hidden Vally ranch and not even think of movies. That was August. On September 13, still at the North Mapleton Drive house and still feeling out of sorts, he told Hedda Hopper that he and Sue were driving down to Rancho Santa Fe and spending a week there without the children. But a few days later there was still another change of plan and the entire family took off for Santa Fe to stay until it was time for the children to go back to school. He tried to relax, to enjoy the opportunity for some close companionship with David. But even in these idyllic surroundings, he was tense, disturbed.

MGM, aware of another spate of Westerns that would be crowding the TV airwaves in the fall and winter of 1958, did not even try for prestigious bookings for *The Badlanders.* Instead the film was given a saturation release in neighborhood theaters before the TV season officially started. For Alan Ladd it was the greatest comedown in sixteen years.

He was to have an even greater one. *Man in the Net* would also be relegated to "the nabes," but the humiliation would be compounded—in New York it would be the bottom half of a double bill with an Ava Gardner disaster, *The Naked Maja*.

The handwriting was too clear on the wall.

Nothing could save him now but a great picture. On his forty-fifth birthday, he realized how slim the chance of getting one was....

Part Five

1958-January 29, 1964

Maybe I thought too much about picking up the money and not enough about the really good parts. Now I don't care how small the parts are as long as they're good.

—ALAN LADD, three months
before his death

CHAPTER 28

Alan Ladd, actor, wasn't slipping. He had already slipped.

The disappointing box-office grosses of his last few pictures were proof of that. What Alan had feared most for sixteen years had happened: with the exception of a pocket of die-hard fans, the public simply wasn't buying.

Disturbed by the string of flop movies and his sharp fall in both box-office and popularity polls, under constant pressure from the everyday problems of a TV production unit in addition to the strain of getting his next picture underway, he was now unable to go to sleep at night without the aid of sleeping pills—often washed down by a stiff drink. He had virtually no tolerance for alcohol, yet his need for it kept growing. It was only by staying busy that he was able to control his craving.

Twenty years later David Ladd would say, "My father didn't drink as much as people have said. Two drinks and he was smashed. He was allergic to liquor. My mother will hate me for saying this, but in the truest sense, my father was an alcoholic."

Sue, aware of the problem, remained silent. She knew that nagging would do little more than cause additional tension and irritation. The marriage, having weathered the storms of a few years earlier, seemed back on a more even keel, with Alan's dependence on her on the rebound, if anything. Inwardly he may have despised himself for not being his own man, but overcome by a sense of guilt at his ingratitude, as he saw it, he buried whatever resentments he may have felt. Indeed, he tried to atone for them. When Sue's fifty-fifth birthday came on October 30, 1958, he marked it by sending her a present every day that week. And there was the usual lavish family get-together at Christmas, when Sue gave him a Thunderbird.

For the most part, however, Alan's thoughts were focused on plans for the TV series *Ivy League* and *Box 13*. Although *Ivy League* required a young boy actor as Bill Bendix's vis-à-vis, and David was now considered the hottest young child star in Hollywood, Alan resisted the temptation to co-star his son in the pilot. He told Bendix, "I don't want David working so hard," and with obviously mixed emotions he signed young Tim Hovey for the part. Casting another actor for his own original role in *Box 13* was equally difficult, and he interviewed dozens before deciding on Bill Leslie.

After engaging the services of Aaron Spelling, Alan was filled with uncharacteristic optimism about his pet series. He had become friendly with the young actor-writer Spelling while working with his wife Carolyn Jones in *The Man in the Net*. "Then," Spelling now recalls, "Alan called me with the assignment to do an overnight rewrite on *Timberland*." Impressed with Spelling's talents and still hurt by Rankin's defection, Alan offered him a spectacular deal: Spelling would oversee *Ivy League* as executive producer, and in the same position write the pilot episode of *Box 13*. For this he would get forty percent of the profits, with Alan perfectly amenable to the suggestion that Carolyn Jones "guest star" in *Box 13*. Spelling would also be in charge of a third series—a Western Alan was contemplating.

Alan was adamant about *not* appearing in any of his own company's TV projects. Although he'd come across impressively in the three "General Electric Theaters" he had done in the past, he had disliked the three-to-five-days-per-episode shooting schedules, the black-and-white photography and the lack of character development in half-hour scripts. Those conditions were all too reminiscent of the ones he'd endured during his days as an actor in "quickie" B's. Although he didn't say it to the actors he was hiring, he felt that television was more suitable to a performer on the way up or the way down. It was a view shared by many in Hollywood at the time, although Alan's own studio, Warners, was the first "major" to succumb to what it rightly perceived as the inevitable.

On February 1, 1959, Carol Lee gave birth to a son Jonathan, nicknamed Jody. By marriage, at least, Alan was officially a grandfather, a situation he accepted with mixed emotions.

Carol Lee recalls: "We went down to Palm Springs right after Jody was born, and I'd get up with the baby early in the morning. Dad would be lying on the couch, and when I went to fix the baby's bottle I'd put the baby cradled up in his arms. From the kitchen I'd hear him talking to this tiny thing, this seven-day-old little thing. He'd tell him all about me and about him. It was adorable."

Yet despite his affection for the new baby, Alan saw the "grandfather" label as one more indication of the frighteningly swift passage of time. The "young Greek god" was long gone and forever relegated to a round tin can stored in the Paramount vault or bound volumes and dog-eared photos in some archivist's storerooms....

Leaving the TV production details in Spelling's hands, Alan now turned to movie making again in May with Jaguar's *Guns of the Timberland*. And once again he reached into the past for security. Jeanne Crain, Twentieth-Century-Fox's answer to June Allyson in the 1940s, was cast in the romantic lead. Gilbert Roland, Lyle Bettger, Noah Beery, Jr., and Frankie Avalon completed the cast, but not even Spelling's rewrite could do enough for Louis L'Amour's story of a feud between ranchers and lumberjacks. Nor could Robert Webb's direction succeed in lifting the film from the damning category of "minor Western"—so minor, in fact, that it was the only Alan Ladd movie the *New York Times* failed to review after Bosley Crowther's rave for *This Gun for Hire*. Hearst columnist Dorothy Kilgallen would add to that insult by later commenting: "Audiences viewing *Guns of the Timberland* express surprise at Alan Ladd's initial appearance; he's gained so much weight he looks quite different from the actor they remember as the star of other films." (Kilgallen would also note that "Alan Ladd's liver trouble is serious"—an obvious allusion to his drinking.)

The *Timberland* project was a bad-luck one from the start. Location shooting outside Reno was held up by Alan's case of the flu, his snakebites, and a fall off a horse. (Self-destruct was the only one firmly in the saddle.) For Alan the one bright note was the fact that he had cast Alana, now sixteen, in the ingenue lead (opposite Frankie Avalon), and that she was living up to his expectations as an actress.

It was David, however, who had captured the country's imagination. Every major child role was offered to him first. Early in the year Alan had permitted him to do a "Playhouse 90," but he had stayed away from the set because, as he told a friend, "It makes me too nervous to watch David if I'm not acting with him." He did agree to allow his son to appear with Donald Crisp and Theodore Bikel in *A Dog of Flanders*, reluctantly because the film was to be shot on location in Belgium and his commitments prevented him accompanying his son. Sue chose to remain home with Alan and sent teacher Jean Martin abroad as chaperone.

When Alan was in Reno his old friend Kirtley Baskett, having been unable to sell an Alan Ladd piece to anyone for several years, uneasily approached him with a suggestion that he write an "Open Letter" to his son for *Modern Screen*. The collaboration was at least a touch beyond the usual fanzine material, expressing Alan's unspoken feelings about the boy. The letter read:

Dear Davy,
    Time scoots along pretty fast when you grow up. That's why it's hard for me to realize you're twelve years old.
    ...I didn't have the things you have when I was a kid....We were poor, very poor. So it's natural, I suppose, to want your kids to have all the things you didn't have. The less you have the more you want to give them. If there is anything you kids have lacked, I don't know what it could be. Sometimes that worried me. I

thought I was spoiling you rotten until I found out that none of you were the spoiling kind.

But I've been strict. You know it, Davy. I don't think I've ever had to lay a hand on you. Most of the times I never even had to say a harsh word. Just a look and you knew what I meant. I figure that's my duty to you. I believe discipline is good for children, David. I think it gives them character and security.

But you were never a Hollywood kid in the obnoxious sense of that word. You were all boy—jeans, T-shirts, scraps and everything.

I'm pretty proud of those A's, David—as I am of your spot on the swimming team, the baseball squad and in the band... You've had all the advantages, I suppose, a boy could ask for. But that doesn't necessarily make a gentleman. Consideration for others does.

You've never let me down, Davy—not for a minute. Even though all that fan mail you're dragging in makes our secretary, Muriel, work nights, even though you've already copped a lot of awards. Neither all these radio and TV interviews, nor those rock 'n roll records that are wowing the teen-agers have given you big ideas. On that p.a. tour, Carol Lee tells me you worried more about your collie, Lance, back at the ranch than you did about how you looked to kids mobbing you for autographs. I know you aren't exactly living it up on a dollar-a-week allowance either. And that twenty-five cents an hour dusting shelves at Higgins-Ladd hardware store in Palm Springs isn't exciting alongside a movie check. But, believe me, those are the things that make it all right with me.

I know now I wouldn't have missed doing that picture with you, Davy. Frankly, I didn't want to play your dad on the screen at first. I wanted to *be* your dad, not play him. But not every father gets a chance to start his son off in his own footsteps.

I've always had a great respect for the picture business, David. It's been good to me. I didn't have anything and it's given me everything. Not only security but the satisfaction of doing what I wanted to do and being what I wanted to be.

I'm proud of your career. But the important thing I
want you to know is this: It's great to see you make movies
as long as it is fun for you. But nobody's pressing and
there is no sweat. You can stop whenever you want to.
Like me, you're a guy who can't sit still. You want to do
everything now, all at once. But there's school and sports
and fun and just growing up too, to think about. We don't
want to gain a star in the Ladd family and lose a boy.
You're the last one we have. . . .

I guess that about wraps it up. It's late and tomorrow's
a rough day, but I'm glad I had this talk with you because,
to tell the truth, I needed it more than you did. I say I'd
rather be David Ladd's dad than Alan Ladd any day.

The Ladd family had gained and lost a star. That's what Alan
wasn't quite able to say to his son, or to anybody else. Alan had
no illusions about *Timberland,* nor about his performance in it.
He was a man floundering, looking for the lifebuoy that would
save him from sinking into oblivion. He had high expectations
for a property he had bought called *The Cavalryman,* and he
had entered into negotiations with director John Ford in the
hope that Ford's genius could somehow work the same magic
with him as George Stevens' had.

Too late. Warners now considered Jaguar a drain on their
resources, judging the company's output as neither a financial
nor artistic credit to the studio. The failure of Alan's TV pilots to
generate interest at any of the three networks had convinced
Jack Warner that it would be best to end the association with
Jaguar and Alan as quickly and quietly as possible, with the
usual face-saving "by mutual consent" statement issued to the
trade papers.

In 1959 Warner was concentrating on Broadway plays that
could be adapted to the screen, and he alternated these with
fresh-young-love stories starring Troy Donahue (the studio's
new blond hope), Sandra Dee, Connie Stevens and Natalie
Wood—popular favorites whose salaries didn't put too much
strain on his budget. Alan Ladd cost too much for far too little
now, and Warner was not a sentimental man.

Nor did Alan have any strong sentimental attachments to the
Brothers Warner or their studio. For him the Burbank lot had
been mainly a working headquarters. He had no sense of loss

such as he had felt at leaving Paramount. The fact that his own production efforts had all failed was a devastating blow to his pride, but he saw no reason to dissolve Jaguar, so he moved its office to the building he owned on Wilshire Boulevard with the idea of reactivating the company at some future date.

True, the ranch was now self-supporting, and whatever money Alan had invested in the television pilots could be absorbed as a tax loss. But still, he found himself subject to assaults of depression, and his periods of insomnia were increasing. Even with the aid of pills he'd still wake up in the middle of the night and toss and turn for hours. During the summer of 1959 his energy level was at an all-time low. He rarely went into the swimming pool and even his passion for golf cooled. At a time when he should have been sticking to a strict exercise regimen, he rejected all the activities he had once enjoyed. He had never been much of a reader, so time was very heavy—very heavy indeed—on his hands....

Meanwhile Laddie was busy making plans. Not quite twenty-two, he had fallen in love with Patty Beazley, an attractive blond dental technician he'd met while still at U.S.C. Alan wanted him to wait until he was established before plunging into marriage, but Laddie, impatient to have his own life and home, rejected any notion of waiting. The formal church wedding was scheduled for late August, with a small reception afterward to be given by Dr. Joe Farber, the Ladds' next-door neighbor in Holmby Hills.

Alan woke up that morning seriously ill—a victim of a "virus attack," according to the family. He was in no shape to make it to the church or any other festivities.

One can only speculate at the thoughts that had to be going through Alan Ladd's head on the day of his firstborn's marriage. Memories of his and Midge's impetuous elopement twenty-three years earlier?... If Midge had lived just two years longer, she undoubtedly would have attended her son's wedding, and how many questions would that have provoked...? Alan (Sue?) was still obsessively anxious to avoid those kind of questions. Bob Harrold recalls: "Laddie had invited my wife Helen and me to his wedding. We had always been close. A few days before the event, he called, very contrite. 'Uncle Bucky,' he said. 'Dad told me he wouldn't come to the wedding if *any* member of the

Harrold family was there.' I understood and told him we would stay away. It was sad because Alan and I had been such good friends in our youth. But the irony was that Alan couldn't attend anyway." Alan somehow did manage to pull himself together in time to make a brief appearance at the reception—his haggard face explanation enough for his failure to attend the ceremony. He looked like a very sick man, and he stayed at the Farbers' just long enough to pose for a few pictures with the bride and groom.

Those photographs gave the public its first real look at the Ladd mystery son who had aroused so much curiosity during the years when he was so carefully kept out of the picture. No longer awkward or overweight, Alan Ladd, Jr., was now a handsome young man with Ina Beavers' dark coloring (which had led to the belief that he was Sue's son), and with Midge's dazzling smile and shy, gentle manner.

Photoplay, in something of a snit over the fact that *Modern Screen* had gotten an Alan-David "first-person" story, had asked a veteran reporter named Sara Hamilton to come up with a similar piece on Laddie entitled, "The Things I Really Wanted to Tell My Son." It was, in fact, an attempt to find out the story of Alan Ladd's first marriage, but they got something quite different. The story that accompanied Laddie's wedding picture was pretty much a reworking of every Sue-Alan anecdote the magazine had printed throughout the 1940s. The sum total of Ladd's advice repeated a familiar refrain: If Laddie and Patty "have the same kind of wonderful marriage that Sue and I have had for seventeen years" they would indeed live "happily ever after." Nowhere in the story was Sue referred to as Laddie's mother, but nowhere either was there a clue to Laddie's age, thereby allowing the presumption that she was.

Alan had still not acknowledged Laddie's natural mother, even though there was no longer, in fact, a star image to protect—which of course is easier to say now than it was for him to acknowledge at the time. The unretouched photo of Alan with the newlyweds was of a tired-looking middle-aged man with puffy cheeks and sagging jowls.

On her stepfather's forty-sixth birthday Carol Lee Veitch surprised him with the news that she was expecting her second child the following January. That same afternoon he must have died a little as he read an item in Dorothy Kilgallen's column that said, "Alan Ladd's ailment has his friends worried." He wondered just *which* ailment the vitriolic New York columnist was referring to. He had more than she knew....

In October Alan reported to Columbia for *All the Young Men*, which he had agreed to do before he left Warners. Had the movie been filmed a decade earlier, at the time of the racial breakthroughs made by *Pinky, Home of the Brave*, and *No Way Out*, its flaws might have been forgiven for its "courage." As it stood, the Korean War drama—about the conflict between a veteran Marine (Ladd) and a black (Sidney Poitier) who becomes his superior when their commander is killed in battle—was called "a sluggish variation on a well-used Western plot." Not even the "daring" twist—which had Alan's life saved by the transfusion of Poitier's black blood—was able to lift the film from mediocrity.

Alan and Poitier maintained a cordial but cool relationship on the set, with Alan very much aware that Poitier was well on his way to becoming Hollywood's first black superstar; having left the celebrated Broadway production of *Raisin in the Sun* a few weeks earlier to return to Hollywood for the film, he was, perhaps justifiably, protecting his own interests.

Alan's spirits did improve some throughout October and November, mostly because of the friendship he developed with world heavyweight boxing champion Ingemar Johansson, who was making his film debut in *All the Young Men*. The two became close companions while the film was on location at Glacier National Park. Alan taught "The Hammer of Thor" how to be a fast draw with a gun, and the young Swede reciprocated with stories of his adventures before winning his title from Floyd Patterson. In Johansson's life, Alan thought he recognized the dramatic qualities that could be turned into a commercial film property, and he made no secret of wanting to buy the rights for a forthcoming Jaguar production. As location shooting drew to an end, Alan insisted that Johansson move into the Holmby Hills house for the remainder of the filming. With Carol Lee and Laddie now gone, Sue was able to arrange a comfortable suite for their guest. Having the young athlete around seemed to give Alan a new zest for living—he was accustomed to friends many years his senior. David, too, was

excited about the champ's teaching him to box. When
Johansson returned to Sweden in early December, it was with
Alan's invitation to use his ranch in Hidden Valley for training
quarters. Alan wanted to convert the barn—put a ring, steam
room and showers. Johansson, in turn, insisted that Alan join
his wedding party when he married his Swedish fiancée, Birgit
Lundgren, after his next championship bout the following May.

But Johansson's departure, along with the finish of the
movie, brought Alan down to another depression. Restless and
moody, he counted the days before starting his next picture: a
Western written by Aaron Spelling and Sydney Boehm
scheduled to be filmed by Twentieth-Century–Fox in September. Alan had frequently and defiantly protested, "I've studied
movies all my life and I know what's good for me. I can't play
black or gray. I can't be a villain or anything close to one. I have
to play white." An odd remark, considering that he had first
become a star by—to extend the metaphor—playing pitch
black.

In any case, white no longer worked . . . Spelling, realizing
that, wrote in a psychotic, sadistic role for him in *One Foot in
Hell* that rivaled Raven in ice-cold menace while providing an
excuse for plenty of butchery and bloodshed. Alan's character
was an embittered sheriff who plots a terrible revenge against the
people of the small town responsible for the death of his
pregnant young wife years earlier. The part called for a
"character performance." In the hands of another director it
might have enabled Alan to make a graceful transition to the
type of roles being played so successfully by such friends and
contemporaries as Edmond O'Brien and Van Heflin. But his
old-time Paramount rivals—Bill Holden, Burt Lancaster, and
Kirk Douglas—were still playing romantic leads opposite
young, beautiful women, and Alan could no more face making
the transition that he could give up his acting career.

One Foot in Hell (Alan's third picture with a demonic title)
was just starting production when the Screen Writers Guild
called a strike that shut down activity at all the major studios,
and a few days later, while at home, Alan "lost his balance,"
slipped and broke his hand. His doctor warned him it would be a
minimum of six weeks before the cast could be removed, so he
called Bill and Tess Bendix, asking them to join him and Sue on
a Hawaiian vacation.

Bendix's career was also going through a readjustment. Television's *The Life of Riley* had made him a major star, but he was essentially a character actor and there were few starring roles in films suitable for him. The failure of *Ivy League* to make it with the networks was a great disappointment, and he was seriously considering a return to Broadway. Alan was upset about Bendix's leaving Hollywood, though fully aware his attitude was selfish. Of all his friends, he still felt the most comfortable with Bendix, possibly because he had known him the longest, and both men regretted what they now considered the wasted years of their estrangement. . . .

His hand almost healed, Alan was tanned and well rested when he returned to work. Nonetheless he was unenthusiastic about *One Foot in Hell,* and as *New York Times* critic Howard Thompson put it, "mumbled through his role with one [foot] in his mouth."

In the late spring of 1960, the movie colony, long sensitive about being considered a "cultural wasteland" by the Eastern establishment, took up art collecting. The works of old and new masters were gobbled up by the monied residents of Beverly Hills and Bel Air as if they were popcorn at a Saturday matinee. Sue, who had an interior decorator's license, persuaded Alan to buy paintings as a hedge against inflation—and once again her *business* judgment was near-infallible. Within a short time visitors to the house on North Mapleton Drive were treated to the works of Dufy, Buffet, Chapell, Utrillo, Vlaminck, Braque, and Matisse hanging from nearly every wall.

In early June, while digging another water well at Hidden Valley, Alan struck oil and promptly ran into a barrage of protest from neighbors who were appalled at the notion of derricks sprouting up on the lush countryside. The "find," however, considerably increased the value of his property. It was almost as though the Fates were playing determinedly capricious games. Alan, who once thought money was the answer to everything, was, literally, being showered with it from every direction, while at the same time his career as an actor—of far greater importance to him now—his looks, his peace of mind and his health were all rapidly going to pieces.

Even Ingemar Johansson's managers got into the act, vetoing the idea of the champ's training at Hidden Valley, a disappointment for Alan and David. But in mid-June, as they had promised David, Alan and Sue took the boy east by rail to see Johansson's championship bout and watched as Floyd Patterson avenged his earlier defeat by flattening the champion in five rounds on June 20.

In August, Alan was due to leave for Brazil to shoot *Captain of the Sands,* but the threat of a revolution in South America delayed the picture indefinitely. So, finding himself with that *bête noire,* free time, he agreed to personal appearances on behalf of *All the Young Men.* Critics had predictably damned the picture but early box-office returns were good—though exhibitors attributed this to Poitier's appeal rather than Alan's.

While touring in the East, the Ladds stopped in West Virginia for a few days to visit with David. The youngster, on summer vacation from school, was filming *Misty,* a story of a boy and a pony produced by Robert Radnitz. Radnitz had been responsible for *Dog of Flanders,* which was now in general release. David's performance as Nello, the orphaned farm boy who yearns to be an artist, seemed to enchant both critics and public—a confirmation of the promise he'd shown in *The Proud Rebel.*

Questioned about his own plans, Alan Ladd smiled his Alan Ladd smile. "I'll go back to work when a good script comes along. In the meantime I'll just go and see David's pictures." He returned to Los Angeles in time to celebrate his forty-seventh birthday and to say good-bye to Laddie, who had just enlisted in the Air Force. Time was not only passing, it was flying—and the landmarks were all too clear . . .

Alana, now seventeen, was totally caught up in her acting career. She was dating other Hollywood movie sprigs such as Peter Fonda and Robert Walker, Jr., though assuring her parents she had no intention of becoming serious with anyone for a long time.

In early fall Alan received an offer to do a film that he told himself would revive his career. Terence Young, who had directed *The Red Beret (Paratrooper),* wanted him for the starring role in *Horatio*—a multinational collaboration scheduled for production in Titograd, Yugoslavia, and in Rome.

After his experience with *Boy on a Dolphin,* Alan had sworn off working abroad, but he respected Young's talents. And there was an excellent role for Alana. So, subjecting himself, Sue and Alana to still another turbulent Atlantic crossing, in early November 1960 he headed for Europe.

And sailed into the most humiliating fiasco of his career.

CHAPTER 29

Aware of the cruel Hollywood bromide that "an actor is as good as his last picture" and unable to fool himself about the outcome of *his* last five pictures, Alan still felt that one blockbuster could put him back up in the polls again.

Horatio would be his first spectacle—complete with lavish sets and the obligatory "cast of thousands." The screenplay, dramatizing the details of the celebrated feud between Horatio and his brothers and the Curati family of early Rome, complete with a Romeo and Juliet-type love story, appeared to have greater substance than most of the genre. The finale, depicting the legendary duel unto death (the film title would eventually be Americanized to *Duel of Champions*), was written to contain the dash and derring-do likely to show off Alan Ladd to best advantage.

"My father," David Ladd recalls, "did not make that movie because he thought, 'Hey, I got a movie, so I'm going to do it.' It was made because the elements in that movie seemed right. My God, working with director Terence Young in those days was an honor. This was meant to be Terence's *Spartacus,* but as it turned out, it was his disaster."

Sue agreed. In mid-January she wrote *Hollywood Reporter*

columnist Mike Connolly from Yugoslavia: "It was so cold today that the extras refused to work and I can't blame them. Those togas are cold. Ask Alan!"

A month later, chilly togas were the least of the Ladds' problems. From Rome, Sue called Louella Parsons to explain why Alan, for the first time in his career, had walked off a picture in the middle of production. Louella printed her account:

> "Alan has worked eleven weeks without a cent. He reported on the set every day and performed under the most grueling locations in Yugoslavia. Alan's agent, MCA, and his lawyer were given a check for $50,000 by the company, partial payment for his services, which MCA has not been able to cash. We have informed Tiberia (Productions) we are leaving for Paris tomorrow to board the S.S. *United States* for home."

Louella sympathetically observed that she was "sure Alan's previous fine record as a dependable performer will stand him in good stead in the legal fireworks bound to explode." A couple of days later, however, Sue was back on the transatlantic wire, and Louella dutifully reported:

> Alan Ladd, who walked out of his Italian picture, *Horatio,* and sent all his luggage home, is staying in Rome to finish the picture. Lux Pictures have assumed payment of his salary. It's fine with Alan, only he hasn't any clothes—just one suit. Everything else was sent on ahead."

The lack of a wardrobe was distinctly underwhelming—by now Alan knew that *Horatio* was easily the worst movie he had ever made, and that critics would most likely savage both the picture and his acting. "And I had wanted so much for it to be a good picture," he would tell friends later.

And in Rome a sinus infection that had bothered him for years flared up, and he retched so long and so violently that an Italian doctor predicted gloomily, "If you don't stop soon, you'll die before morning." At the moment it seemed a benediction.

But he went on working. It was what he did.

On the last day of shooting his beloved dachshund pup Ciao,

which he bought in Italy, suddenly died—which was one straw too many. A local socialite, Gilda Dahlberg, had planned a large cocktail party in Alan's honor, and he was finally persuaded to make a brief appearance, even if two hours late. Broadway columnist Earl Wilson, in Rome at the time and a guest at the party, recalls Alan mournfully telling him, "Never fall in love" (with a dog).

On March 23 Alan, Sue and Alana boarded the S.S. *United States* and gratefully sailed for home. Arriving in New York on the twenty-seventh and still bitter about the whole experience, Alan grimly told Hy Gardner of the *Herald Tribune,* "It rained steadily for twelve weeks, and I broke my hand and hurt my knee in a dueling scene because of a peculiar Yugo custom—they don't believe in using wooden swords there, just steel." (One reasonably suspects by now that he would have found a way to afflict himself if they'd been made of feathers.)

Back in Los Angeles on April 1, he told Hedda Hopper, "This has taught me a lesson. I'll only make pictures abroad for major American companies, but I'd rather make them here." Hedda further reported that Alan had not yet received compensation for the picture, though the money was being cleared through an Italian bank, and that he had given the company an extra week without pay so they could finish the picture.

He needn't have bothered. *Ojario, Horatio,* or *Duel of Champions*—whatever the title—was trimmed from its projected running time of more than two hours to ninety-three minutes and then to a humiliating seventy-one. No major studio wanted to release it at any length or price. Eventually it was shown at the E. M. Loew Center Theater in Boston in August 1964, booked by little-known Medallion Pictures. The trade journal *Motion Picture Herald* reviewed it from Boston, noting that "with any kind of exploitation endeavor on the community level [it] can be depended on for satisfactory grosses." About Alan's performance, the *Herald's* critic observed kindly, "Ladd impresses as the grim-visaged warrior." (*That* wasn't acting.)

Medallion, however, still found no buyers, and six months later, in February 1965, Allen Eyles' review in *Films and Filming* made sure the movie would never be bought. Eyles wrote that "...[the] film is a thoroughly indifferent spectacle, and there is little pleasure in watching [Alan Ladd] rather spent and ill-at-ease, reduced to playing a part for which he is many years too old in a setting that is cheap and unfamiliar." After this, *Duel of Champions* vanished forever. It would not even be considered fodder for the "Late Late Show" at three o'clock in the morning. However, Alan would be mercifully spared this knowledge. . . .

But he wouldn't be spared the disappointment of seeing another pet project of his—*13 West Street*—open in New York on the bottom half of a double bill. *13 West Street*, originally titled *The Tiger Among Us,* was produced by "Ladd Enterprises" for Columbia Pictures. Its story, presenting Alan as a rocket engineer terrorized by a gang of wealthy, thrill-seeking thugs, had considerable going for it with co-star Rod Steiger giving a strong performance as a detective. But there was no offstage communication between the two men . . . Steiger remembers: "Alan was a very sweet and a very kind and a rather sad man. He was exhausted, really. The man was an exhausted human being. He was never unkind or had an unkind word. He never gave anyone any trouble. He was always there on time and he always left on time, but one had a feeling he was waiting for it all to end."

The news of actress Gail Russell's death on August 26, 1961, undoubtedly hit Alan hard. Although the two had the most superficial relationship when they had co-starred in *Salty O'Rourke* and *Calcutta* back in the Forties, like everyone else at Paramount at the time Alan admired Gail's beauty and warmth. And he was keenly aware of an insecurity not so unlike his own. After learning that her body had been found on the floor of her apartment surrounded by empty vodka bottles, and concerned that thirty-seven-year-old Gail would be deserted in death—as she was in the last years of her life—Alan was determined to attend the funeral.

By the time he arrived at the Westwood Church he was noticeably drunk. Surprisingly, a large contingent of Gail Russell's friends from her Paramount days had come to pay their last respects. Old co-stars Diana Lynn and Bill Edwards were among them, and both were shocked to see the condition Alan Ladd was in. Equally shocked was Robert Osborne, now a noted author and lecturer as well as a columnist for the *Hollywood Reporter.* At that time he was an actor and great admirer of Gail's, and he was seated in a pew directly behind Alan and Sue. Alan had staggered to his pew, and throughout the service kept talking to himself, muttering under his breath. Sue kept nudging him, urging him to be quiet, but he continued to mumble, his words unintelligible to those around him. Osborne, who caught a glimpse of Alan's face when he left the chapel, recalls, "He was devastated." Fortunately for him there were no photographers waiting outside.

13 West Street was not scheduled for release until the following summer, and for the first time since he'd become a star Alan faced a complete void as far as work was concerned. Looking back on that period Sue insists that "Alan had lots of chances to work in things that he did not want to work in."

No doubt true. But for the important pictures of the year—the *Lawrence of Arabia* that he had once dreamed of doing, *To Kill a Mockingbird, The Counterfeit Traitor*—he wasn't even considered. . . .

Whatever frustrations he felt, though, were hidden from his children. He remembered the effects of Ina Beavers' deterioration on himself. "Around the family," as Sue tells it, "he was a very sweet, happy, easygoing man. You know you can't be that unhappy when you have four lovely children who love you and adore you. He might have shown some unhappiness to some of his friends or they might have felt they detected it, but not around the family."

Alan's friends did indeed detect it, particularly Van Heflin, who needed no special invitation to come by the Ladd house. Along with Bill Bendix and Edmond O'Brien he was one of three men with whom Alan could be totally relaxed and who, in turn, could sometimes snap him out of his black moods.

One afternoon in the early autumn of 1961, Van Heflin came by just as Alan was completing an interview with a New York-based reporter. The session had gone badly for both the reporter and Alan, who had turned surprisingly hostile when the woman, refusing his invitation to join him in a drink, accepted Sue's seemingly diversionary offer of apple pie and coffee instead. Van Heflin's appearance broke the tension, and he reminisced with humor about his days as a starving actor in New York. Which prompted Alan to tell some of his own experiences during his early job-hunting days with Sue. In the middle of one such story, Sue interrupted to correct a small detail in her husband's story. Alan abruptly jumped to his feet. "Okay," he shouted, "if you want to tell it so badly, *you* tell it," and exited the room, leaving his guests and his wife in silent embarrassment.

Van Heflin went after him, and after a while he came back, apparently calm and apologetic. A few minutes later the reporter, still shaken by the scene she had just witnessed, made her excuses and left.

Before, whatever problems Alan may have had, he always at least hid them from the press. Now he no longer bothered—or was able to. Or both. The reporter didn't use the incident in her story, but she told her editor that she thought Alan Ladd was "the most defeated man" she'd ever seen.

CHAPTER 30

Nineteen sixty-two: it started as the old year had ended—with a drink.

Too much to drink on New Year's Eve, the image in the full-length mirror revealing the ravages of illness, accidents, and alcohol. The once-muscular body was flabby, the once-handsome face puffy almost beyond recognition, its color sallow. Now when he spoke the deep, resonant voice was slurred and indistinct. And he seemed to feel no reason to shape up, to start living again....

A few of the New York columnists such as Walter Winchell and Dorothy Kilgallen had made comments about his appearance, but Hollywood writers generally maintained the charity of silence. Ladd column-items were down to a trickle. The fan magazines were turning somersaults over another blond actor named Richard Chamberlain, who was suddenly being referred to as "a *young* Alan Ladd" or "a *tall* Alan Ladd." Vince Edwards and George Maharis were the hot new "tough guys," and Warren Beatty the exciting new sex image. On the Western front, they were dusting off adjectives once saved for Alan to describe a grim-lipped newcomer named Clint Eastwood who was co-starring in a TV series called *Rawhide*.

There was no one Alan felt he could open up to, with the exception of Van Heflin. Willing as he might have been to advise and comfort, in 1962 Heflin had his own share of personal and professional problems. Like Alan, he hadn't appeared in a picture for over two years, and his last, *Under Ten Flags* for Dino DeLaurentiis, had been a failure.

"However," Heflin recalled, "Alan would argue that *I* could always return to the stage. Growing older would never prevent *my* getting work, but it could wipe him out completely."

Troubled by Alan's state of mind, Van Heflin suggested that his friend give some thought to undergoing therapy, but to Alan that idea was terrifying. He continued to confide in his friend—about the loss of his looks, lack of self-esteem, and his fears of diminishing sexual potency, and Heflin tried to assure him that what he was going through was normal for most men in midlife—par for the course. But at no time did he suggest that Alan indulge in extramarital affairs, like some of their peers. "Alan's guilt feelings were so intense as it was," Van confided to a friend, "that any additional burden would have driven him only further into the abyss."

On March 15, 1962, the Ladds had their twentieth wedding anniversary, but Alan Ladd was in no mood to celebrate the occasion. He was growing increasingly morose, and had told his agents not to bother sending him any more scripts for TV Western series. His experience with his own pilots had soured him on television. He'd turn on the "tube," watch what he considered the badly written, poorly directed material that had made it onto the networks, and wonder where he had gone wrong. European producers did try to induce him to return to the Continent with extravagant percentage deals, the offers mainly involving action-adventure pictures or "spaghetti" Westerns, but after his experience with *Duel of Champions,* he wanted no part of them.

The Ladd offspring were preoccupied with their own lives—in the case of Carol Lee and now Laddie too, with their own children. Alan enjoyed his grandchildren when they came to visit, but couldn't help also seeing them as still another reminder of the inexorable passage of time. For him the Holmby Hills house had become a glorified prison, and to break out he'd make frequent trips to Hidden Valley, though the role of gentleman farmer was also getting on his nerves.

On Thursday, November 1, feeling particularly low, he drove to Alsulana—alone. He prowled around the place, aimlessly checking on the damage that had resulted earlier in the year when a pipe had broken and caused extensive flooding. After a few drinks, he gloomily retired to his bedroom. The next day, in the early-morning hours, he was found unconscious, lying in a pool of his own blood. His three dogs were hovering over him, whining.

When he came to momentarily he saw the room filled with policemen and ambulance attendants. Sue and his Holmby Hills neighbor, Dr. Joe Farber, were bending over him, calling his name. He was too weak from loss of blood to move or speak a word. There was only a thin thread of pulse. Again he passed out.

When he regained consciousness he was in the Woodland Park Community Hospital being prepared for surgery. A .38-caliber bullet had penetrated his chest, punctured his left lung, ricocheted around his rib cage, and come to rest in the muscles on his back. If it had gone through to pierce his spine, he would have been totally paralyzed. If it had entered one-eighth of an inch to the right, it would have drilled his heart and killed him.

He was alive—but only just. Sue had called in one of the finest surgeons available, who operated while Dr. Farber assisted. The press was notified. Louella Parsons told her readers that "Alan Ladd had been close to death after accidentally shooting himself while cleaning his gun." Other writers went along with this story, rather too preoccupied with the aftermath of the Cuban missile crisis to be concerned about a near-fatal mishap to a fading movie star.

On Monday, November 5, Sue permitted an Associated Press photographer to enter the hospital room. The picture he took of Alan smiling wanly while his perfectly groomed wife hovered over him was a throwaway.

Sue's own accident a few weeks later barely made a column item. She was being chauffeured to the hospital for her daily visit to Alan when a reckless driver went through a red light and smashed into her Cadillac, demolishing the car. It was remarkable that either she or her driver survived. She arrived at the hospital with a bloody gash across her face and one badly swollen knee, given emergency treatment and, after assuring her husband she'd be fine, returned home, still badly shaken. It was her second near-miss with death. "Accidents" were becoming, it seemed, a kind of family curse.

Other than the immediate family, Alan allowed few visitors, to whom he tried to be casual, insisting it was all a "silly accident." But while the press was not exactly crowding his hospital room, there were still questions that had to be answered before the police could close their files.

Alan stayed in the hospital for a month, and during the long, sleepless hours alone, he was taken by moods of deep depression. Though he also lost much of the excess weight he'd been carrying, that once-muscular body was permanently damaged. An ugly, purplish scar now laced halfway around his body from a white spot the size of a bullet almost directly over his heart.

He came home for Christmas, and by then the account of the "accident" had undergone major revisions. Louella Parsons' story about "cleaning a gun" was discarded. Visited by writer Kirtley Baskett, whom he still trusted implicitly, Alan finally agreed to reveal all the "details." After an exhausting day at the ranch, his story went, he had turned in early. Beside his bed was the .38 pistol he always kept handy because the state mental hospital at Camarillo was only three miles away. Alan told Baskett:

"I must have heard a noise, because something woke me suddenly. I was plenty groggy, but I grabbed the gun, instinctively lurched across the room, and tripped over one of the dogs in the dark.

"I must have landed on my head and got knocked out, because I don't remember anything about a shot—no report, no pain—nothing.

"I got to my feet, still not knowing anything had happened. I turned on the light, put the revolver back in the drawer and got back into bed. That's when I saw the blood spurting from my chest. I reached for the phone and called Sue. 'Migosh,' I told her, 'I think I've been shot!'

"Then I passed out, with the receiver still off the hook.

"Now wasn't that a damn fool performance?"

The story that Baskett related, exactly as Alan told it—in "The Man Who Came Back" in the February 1964 issue of *Motion Picture*—has never been explicitly refuted. But the obvious questions still remain....

June Allyson's comments seem at least to provide a clue: "Richard told me that Alan had telephoned him the afternoon of the accident," she says. "I honestly don't know why—or what Alan talked to Richard about. My husband never told me; he just mentioned the fact that he had received the call—and that's all he wanted to say about it. Years later I would wonder about the call and the accident. But at that time I was concerned only with the way Richard was feeling."

Afterward Alan always did his best to treat the matter lightly. He told Kirtley Baskett, "Here I am, making my living with a gun. Then I go plug myself. How dumb can you get?" And added, with a straight face, "I guess my time just wasn't up."

But Dick Powell's was. On January 2, 1963, while still recuperating from his wound, Alan heard the news on radio that Powell had lost his battle against cancer. He knew that Dick had had the disease, but he was still shocked and perversely guilt-ridden. Eight years had passed since the episode with June Allyson, but he had always been uncomfortably aware of how much her husband had been upset by Sue's outburst. He sent June a brief condolence note, then went to his bar and built himself a drink. A large one. Sue tried to get him to eat something, but he was hardly interested in food. It was a scene that had taken place too often in the Ladd household....

From the start of the new decade, so many people who had passed through Alan's life had died—Gail Russell, Marilyn Monroe, and now Dick Powell.

Before his own time would run out there was one more part to play. And one final return to the place where the gates had first opened up for him.

CHAPTER 31

The way Alan Ladd was selected for *The Carpetbaggers* sounded like a movie scriptwriter's dream.

Publicity releases of the time credit Joseph E. Levine, president of Embassy Pictures, with, as they say, a stroke of casting genius for assigning Ladd the Nevada Smith role. But Mr. Levine passes. "I didn't know the man," he says, "and we had very little contact during production. He was Edward Dmytryk's personal choice." Dmytryk, however, says it was producer Marty Rackin who insisted upon Alan—overriding *his* objections.

Dmytryk had been the neophyte thirty-year-old director who had given Alan the juvenile lead in *Her First Romance*. When he was signed to direct *The Carpetbaggers* he was fifty-five, with credits that included such powerhouses as *The Caine Mutiny, Raintree County,* and *The Young Lions*. He was the first really strong director Alan had had since George Stevens in *Shane*

In his recent book, *It's a Hell of a Life But Not a Bad Living,* Dmytryk wrote:

> Alan Ladd was not the man I had known in 1940. Then he had been a non-drinker and an athlete of Olympic calibre.

Now he was a heavy closet drinker and physically not even a caricature of his old self....Size has rarely been a requisite for stardom. Men like James Cagney and Edward G. Robinson were short and couldn't have cared less....Ladd, at one time the top draw in the business just couldn't handle it....I had serious doubts about Ladd's ability to handle the part of Nevada Smith. My fears proved well founded but somehow we nursed him through the film and what eventually appeared on the screen was one of the best performances of his life. It was also his last....

A few days before Alan had reported to the Paramount lot, for the first time since 1954, he had seen his "baby" son off on his first vacation without the family. Now sixteen, David had decided to fly to Hawaii with some of his friends; unlike his father, he was not afraid of planes. Alan had agreed to David's plans, but the idea of David now being old enough to go off on his own was upsetting. He insisted on driving his son to the airport, and David remembers that as the two sat talking before flight departure was announced, his father suddenly broke down and began crying.

When the plane left the ground David could only think of his father standing there...crying. Turning his back on his happy companions, he picked up a pen and paper and wrote:

Dear Dad,
   I don't know exactly what I'm going to write. I only know what I feel. For the first time I realize how much I really do love you and how much you really must love me. When I got on the plane I felt like crying in happiness and even crying because I wished you were coming along with me.
   Both you and mother have been the best parents any son could ever want. I feel bad because I have never told you this before and I hope someday I can make you proud enough of me to return the love you have given me. I will do anything to make you happy.
   At times I haven't understood some of the things you have done in raising me but now I realize your ways will have trained me in the best way to make a better man of

me and that your strictness and the training you have given me come from love.

You are to me a father, a friend, a great man. If I had one wish in life, I wish I could be like you.

Love,
David

Returning to Paramount for *The Carpetbaggers* was even more upsetting to Alan than seeing David off—but it was also exhilarating. He received deferential superstar treatment during the months he spent filming at Paramount, but it was due more to the memory of the star that was than to the actor whose role was secondary to the movie's central story line.

"It's Peppard's picture, you know," he quietly told visitors to the set. It was, of course. And the George Peppard role of Jonas Cord was the kind Alan Ladd could have played twenty, perhaps fifteen years earlier. Alan's character, Nevada Smith—of equal importance in the book—is seen only in his later years in the film. (In 1966, a pre-sequel to *The Carpetbaggers* was made—*Nevada Smith,* starring Steve McQueen. Publicity releases from the studio in 1963 hinted Alan would return to play the role, but no one was fooled. The pre-sequel had called for a young man, and Alan, who had turned fifty during the shooting of *The Carpetbaggers,* was no longer young. Not even careful photography could conceal the damages alcoholism and the years had inflicted.)

The Eastern press, as usual, took their shots at Alan. Walter Winchell asked, "Did Alan Ladd have his face elevated?" And Frank Farrell: "When you see the movie *The Carpetbaggers,* try to spot the male star who recently underwent a complete facial up-lift."

Alan never issued a denial. The evidence against was, he thought wryly, pretty overwhelming. When asked about it recently, Carol Lee Veitch said, "That's not so, my father never had a face-lift. I swear to that. And I should know."

Other than a few column items, the press seemed indifferent to Alan Ladd's "comeback"—he had only half a dozen scenes in the film worth noting. Reporters were more interested in the romance developing between the still-married George Peppard and his still-married leading lady, Elizabeth Ashley. Although the two maintained separate residences for appearance sake, they were, in fact, sharing a hideaway to which they retreated evenings when the cameras stopped rolling. Everyone on the lot knew they were lovers, and the studio gave the affair its tacit approval, presumably thinking that a touch of real-life scandal could further hype the film. The movie industry had come a long way since that time twenty-two years earlier when a word about Alan and Sue's relationship could well have ended his career before it even got started. . . .

When his scenes in *The Carpetbaggers* were finished, Alan once more faced a void. And his energy level was at an all-time low—a fact painfully brought home to him during his fight scene with Peppard that was the climax of the film.

In spite of his physical exhaustion from work—or perhaps because of it—he was having greater difficulty than ever in sleeping. His body had built up an immunity to the pills he had taken nightly for years, and often it would be daylight before he fell asleep.

David and Alana were still living at home, but neither their company nor Sue's constant attention could relieve the awful letdown and loneliness he experienced after winding up at Paramount.

To compound his depression, a close friend, studio grip Coley Kessinger, was dying of cancer. Alan's frequent visits to Kessinger were also taking their own toll on his fragile emotional condition. And his two best friends were thousands of miles away: Van Heflin had begun what appeared to be a long Broadway run in the Louis Nizer play, *A Case of Libel*; Bill Bendix was in Chicago, committed to a long national tour with *Never Too Late*. The telephone was now his only link— lifeline?—to them.

Tess Bendix remembers: "During the last months of Alan's life, he just seemed to hang on to Bill all the time. He'd call Bill at two and three in the morning and say, 'Come home, I need you.' And Bill would say, 'I can't come home, I have a contract.' And then one night not long before he died, Alan called Bill and said, "Look, I'll buy out your contract. Just come home.' Bill of course, had a responsibility to the rest of the company and to his producer. He was worried about Alan, but he just couldn't leave the show. . . ."

Even the fact that Laddie's wife Patty was expecting her second child in December did little to help Alan's sinking morale. Sober throughout the filming of *The Carpetbaggers,* he began drinking again. Nevertheless, Christmas came and went without anything to set it apart from past holidays spent on North Mapleton Drive. Neither Sue nor Alana remember anything unusual. Carol Lee says, "The only difference I can think of is that there were now young children again to fuss over—Laddie's oldest and my Jody and Janna. But Christmas was always a special time for us." (A time of tinsel, of good cheer, of make-believe...)

No one in the family admits to even a premonition that the Christmas of 1963 was to be Alan's last.

Nonetheless, in slightly more than a month, he would be dead.

CHAPTER 32

The last ten days of Alan Ladd's life are clouded by mystery and contradiction. (His death certificate places him in "county of death"—Riverside—for two weeks. Years later Sue would say he went to Palm Springs for a "couple of days." David would remember him gone "no more than three days." The police reported ten days.)

Except for his butler, Wendell Tyler, he was alone at 323 Camino Norte in Palm Springs, sleeping poorly, drinking, watching television, speaking fitfully on the telephone to Sue and friends.

In addition to Bill Bendix, he was in touch with Samuel Vorzimer, who now ran the hardware store for him, and a few nights before he died a local resident recalls seeing him walking alone in the center of town. Mostly though, he stayed in seclusion.

On Tuesday, January 28, he became abruptly enervated. Although Sue would tell the press that she "spoke to Alan three times on Tuesday and he seemed in fine spirits, as always," he was, in fact, so upset about his fatigue that he complained to his butler about his condition and then, later in the evening, called in a local physician, Dr. Joseph Sage. Finding nothing wrong,

Sage administered a vitamin shot and told him to get a good night's sleep.

Which he found impossible. As had become his habit, he sought assistance from the small bottle of pills on his night table.

He awoke in the early morning, still feeling debilitated. Unable to go back to sleep, he called Tyler, asking for breakfast in bed. He also said something to the butler about wanting to take a nap and told him not to disturb him under any circumstances.

Once again he reached for the bottle on the night table.

Tyler went about his business the rest of the morning and through the early afternoon. At three-thirty P.M. he went into the master bedroom. He found Alan in bed, wearing his robe over his pajama top.

It took a few minutes before the butler realized Alan Ladd was dead.

Shocked, panicked, Tyler called neither Dr. Sage nor the police. Instead he contacted Samuel Vorzimer. Vorzimer called Sage and then notified the police. They dispatched a resuscitator squad. Firemen attempted to revive Alan, but Sage pronounced him dead at the scene.

Deputy Coroner Robert Drake told reporters that an autopsy to determine the cause of death would be performed on either January 30 or 31, since Dr. Sage felt he hadn't known Alan Ladd long enough to sign a death certificate.

But Alan's death certificate was signed by Drake on January 29. According to the certificate, an autopsy had been performed and the cause of death was officially listed as "Cerebral Edema due to Synergistic Effects of C.N.D. Chemical Depressants." When Drake was asked to specify "accident," "suicide," or "homicide," his verdict was "Accident due to a reaction to combination of Depressant and Ethonal."

The coroner stated that the "accident" had taken place on the night of January 28, and the official hour of death—when Dr. Sage arrived on the scene—was three fifty-five P.M. on January 29. Alan, of course, had been seen alive by his butler at ten o'clock that morning. Confusion, contradiction, but the *real* mystery was—is—not in the facts of the cause of death, but rather whether it was "accident," as reported, or the decision of a man who had come to the end of his string.

To Samuel Vorzimer went the burden of notifying the family. Sue Ladd remembers sitting with a man from the Internal Revenue Department when the call came in from Vorzimer, informing her as gently as possible that her husband had died from an "apparent" heart attack—Dr. Sage's immediate diagnosis when he arrived on the scene, and the one sent over the wire services. Fortunately Alana was home to help her mother through those first dreadful hours. Carol Lee, informed by her husband, arrived soon after.

David Ladd was driving home along the freeway when he suddenly heard the news on the car radio. "I just pulled across four lanes of traffic and went to a friend's house," he remembers. "I really didn't believe my father was dead until I heard my mother's voice on the phone."

By coincidence, Van Heflin and Robert Preston, both appearing on Broadway, had had plans to meet for dinner in New York at a small theatrical restaurant called Frankie and Johnny's after their respective curtains came down. Over a drink Heflin confided to Preston, "I'm terribly saddened. But I'm not really surprised. He tried it before, you know." Heflin was, presumably, referring to the shooting "accident." Before retiring for the night, Heflin telephoned his wife, Frances Neal, in Los Angeles. She later told friends, "It was only the second time I ever heard Van cry. Alan was so simple and sweet, I wish he'd stayed on a farm and never become an actor."

Bill Bendix learned of his old friend's death when he went back to his hotel after an evening performance of *Never Too Late* in St. Paul, Minnesota. Unable to sleep, he kept repeating hoarsely to Tess, "If only I had gone home, maybe he wouldn't have died." There was nothing Tess could say to console him or relieve him of what she considered his unrealistic feelings of guilt.

June Allyson can't recall exactly where she was or how she heard of Alan's death. "Things were all blurry for a year or more after Richard died, but I do remember being terribly, terribly shocked." And then, remembering the call Alan had made to Dick Powell from Hidden Valley fourteen months earlier, June would ask sadly, "Did Alan commit suicide?"

A great many people would ask that question, or would wonder. . . .

"My father didn't commit suicide," David Ladd says. "It was the combination of liquor and sleeping pills. He often took sleeping pills and he often took liquor. As history has now proved to us with a great many people, there's a 'magic' number that causes death. I spoke to the coroner in Palm Springs myself and he told me, 'There was neither enough liquor or enough sleeping pills in your father's system to call it a suicide.' It was just that magic number, that magic combination—whatever it is—that you just don't wake up from."

Since Alan Ladd's death, medical research has given considerable backup to David's statement. Dr. Frank Seixas, medical and research executive of the National Council on Alcoholism, recently told a *New York Times* reporter that some drugs react synergistically with alcohol—that is, one plus one equals ten or even fifty. Alcohol and phenobarbital, a sedative, are a classic bad-news pair. Says Dr. Seixas in the *Times*, "You can take much less than a lethal dose of alcohol and very much less than a lethal dose of phenobarbital and together they can kill you."

Barbara Harrold Grether never believed the rumors that Alan had taken his own life, but although she was Laddie's aunt never attended the funeral.

Kirtley Baskett, who did go to the service, scoffed at the rumors too. Ironically, Baskett's final story on Alan, an optimistic-sounding piece in *Motion Picture* about Alan's "comeback," was still on the newsstands. Baskett, whose words had given rise to and helped perpetuate the so-called Ladd legend, said he'd never write another word about his friend. He made plans to go to the service, but couldn't bring himself to view the body.

Virginia Mayo remembers: "I was devastated by the news of Alan's death. It was just tragic that he died so young. But I'm sure it was an accident. I don't think he committed suicide. At the time I had just gone through a terrible thyroid removal and my husband was having a serious operation. That was a very low year for me. We didn't go to the funeral, which I deeply regret. Sue probably thought it was terrible of us."

Alan's close friend Edmond O'Brien agreed to read the eulogy, which consisted for the most part of the letter David had written to his father on the plane enroute to Hawaii. Sue made arrangements to have the original placed in the coffin with Alan.

Makeup man Hal Lierley wasn't able to attend, but he wanted to perform one final service for his longtime friend. Although he hadn't seen Alan for several years, he phoned Sue to ask if he could make up Alan for the burial. Arriving for this grim task, Lierley was shocked to find what time and illness had done to Alan. "He was all bloated," Lierley says. "He must have had a liver ailment. Alan was a proud man in life. I wanted to do my best for him, to make him look the way people remembered him..."

The funeral services were scheduled for two-thirty P.M. on Saturday, February 1, at the Church of the Recessional in Forest Lawn Memorial Park. Alana recalls: "The chapel was filled to capacity with friends of my father, but the funeral was so enormous that everything was delayed and delayed and delayed. It was February, and it was getting dark. We were all in the family room, and the head of Forest Lawn came to my mother and said, 'There are three thousand people out there waiting to get in to see him. Shall I let them in?' I said, 'Oh no, Mama. It will be dark when we bury him.' But she looked up at the man with those huge brown eyes of hers and said, 'Let them in. They loved him too.' So we sat there for hours as the fans walked by to take a last look...."

They saw Alan Ladd as they remembered him.

Hal Lierley had done his work well. Alan Ladd in death looked like what he wanted most of his life to be—and was.

He looked like a movie star.

Epilogue: The Legacy

A memorial service for Alan Ladd was held on September 3, 1964—his fifty-first birthday. Sue Carol Ladd unveiled a bronze bust of her late husband and placed it on a pedestal to the left of his crypt in the Sanctuary of Heritage in Forest Lawn.

On a plaque beneath the bust a poem—"Success"—had been inscribed, its irony only for those who knew:

ALAN LADD
SEPTEMBER 3, 1913–JANUARY 29, 1964
I HOLD NO DREAM OF FORTUNE VAST,
NOR SEEK UNDYING FAME.
I DO NOT ASK WHEN LIFE IS PAST
THAT MANY KNOW MY NAME.
AND I CAN LIVE MY LIFE ON EARTH
CONTENTED TO THE END
IF BUT A FEW SHALL KNOW MY NAME
AND PROUDLY CALL ME FRIEND

—Edgar A. Guest

At the time of the unveiling, *The Carpetbaggers*, having premiered in early July, was playing in local theaters throughout the country. Although the critics had attacked the Joseph E. Levine production—reliable Bosley Crowther of the *New York Times* had called it "a sickly, sour distillation of the big-selling Harold Robbins novel"—most were kind to Alan Ladd, sparing him the sarcasm inflicted on the film and its other performers.

On December 10, 1964, William Bendix entered the Good Samaritan Hospital in Los Angeles suffering from lobar pneumonia and malnutrition. Five days later, a month and a half short of the first anniversary of Alan's death, Bendix joined his best friend. He was fifty-eight. *Lucky Jordan*'s director, Frank Tuttle, and its female star, Helen Walker, both died in 1968.

On July 24, 1971, twenty years after *Shane* began, Van Heflin suffered a fatal heart attack while swimming in the pool of the Los Angeles apartment hotel where he had moved shortly after his divorce from his wife of twenty-five years, Frances Neal. He was sixty.

Just a year later, on July 6 in Denver, Colorado, where he was appearing in *Butterflies Are Free*, Brandon De Wilde, the beautiful tow-haired little boy who had broken hearts when he had called out, "Shane, Shane, come back," was killed when his van slammed into a flatback truck parked by the road during a blinding rainstorm. He was thirty.

Shane director George Stevens died on March 8, 1975, at age sixty-nine.

And on July 7, 1973, Veronica Lake, then fifty-three, died in Burlington, Vermont, where she had been hospitalized for eleven days for treatment of acute hepatitis. Ironically, she had written in her autobiography, completed four years earlier: "If I had stayed in Hollywood, I would have ended up like Alan Ladd and Gail Russell—dead and buried by now. That rat race killed them and I know it would have eventually killed me, so I had to get out."

Nick Stuart, Carol Lee Veitch's natural father and Sue Carol Ladd's second husband, died in 1973.

Cynthia Farnsworth, Midge's only daughter, died at age twenty-five in 1972. According to his aunt, Barbara Harrold Grether, Darrick Farnsworth, Midge's younger son, still suffering from cerebral palsy, is a happy and well-adjusted young man. William Farnsworth, Midge's second husband, is still alive and is a successful businessman in Balboa, California.

The four Ladd children, once over the initial grief of losing their father, went on with their lives, and in some ways spectacularly.

The teen-ager who had solemnly told his father that he wanted to be a producer managed to fulfill all his childhood dreams—just like in the movies. Unpretentious, soft-spoken Laddie did it, as they say, the hard way. When he couldn't get into the unions that would enable him to be either a film editor or assistant director, he became an agent, first in Hollywood and then in England. After that he became a partner in a small production company and finally, in January 1973, he was appointed Twentieth-Century-Fox's vice president of creative affairs. A year later he was promoted to vice president of production and in 1975 the then-faltering studio appointed him vice president in charge of worldwide production.

In 1976 Laddie had still another promotion—the big one: he was named president of the feature-film division of Twentieth-Century-Fox Corporation. And following his studio's production of *Star Wars*—the highest-grossing film of all time—the studio notified its stockholders that Alan Ladd, Jr., who in May 1978, was promoted to corporate senior vice-president, was now president, Twentieth-Century-Fox, and a member of the Fox Board of Directors.

In June, 1979, following the successful launching of *Alien,* Laddie shocked the film community by announcing his resignation from 20th-Fox. Explaining he wanted to be exclusively involved in creative producing and free from administrative responsibilities, Laddie then made a deal with Warners, Inc. to finance his future ventures.

So, ironically, Laddie is now associated with the studio where his dad faltered so disastrously—both as an independent producer and an actor. Unlike his father, however, Laddie is not adverse to taking spectacular risks, as his recent actions prove.

Laddie has not adopted the exhibitionist ways of the old-time movie moguls. He seems uncomfortable being interviewed, although on occasion he has spoken to the press on industry topics. He rarely talks about his wife Patricia or discusses his family. He did recently acknowledge that he wanted to have six months off to recapture the time he hadn't spent with Patricia and his three daughters—Kelly, Tracy and Amanda.

A *Crawdaddy* reporter asked him how he had felt when he saw his father on the screen and he answered, "I never really thought about it actually. I just watched the movies, watched him as an actor. I wasn't continually thinking, 'There's my father up there.' He was a personality. Some of his movies I liked better than others. Some, I liked a lot, some I didn't much care for. It was never really a question of being conscious of him all the time."

Still, the hard-hitting investigative journalists of the 1970s—like the "sob sisters" of the 1940s—preferred not to ask about Midge, though Laddie freely admitted to *People* magazine that he lived with his mother until he was thirteen.

His aunt Barbara Harrold Grether is full of pride about her nephew: "Laddie is very much like his mother. He has her gentleness, and her goodness. He is a very fine man. And he got where he got on his own. No one got his job for him. And you know, of all of Alan's children, I have the feeling that Laddie really loved him the most, because he was the most realistic about him. I only wish Midge could have lived to see how successful Laddie has become. She would have been so proud."

Alan would have been proud of Laddie too. And certainly he would have been proud of the way David has handled his life. "My father," David says, "didn't want my career as a child actor to interfere with my education, so I pulled out of it when I was fourteen and went to military school. I did the things most every kid did, I was captain of the swimming team and was into sports..." Soon after Alan's death, David won two medals at the El Segundo swim meet, following his father's tradition. There was a possibility of a part-time scholarship to Princeton, but David decided to stay home to be close to his mother, and enrolled at the University of Southern California. After graduation he began to think about returning to movies, but the transition to adult parts wasn't easy, and there was the inevitable comparison with his father. "You always get that business," David says, "of 'You look like your father,' or 'You don't look like your father.' All I wanted was to be as *good* as my father."

In 1973, David got the lead role in a disastrous movie called

Evil in the Deep, which is memorable to him now only because it was during the filming that he met and fell in love with his co-star—Cheryl Jean Stoppelmoor, a beautiful twenty-two-year-old blond TV actress from Huron, South Dakota. They were married in May 1974 and their daughter, Jordan (named after a character in *The Great Gatsby*), was born the following year. It was David who persuaded his wife to use her married name professionally. Ironically, it was Aaron Spelling, whom Alan had helped get started in television, who gave Cheryl Ladd her break on *Charlie's Angels.* And so once again, the Ladd name was in lights.

Carol Lee Veitch's husband John—the man Alan and Sue had discovered many years before and invited to Hollywood—is now executive vice-president in charge of worldwide production at Columbia Pictures. Their son Jon is a student at Stanford University; their daughter Janna entered U.C.L.A. as a freshman in September 1978. Carol Lee seems a happy, well-adjusted woman who credits her happiness to her husband—and to Alan and Sue ... "My parents always taught us to do the right things. They also taught us the value of the dollar. Which doesn't mean we didn't have everything in the world, but we didn't *expect* to have it. It was never, 'Take my credit cards and go out and buy anything you want.' We weren't given gifts without reason—birthdays, Christmas, Valentine's Day. And we do the same with our children. And all of us have remained very close. I can't say it doesn't have something to do with the way my mother handles us. She's just the most wonderful thing you can imagine. She always has time for every single one of us, every minute of the day, no matter what she's doing. We're quite a family."

Alana Ladd echoes her sister's earnest sentiments, and the years seem to have been equally good to her. Her 1965 marriage to broadcaster Michael Jackson, an Englishman, has been a happy one, resulting in three children—Alan Ladd (Jackson), Alissa Sue, and Devon Michael. Michael Jackson now hosts the most successful radio and television talk shows in the Los Angeles area. The Jacksons live in Beverly Hills, just a few minutes away from the other Ladd children and from the Holmby Hills mansion. "The big house, to me," says Alana, "has always seemed like the center of a wheel of which we're the spokes. It will always be the main house, and we always come back."

Alana remembers her father as a "deeply caring man; a sensitive man, a physical man but always gentle. I have never known a man who was as deeply loved as my father. My husband is constantly interviewing or running into people who knew my father very well. He comes home and says to me, 'My God, the love they had for your father,' and what my father did for them. It's lovely to have that. It's a way for my husband to know my father, even though he never met him."

About her mother, Alana says, "She has a tenderness, a kindness, and a sweetness . . . She's beaten her head against walls for people. She's brilliant. She can do anything. She knows more than anyone when it comes to putting together deals. She's sharp, but she never lost that feminine tenderness. She's just an incredible, wonderful woman . . . My mother never got over dad's death. Never. But she didn't go into a shell. She's a very active, vital woman. And dad just couldn't have dealt with life without her. God only knows what would have happened if she had gone first. He worshipped her. Everything was Susie. Kids were secondary, and I don't mean we got any second-class treatment—but first and foremost was Susie . . . With the love and devotion and the constant supervision we got, all four of us turned out pretty okay."

David agrees. "What I remember most about my father is what he left all of us. He has four very productive, healthy children, and we all have strong family units. It must have come from somewhere." Of his father's relationship with his mother, he says, "I've heard all the bad stories and all the good, and I think my mother is terrific. She adored this man, and she did everything she did with him out of total love, to keep his life together and to try to keep him together. It's very hard to have a woman as your backbone—that I'll concede. But he was crazy about her, desperately in love with her—almost overly so—to a point where he couldn't be without her."

Throughout the large house on North Mapleton Drive there are reminders of Alan Ladd—mementos of times the Ladd family shared together and the places they went, scrapbooks of

Alan's career, photograph albums, bound volumes of the early movie magazines, and a magnificent painting of Alan as he appeared in *Shane*. In airtight containers are prints of all his movies. Almost always, at family gatherings, one is taken out and run, to the delight of the nine Ladd grandchildren.

The way Alan walked, talked, and breathed—all his mannerisms are etched in Sue Carol Ladd's memories. His films, either shown at home or on an "Alan Ladd Week" on local TV, are a tonic for her too. There is *Shane*, with his blond hair glittering in the sun, his green eyes filled with contempt as he confronts Jack Palance. "So you're Jack Wilson. I've heard about you. I've heard that you are a low-down Yankee liar." There is Jay Gatsby, youthful and handsome, staring moodily across the bay at the green light shimmering from Daisy Buchanan's dock. And there is Alan Ladd in a duet of "Tallahassee" with Dorothy Lamour, and Alan Ladd in a mock confrontation with Howard Da Silva over Veronica Lake, and Alan Ladd out to shoot Macdonald Carey with a bow and arrow in those all-star Paramount spectacles. *And* Alan Ladd, heroic and commanding above the square-rigger *Pilgrim* in *Two Years Before the Mast;* self-composed and compassionate as the doctor in *And Now Tomorrow;* rough and ruthless as the oil man in *China;* icy and frightening yet strangely appealing as Raven in *This Gun for Hire*.

"I'll never remarry, I'm still in love with him," Sue recently said. "I'm luckier than most widows because I still have Alan with me. I can see him in one of his pictures ... I hear his voice, I see his face ..."

To his biographer—in a conversation held three days after what would have been his sixty-fifth birthday—Sue Carol Ladd said, "Alan was always a very happy man. My husband had a very happy life."

That's what she said.

Filmography

Note: Alan Ladd appeared in very minor roles in dozens of films before *This Gun for Hire*. In most he received no billing. This filmography is of Ladd's films as a star. The dates refer to New York City openings, except in the case of *Duel of Champions (Horatio)*.

THIS GUN FOR HIRE. Paramount, May 13, 1942. Screenplay by Albert Maltz and W. R. Burnett. Based on the novel by Graham Greene. Directed by Frank Tuttle. Veronica Lake, Robert Preston, Laird Cregar, Tully Marshall, Mikhail Rasumny, Marc Lawrence, Pamela Blake, Roger Imhoff, Victor Killian.

THE GLASS KEY. Paramount, October 15, 1942. Screenplay by Jonathan Latimer. Based on the novel by Dashiell Hammett. Directed by Stuart Heisler. Brian Donlevy, Veronica Lake, Bonita Granville, Joseph Calleia, Richard Denning, Moroni Olsen, William Bendix, Margaret Hayes, Arthur Loft, George Meader, Eddie Marr, Frances Gifford, Joe McGuinn, Frank Hagney, Joseph King.

STAR SPANGLED RHYTHM. Paramount, December 30, 1942. Screenplay by Harry Tugend. Directed by George Marshall. Songs by Johnny Mercer and Harold Arlen. Victor Moore, Betty Hutton, Eddie Bracken, Walter Abel, Anne Revere, Cass Daley, Gil Lamb, Edward Fielding, Edgar Dearing, William Haade, Maynard Holmes, James Millican, Eddie Johnson, Bing Crosby and Bob Hope, Fred MacMurray, Franchot Tone, Ray Milland, Dorothy Lamour, Paulette Goddard, Vera Zorina, Eddie "Rochester" Anderson, William Bendix, Susan Hayward, Jerry Colonna, Macdonald Carey, Marjorie Reynolds, Betty Rhodes, Dona Drake, Lynne Overman, Gary Crosby, Johnny Johnston, Ernest Truex, Arthur Treacher, Sterling Holloway, Cecil B. DeMille, Preston Sturges, Ralph Murphy, Walter Catlett, Katherine Dunham, Walter Dare Wahl and Company, the Golden Gate Quartette, and Slim and Sam.

LUCKY JORDAN. Paramount, January 24, 1943. Screenplay by Darrell Ware and Karl Tunberg. From a story by Charles Leonard. Directed by Frank Tuttle. Helen Walker, Sheldon Leonard, Mabel Paige, Marie McDonald, Lloyd Corrigan.

CHINA. Paramount, April 22, 1943. Screenplay by Frank Butler. Based on a play by Archibald Forbes. Directed by John Farrow. Produced by Dick Blumenthal. Loretta Young, William Bendix, Philip Ahn.

AND NOW TOMORROW. Paramount, November 22, 1944. Screenplay by Frank Partos and Raymond Chandler. From the novel by Rachel Field. Directed by Irving Pichel. Produced by Fred Kohlmar. Loretta Young, Susan Hayward, Barry Sullivan, Beulah Bondi, Cecil Kellaway, Grant Mitchell, Helen Mack, Anthony Caruso, Jonathan Hale, George Carleton, Connie Leon.

SALTY O'ROURKE. Paramount, April 25, 1945. Original story and screenplay by Milton Holmes. Directed by Raoul Walsh. Produced by E. D. Leshin. Gail Russell, Stanley Clements, William Demarest, Spring Byington, Bruce Cabot, Marjorie Woodworth.

DUFFY'S TAVERN. Paramount, September 5, 1945. Screenplay by Melvin Frank and Norman Panama. Songs by Johnny Burke and James Van Heusen. Directed by Hal Walker. Ed Gardner, Victor Moore, Marjorie Reynolds, Barry Sullivan, Charles Cantor, Eddie Green, Ann Thomas, Bing Crosby, Betty Hutton, Paulette Goddard, Dorothy Lamour, Eddie Bracken, Brian Donlevy, Sonny Tufts, Veronica Lake, Arturo de Cordova, Barry Fitzgerald, Cass Daley, Diana Lynn, Robert Benchley, William Demarest, Walter Abel, Billy De Wolfe, Johnny Coy, Miriam Franklin, Howard Da Silva, and Garry, Philip, Dennis and Lin Crosby.

THE BLUE DAHLIA. Paramount, May 9, 1946. Original screenplay by Raymond Chandler. Directed by George Marshall. Produced by John Houseman. Veronica Lake, William Bendix, Howard Da Silva, Doris Dowling, Tom Powers, Hugh Beaumont, Howard Freeman, Don Costello, Will Wright, Frank Faylen, Walter Sande.

O.S.S. Paramount, May 26, 1946. Written and produced by Richard Maibaum. Directed by Irving Pichel. Geraldine Fitzgerald, Patric Knowles, John Hoyt, Gloria Saunders, Richard Webb, Richard Benedict, Harold Vermilyea, Doc Beddoc, Onslow Stevens, Egon Brecher, Gavin Muir, Joseph Crehan, Bobby Driscoll, Julia Dean, Crane Whitley.

TWO YEARS BEFORE THE MAST. Paramount, September 24, 1946. Screenplay by Seton I. Miller and George Bruce. Based on the book by Richard Henry Dana, Jr. Directed by John Farrow. Brian Donlevy, William Bendix, Barry Fitzgerald, Howard Da Silva, Esther Fernandez, Albert Dekker, Louis Van Rooten, Darryl Hickman, Roman Bohnen, Ray Collins, Theodore Newton, Tom Powers, James Burke.

CALCUTTA. Paramount, April 23, 1947. Screenplay by Seton I. Miller. Directed by John Farrow. Produced by Mr. Miller. Gail Russell, William Bendix, June Duprez, Lowell Gilmore, Edith King, Paul Singh, Gavin Muir, John Whitney, Benson Fong.

WILD HARVEST. Paramount, November 12, 1947. Original story by Houston Branch; screenplay by John Monks. Directed by Tay Garnett. Produced by Robert Fellows. Dorothy Lamour, Robert Preston, Lloyd Nolan, Dick Erdman, Allen Jenkins, Will Wright, Griff Barnett, Anthony Caruso, Walter Sande, Frank Sully, William Meader, Bob Kortman.

SAIGON. Paramount, March 31, 1948. Screenplay by P. J. Wolfson and Arthur Shrekman, based on story by Julian Zimet. Directed by Leslie Fenton. Produced by P. J. Wolfson. Veronica Lake, Douglas Dick, Wally Cassel, Luther Adler, Morris Carnovsky, Mikhall Resumny, Luis Van Rooten, Eugene Borden.

BEYOND GLORY. Paramount, August 3, 1948. Screenplay by Johnathan Latimer, Charles M. Warren, and William W. Haines. Directed by John Farrow. Produced by Robert Fellows. Donna Reed, George Macready, George Coulouris, Harold Vermilyea, Henry Travers, Luis Van Rooten, Tom Neal, Conrad Janis, Margaret Field, Paul Lees, Dick Hogan, Audie Murphy, Geraldine Wall, Charles Evans, Russell Wade, Vincent Donahue, Steve Pendleton, Harland Tucker.

WHISPERING SMITH. Paramount, February 14, 1949. Screenplay by Frank Butler and Karl Kamb, based on the novel by Frank H. Spearman. Directed by Leslie Fenton. Robert Preston, Donald Crisp, Brenda Marshall, William Demarest, Fay Holden, Murvyn Vye, Frank Faylen, John Eldredge, Robert Wood, J. Farrell McDonald, Will Wright, Don Barclay.

THE GREAT GATSBY. Paramount, July 13, 1949. Screenplay by Cyris Hume and Richard Maibaum, from the novel by F. Scott Fitzgerald and the play by Owen Davis. Directed by Elliot Nugent. Produced by Richard Maibaum. Betty Field, Barry Sullivan, Macdonald Carey, Ruth Hussey, Howard Da Silva, Shelley Winters, Elisha Cook, Jr., Ed Begley, Henry Hull, Carole Matthews, Nicholas Joy, Tito Vuolo.

CHICAGO DEADLINE. Paramount. November 3, 1949. Screenplay by Warren Duff. Based on the novel by Tiffany Thayer.

Directed by Lewis Allen. Produced by Robert Fellows. Donna Reed, Margaret Field, Harold Vermilyea, June Havoc, Gavin Muir, Shepperd Strudwick, Arthur Kennedy, Irene Hervey, John Beal, Berry Droeger, Celia Lovsky.

CAPTAIN CAREY U.S.A. Paramount, March 29, 1950. Screenplay by Robert Thoeren, based on the novel by Martha Albrand. Directed by Mitchell Leisen. Produced by Richard Maibaum. Wanda Hendrix, Francis Lederer, Celia Lovsky, Angela Clarke, Richard Avonde, Joseph Calleia, Roland Winters, Frank Puglia, Luis Alberni, Jane Nigh, Rusty Tamblyn, George Lewis, David Leonard, Virginia Farmer, Paul Lees, Henry Escalante.

BRANDED. Paramount, January 10, 1951. Screenplay by Sydney Boehm and Cyril Hume. Based on a novel by Evan Evans. Directed by Rudolph Mate. Produced by Mel Epstein. Mona Freeman, Charles Bickford, Robert Keith, Joseph Calleia, Peter Hansen, Selena Royle, Tom Tully, John Berkes, Milburn Stone, Martin Garralaga, Edward Clark, John Butler.

APPOINTMENT WITH DANGER. Paramount, May 9, 1951. Written by Richard Breen and Warren Duff. Directed by Lewis Allen. Produced by Robert Fellows. Phyllis Calvert, Paul Steward, Jan Sterling, Jack Webb, Stacy Harris, Henry Morgan, David Wolfe, Ron Riss, Harry Antrim, Geraldine Wall, George J. Lewis, Paul Lees.

RED MOUNTAIN. Paramount, April 25, 1952. Screenplay by John Meredyth Lucas, George F. Slavin, and George W. George. Directed by William Dieterle. Produced by Hal B. Wallis. Lizbeth Scott, Arthur Kennedy, John Ireland, Jeff Corey, James Bell, Bert Freed, Walter Sande, Neville Brand, Carleton Young, Whit Bissell, Jay Silverheels, Francis McDonald, Iron Eyes Cody, Herbert Belles, Dan White, Ralph Moody, Crane Whitley.

THE IRON MISTRESS. Warner Brothers, November 19, 1952. Screenplay by James R. Webb, based on the novel by Paul I. Wellman. Directed by Gordon Douglas. Produced by Henry

Blanke. Virginia Mayo, Joseph Calleia, Phyllis Kirk, Alf Kjellin, Douglas Dick, Anthony Caruso, Ned Young, George Voskovec, Richard Carlyle, Robert Emhardt, Donald Beddoe, Harold Gordon, Gordon Nelson, Jay Novello, Nick Dennis, Sarah Selby, Dick Paxton, George Lewis, Edward Colmans.

THUNDER IN THE EAST. Paramount, February 3, 1953. Screenplay by Jo Swerling, based on a novel by Alan Moorehead. Directed by Charles Vidor. Produced by Everett Riskin. Deborah Kerr, Charles Boyer, Corinne Calvet, Cecil Kellaway, Mark Cavell, Philip Bourneuf, John Abbott, John Williams, Charlie Lung, Leonard Carey, Nelson Welch.

SHANE. Paramount, April 25, 1953. Screenplay by A. B. Guthrie, Jr., based on the novel by Jack Schaefer. Directed and produced by George Stevens. Jean Arthur, Van Heflin, Brandon De Wilde, Jack Palance, Ben Johnson, Edgar Buchanan, Emile Meyer, Elisha Cook, Jr., Douglas Spencer, John Dierkes, Ellen Corby, Paul McVey, John Miller, Edith Evanson, Leonard Strong, Ray Spiker, Janice Carroll, Martin Mason, Helen Brown, Nancy Kulp.

DESERT LEGION. Universal-International, May 8, 1953. Screenplay by Irving Wallace and Lewis Meltzer. Directed by Joseph Pevney. Produced by Ted Richmond. Richard Conte, Arlene Dahl, Akim Tamiroff, Leon Askin, Oscar Beregi, Anthony Caruso.

BOTANY BAY. Paramount, October 29, 1953. Screenplay by Jonathan Latimer, based on a novel by Charles Nordhoff and James Norman Hall. Directed by John Farrow. Produced by Joseph Sistrom. James Mason, Patricia Medina, Sir Cedric Hardwicke, Murray Matheson, Dorothy Patten, John Hardy, Hugh Pryse, Malcolm Lee Beggs, Anita Bolster, Jonathan Harris, Alec Harford.

PARATROOPER. Columbia, December 30, 1953. Screenplay by Richard Maibaum and Frank Nugent, based on a novel by Hilary St. George Saunders. Directed by Terence Young. Produced by Irving Allen and Albert R. Broccoli. Leo Genn,

Susan Stephen, Harry Andrews, Donald Houston, Anthony Bushell, Patric Doonan, Stanley Baker.

SASKATCHEWAN. Universal-International, March 10, 1954. Screenplay by Gil Doud. Directed by Raoul Walsh. Produced by Aaron Rosenberg. Shelley Winters, J. Carroll Naish, Hugh O'Brian, Robert Douglas, George Lewis, Richard Long, Jay Silverheels, Antonio Moreno, Frank Chase, Lowell Gilmore, Anthony Caruso, John Cason, Henry Wills.

HELL BELOW ZERO. Columbia, July 16, 1954. Screenplay by Alec Coppel and Max Trell. Directed by Mark Robson. Produced by Irving Allen and Albert R. Broccoli. Joan Tetzel, Stanley Baker, Basil Sydney, Jill Bennett, Niall MacGinnis, Joseph Tomelty.

THE BLACK KNIGHT. Columbia, October 28, 1954. Story and screenplay by Alec Coppel. Directed by Tay Garnett. Produced by Irving Allen and Albert R. Broccoli, Patricia Medina, Andre Morell, Harry Andrews, Peter Cushing, Anthony Bushell, Patrick Troughton.

DRUM BEAT. Warner Brothers, November 17, 1954. Written and directed by Delmer Daves. Audrey Dalton, Marisa Pavan, Robert Keith, Charles Bronson, Warner Anderson, Elisha Cook, Jr., Anthony Caruso, Richard Gaines, Hayden Rorke, Frank De Kova, Rodolfo Acosta, Perry Lopez, Willis Bouchey, Peter Hansen, George Lewis, Isabel Jewell, Frank Ferguson.

THE MC CONNELL STORY. Warner Brothers, September 29, 1955. Screenplay by Ted Sherdeman and Sam Rolfe, from a story by Sherdeman. Directed by Gordon Douglas. Produced by Henry Blanke. June Allyson, James Whitmore, Frank Faylen, Robert Ellis, Sarah Selby, Willis Bouchey, Gregory Walcott, Frank Ferguson.

HELL ON FRISCO BAY. Warner Brothers, January 6, 1956. Screenplay by Martin Rackin and Sydney Boehm, from the novel by William P. McGivern. Directed by Frank Tuttle. Edward G. Robinson, Joanne Dru, William Demarest, Paul

Stewart, Perry Lopez, Fay Wray, Renata Vanni, Nestor Paiva, Stanley Adams, Willis Bouchey, Peter Hansen, Anthony Caruso, Tina Carver, Rodney Taylor, Peter Votrain, Jayne Mansfield.

SANTIAGO. Warner Brothers, July 13, 1956. Screenplay by Martin Rackin and John Twist, based on a novel by Mr. Rackin. Directed by Gordon Douglas. Produced by Rackin. Rossana Podesta, Lloyd Nolan, Chill Wills, Paul Fix, L. Q. Jones, Frank De Kova, George J. Lewis, Royal Dano, Don Blackman.

THE BIG LAND. Warner Brothers, March 1, 1957. Screenplay by David Dortort and Martin Rackin, based on a novel by Frank Gruber. Directed by Gordon Douglas. Virginia Mayo, Edmond O'Brien, Anthony Caruso, June Bishop, John Qualen, Don Castle, David Ladd.

BOY ON A DOLPHIN. Twentieth-Century-Fox, April 19, 1957. Screenplay by Ivan Moffat and Dwight Taylor, based on a novel by David Divine. Directed by Jean Negulesco. Produced by Samuel G. Engel. Sophia Loren, Clifton Webb, Jorge Mistral, Laurence Naismith, Alexis Minotis, Piero Giagnoni, Charles Fawcett, Gertrude Flynn, Charlotte Terrabust, Margaret Stahl, Orestes Rallis.

THE DEEP SIX. Warner Brothers, January 15, 1958. Written by John Twist, Martin Rackin, and Harry Brown, from a novel by Martin Dibner. Directed by Rudy Mate. Dianne Foster, William Bendix, Keenan Wynn, James Whitmore, Efrem Zimbalist Jr., Joey Bishop.

THE PROUD REBEL. A Buena Vista release, July 1, 1958. Screenplay by Joe Petracca and Lillie Hayward from a story by James Edward Grant. Directed by Michael Curtiz. Produced by Samuel Goldwyn, Jr. Olivia de Havilland, Dean Jagger, David Ladd, Cecil Kellaway, Dean Stanton, Thomas Pittman, Henry Hull, Eli Mintz, James Westerfield, John Carradine, (the dog) King.

THE BADLANDERS. Metro–Goldwyn–Mayer, September 3, 1958. Screenplay by Richard Collins, based on a novel by W. R. Burnett. Directed by Delmer Daves. Produced by Aaron Rosenberg. Ernest Borgnine, Katy Jurado, Claire Kelly, Kent Smith, Nehemiah Persoff, Robert Emhardt, Anthony Caruso, Adam Williams, Ford Rainey, John Day.

THE MAN IN THE NET. United Artists, June 10, 1959. Screenplay by Reginald Rose, based on a novel by Patrick Quentin. Directed by Michael Curtiz. Produced by Walter Mirisch. Carolyn Jones, Diane Brewster, Charles McGraw, John Lupton, Tom Helmore, Betty Lou Holland, John Alexander, Kathryn Givney, Edward Binns, Alvin Childress, Barbara Beaird.

GUNS OF THE TIMBERLAND. Warner Brothers, February 1, 1960. Screenplay by Joseph Petracca and Aaron Spelling, based on a novel by Louis L'Amour. Directed by Robert D. Webb. Produced by Aaron Spelling. Jeanne Crain, Gilbert Roland, Frankie Avalon, Lyle Bettger, Noah Beery, Verna Felton, Alana Ladd, Regis Toomey, Johnny Seven, George Selk, Paul E. Burns, Henry Kulky.

ALL THE YOUNG MEN. Columbia, August 26, 1960. Written, produced, and directed by Hall Bartlett. Sidney Poitier, Ingemar Johansson, James Darren, Glenn Corbett, Mort Sahl, Ana St. Clair, Paul Richards, Dick Davalos, Lee Kinsolving, Charles Quinlivan.

ONE FOOT IN HELL. Twentieth-Century-Fox, October 19, 1960. Screenplay by Aaron Spelling and Sydney Boehm, based on a story by Spelling. Directed by James B. Clark. Produced by Boehm. Don Murray, Dolores Michaels, Barry Coe, Dan O'Herlihy, Larry Gates, Karl Swenson.

13 WEST STREET. Columbia, June 6, 1962. Screenplay by Bernard Schoenfeld and Robert Presnell, based on a novel by Leigh Brackett. Directed by Philip Leacock. Produced by William Bloom. Rod Steiger, Dolores Dorn, Michael Callan, Margaret Hayes, Kenneth MacKenna.

DUEL OF CHAMPIONS (HORATIO). Medallion, 1964. Screenplay by Vincenzoni, Lizzani, De Concini, and Montaldo. Directed by Ferdinando Raldi. Produced by Domenico Fazzari. Franca Bettoja, Franco Fabrizi, Robert Keith, Jacqueline Derval, Alfred Varelli, Alana Ladd.

THE CARPETBAGGERS. Paramount, July 1, 1964. Screenplay by John Michael Hayes, based on a novel by Harold Robbins. Directed by Edward Dmytryk. Produced by Joseph E. Levine. George Peppard, Carroll Baker, Bob Cummings, Martha Hyer, Elizabeth Ashley, Lew Ayres, Martin Balsam, Ralph Taeger, Archie Moore, Leif Erikson, Arthur Franz, Tom Tully, Audrey Totter, Tom Lowell.

A Partial Listing of
Alan Ladd's Radio Credits
(STARRING ROLES)

Lux Radio Theater

This Gun for Hire	Joan Blondell	January 25, 1943
China	Loretta Young	November 22, 1943
Casablanca	Hedy Lamarr,	
	John Loder	January 24, 1944
Coney Island	Dorothy Lamour	April 17, 1944
Disputed Passage	Dorothy Lamour	March 4, 1945
And Now Tomorrow	Loretta Young	March 5, 1945
Salty O'Rourke	Marjorie Reynolds	November 26, 1945
Whistle Stop	Evelyn Keyes	April 15, 1946
O.S.S.	Veronica Lake	November 18, 1946
Two Years	Macdonald Carey,	
Before the Mast	Wanda Hendrix	September 22, 1946
Shane	Van Heflin	February 22, 1955

Screen Guild Players

Lucky Jordan	Helen Walker,	
	Marjorie Main	January 31, 1943
This Gun for Hire	Veronica Lake	April 2, 1944
The Glass Key		July 22, 1946
Blue Dahlia	Veronica Lake	April 21, 1949
Saigon	Veronica Lake	July 29, 1949
Whispering Smith		September 16, 1949

Take a Letter, Darling	Bob Hope, Rosalind Russell	February 1, 1950
Chicago Deadline		March 24, 1950
Lucky Jordan		February 8, 1951
Beyond Glory		May 31, 1951

Suspense

A Killing in Abilene	December 14, 1950

Screen Director's Guild Playhouse

Saigon	Veronica Lake	July 29, 1949
Whispering Smith		September 16, 1949
Take a Letter, Darling	Bob Hope, Rosalind Russell	February 1, 1950
Chicago Deadline		March 24, 1950
Lucky Jordan		February 8, 1951
Beyond Glory		May 31, 1951

Box 13

(Syndicated by Alan Ladd Productions 1948/49)
Note: Alan Ladd was also a guest on the Kate Smith Hour (1942), The *Bob Hope Show* (1943), and the *Milton Berle Hour* (1945). As an anonymous freelance radio performer he was heard as either a featured performer or a bit player in hundreds of shows over a period of five years. These records no longer exist.

Television Credits

The *General Electric Theater* Productions of:

Committed	December 1954
Farewell to K.	November 12, 1955
Silent Ambush	January 25, 1958

Index

Glittering lives of famous people!
Bestsellers from Berkley

____ **DOLLY**   04221-9—$2.50
Alanna Nash

____ **HITCH: THE LIFE AND TIMES OF**
ALFRED HITCHCOCK   04436-X—$2.75
John Russell Taylor

____ **LADD: A HOLLYWOOD**
TRAGEDY   04531-5—$2.75
Beverly Linet

____ **LIVING IT UP**   04352-5—$2.25
George Burns

____ **MERMAN:**
AN AUTOBIOGRAPHY   04261-8—$2.50
Ethel Merman with George Eells

____ **MOMMIE DEAREST**   04444-0—$2.75
Christina Crawford

____ **MOTHER GODDAM**   04119-0—$2.50
Whitney Sune with Bette Davis

____ **MY WICKED, WICKED WAYS**   04686-9—$2.75
Errol Flynn

____ **NO BED OF ROSES**   04241-3—$2.50
Joan Fontaine

____ **SELF-PORTRAIT**   04485-8—$2.75
Gene Tierney, with Mickey Herskowitz

____ **MISS TALLULAH BANKHEAD**   04574-9—$2.75
Lee Israel

Available at your local bookstore or return this form to:

Berkley Book Mailing Service
P.O. Box 690
Rockville Centre, NY 11570

Please send me the above titles. I am enclosing $_____
(Please add 50¢ per copy to cover postage and handling). Send check or money order—no cash or C.O.D.'s. Allow three weeks for delivery

NAME_____

ADDRESS_____

CITY_____STATE/ZIP_____ 6

Bestsellers from Berkley
The books you've been hearing about—and want to read

___**THE BIDDERS**	04606-4—$2.75
John Baxter	
___**TROIKA**	04662-1—$2.75
David Gurr	
___**ZEBRA**	04635-4—$2.95
Clark Howard	
___**THE FIRST DEADLY SIN**	04692-3—$2.95
Lawrence Sanders	
___**THE THIRD WORLD WAR:**	
AUGUST 1985	04477-7—$2.95
General Sir John Hackett, et al.	
___**THE PIERCING**	04563-3—$2.50
John Coyne	
___**THE WINNER'S CIRCLE**	04500-5—$2.50
Charles Paul Conn	
___**MOMMIE DEAREST**	04444-0—$2.75
Christina Crawford	
___**NURSE**	04685-0—$2.75
Peggy Anderson	
___**THE SIXTH COMMANDMENT**	04271-5—$2.75
Lawrence Sanders	
___**SINCERELY, RONALD**	
REAGAN	04885-1—$2.50
Edited by Helene von Damm	
___**A TIME FOR ACTION**	04840-3—$2.75
William E. Simon	

Berkley Book Mailing Service
P.O. Box 690
Rockville Centre, NY 11570

Please send me the above titles. I am enclosing $ _____
(Please add 50¢ per copy to cover postage and handling). Send check or
money order—no cash or C.O.D.'s. Allow six weeks for delivery.

NAME _____

ADDRESS _____

CITY _____ STATE/ZIP _____

1